Share My
Pleasant
Stones

2 008

EUGENIA PRICE

Share My Pleasant Stones

Meditations for
Every Day of the Year

DOUBLEDAY

NEW YORK   LONDON   TORONTO   SYDNEY   AUCKLAND

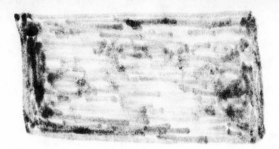

PUBLISHED BY DOUBLEDAY
a division of Bantam Doubleday Dell Publishing Group, Inc.
666 Fifth Avenue, New York, New York 10103

DOUBLEDAY and the portrayal of an anchor with a dolphin
are trademarks of Doubleday, a division of Bantam Doubleday Dell
Publishing Group, Inc.

Share My Pleasant Stones was originally published in hardcover
by Zondervan Publishing House in 1957. The Doubleday edition
is published by arrangement with Eugenia Price.

Library of Congress Cataloging-in-Publication Data
Price, Eugenia.
    [Share my pleasant stones every day for a year]
    Share my pleasant stones : meditations for every
    day of the year / Eugenia Price.
        p. cm.
    —(The Eugenia Price treasury of faith)
    Includes index.
    1. Devotional calendars.   I. Title.
II. Series: Price, Eugenia.
Eugenia Price treasure of faith.
[BV4811.P75   1991]   90-20896
242'.2—dc20   CIP
ISBN 0-385-41712-8

BVG 01

For the late Dr. Anna B. Mow

CONTENTS

Share My Pleasant Stones

PREFACE

For this author to reread a book written thirty years ago is nothing less than a mental *and* spiritual adventure! I well remember that after my adored father's death in 1958, Mother and I clung to what I had been given from these meditations in the section I called Purple Stones. They came through my mind, but the inner strength they brought in our blank grief plainly had another Source beyond me.

I have just browsed through some of these Pleasant Stones as I write these lines. I have also just reread my original Preface. My publisher has allowed me full freedom to use or to alter anything I care to, and for the most part in *Share My Pleasant Stones* I have chosen to leave much of my original Preface as it stands. After all, that is where I was back in 1955 and 1956 as I was writing these daily meditations. Evidently, I had been a Christian only seven years. I rather marvel now that in such a short period of time, He had so captured my attention. This is some of what I wrote in that early Preface, including the Bible verse from which I took my title:

O thou afflicted, tossed with tempest, and not comforted, behold, I will lay thy stones with fair colours, and lay thy foundations with sapphires. And I will make thy windows of agates, and thy gates of carbuncles, and all thy borders of *pleasant stones*.

"These are the eleventh and twelfth verses of the fifty-fourth chapter of Isaiah. In a way I could never put into words, this passage took me by the heart during the first sometimes frightening months of my new life in Christ.

"Those two verses of beautiful imagery became a firm wall to which I could cling when the currents of temptation and fear of the strange newness threatened to pull me back into the familiar darkness of my old life.

"They were a wall of 'pleasant stones.'

"And I clung to them, not knowing all God meant by 'pleasant stones,' but somehow deriving new comfort and courage as I grew more and more convinced that God knew all that He meant, even if I did not.

"He *has* made my borders of 'pleasant stones' during these first seven years. *Within* the borders of my new life have whirled the confusions and the storms that have whirled within the borders of your life. But those borders have been laid firmly and forever with the 'pleasant stones' God promised the first time I ever read the book of Isaiah.

"I am convinced that I have only glimpsed the meaning of these stones which He has laid and is laying in my life. Some are new thought patterns formed in my once self-occupied mind. Some are the new desires created by His very presence within me. The 'corner stone' is Christ Himself and among these 'pleasant stones' are the verse and thoughts I want to share with you here. This book is written from notes scribbled in the margins of the Bible given me by Mother shortly after my conversion in 1949. Light keeps coming into them. Where God's Word is, there is new light and growth because living Water streams forever over the words He chose to use. And because this living Water is a 'well of water *springing* up into everlasting life' everlastingly, continuously, even the 'pleasant stones' of God's written-down Word grow in meaning to us as the Water continues to flow over them.

"My understanding has been deepened through even a little knowledge of the formation of natural stones. Think of the crystalline wonder in precious and semi-precious stones—in the so-called ordinary formations known as geodes or the fairyland of crystallization in underground caves where hanging stalactites and towering stalagmites 'grow' from commonplace ugly lumps of limestone! Break open an ordinary geode and inside you may find it is lined with lovely agate or chalcedony instead of crystals, but they have all 'grown' in the same way: Somewhere in the common rocks there were little openings filled with sand or clay, and into these openings seeped water—water that dissolved away certain minerals and salts through the ages and caused the formation of 'pleasant stones.'

"God's presence in my life has caused my 'pleasant stones' to grow.

"Spend the next year with me and 'share my pleasant stones'— Clear stones, Red stones, Blue stones, Purple stones, Green stones and stones that are many-colored—each one of which I have been given by the One who gave Himself."

EUGENIA PRICE
St. Simons Island, Georgia

CLEAR STONES

When I think of "clear stones," I think first of diamonds. There are diamonds of almost every color. But those known as "water-white" stones are the rarest and most to be desired WHEN *they are perfect and free from flaws.*

God's Word is perfect and so we include in our collection of "clear stones," some of the verses which strike me as having the properties of "water-white," flawless diamonds.

Verses which cut right through to the deepest meaning. Verses which could be called "hard" in the sense that the diamond is the hardest of all materials and is used to cut through other stones and to puncture steel as well as to adorn a ring given to prove love for the loved one.

God's love CUTS RIGHT THROUGH.

Without the "diamond" verses in the Bible, there would be no starting place for growth. No amount of criticism can destroy these verses, just as no acid or any other solvent can eat away a diamond.

But — when a diamond is tapped even lightly at exactly the right place, it cleaves easily and exposes beautiful hidden facets of itself. To me, these verses "cut right through" without compromise. I need them to do that. But together under the direction of the Holy Spirit, we can also "tap them lightly" and let them cleave quickly to show us shining NEW *facets of truth.*

Share my pleasant CLEAR *stones.*

JANUARY 1

In the beginning was the Word, and the Word was with God, and the Word was God. . . . And the Word was made flesh, and dwelt among us (John 1:1, 14a).

THERE is only one place to begin. And that is in the beginning. And let our hearts rejoice that "In the beginning was the *Word*" and that Word became flesh . . . became a Man, in the person of Jesus Christ.

This is the greatest relief I know.

This is the greatest fact in all history. There is no other place to begin except to rest the central confidence of our lives in the *fact* that God *did* reveal Himself in Jesus and that He is alive now. When we begin at any other point, we get lost. More accurately, we realize we *are* already lost. Only *He* is a Redeemer. Only *He* offers forgiveness. Only *He* offers a way out of temptation. Only *He* offers a way to make *use* of suffering.

Only Jesus Christ offers eternal Life, because only He *is* eternal Life.

We are beginning and there is no other place to begin except with the glorious fact of Jesus Christ, who Himself *is* the beginning and the end.

Cutting through all our confusion as to where this year may end, is the "water-white" flawless *fact* of Jesus Christ, who will be there when it ends as He is here now in the beginning!

I am He that liveth, and was dead; and . . . am alive for evermore. I am the beginning and the end.

8

JANUARY 2

I am the Lord: that is my name: . . . and new things do I declare: before they spring forth I tell you of them (Isaiah 42:8a, 9b).

IF we believe Jesus Christ Himself when He declares Himself to be "the beginning and the end," we also believe Him when He declares that "I and the Father are one." So the Prophet Isaiah, writing of "the Lord" wrote of this same Jesus Christ who Himself *is* the beginning and the end.

But we do not begin merely with the miraculous birth of Jesus, nor with the tender healer of mankind's pain and sickness and sin. We do not dare even to begin with the sacrificial death of Jesus.

We dare only to begin with the Living *Lord* Jesus who *was* in the beginning and before it, who got up and walked out of that tomb and who *lives* on this our second day of sharing and forever. And who promises to tell us of the new things before they "spring forth"!

"I am the Lord; that is my name: . . . and new things do I declare: before they spring forth I tell you of them." Does He mean He will warn us exactly of each upcoming failure or tragedy or success? No. If He did, we would begin to depend upon His warnings. Tap this "clear stone" lightly and watch it cleave to show this *new* and deeper truth: "In the world ye shall have tribulation: but be of good cheer; I have overcome the world."

And this Lord has *already* overcome *whatever* comes to us in this or any new year.

If it is tragedy, He has overcome it.

If it is sickness, He has overcome it.

If it is death, He has overcome that.

If it is sudden success, He has overcome that.

Whatever comes, "before they spring forth," Jesus Christ Himself tells us that He has already overcome it!

I am the Lord: that is my name . . .

JANUARY 3

But your iniquities have separated between you and your God, and your sins have hid his face from you, that he will not hear (Isaiah 59:2).

ONENESS with the Living Person, Jesus Christ, is the secret of the victorious *daily* life. Jesus prayed for this oneness in the Garden of Gethsemane just before they killed Him. The most perverted characteristic about us is that we somehow fall into the trap of believing that *we* must persuade God to hear us and then plead with Him to remember our request long enough to grant it.

We are so inclined to put the blame on God when our prayers for a sense of His nearness are seemingly not answered. We have His word for it that He will never leave us nor forsake us and yet in what we hope are "humble phrases," we speak of our spiritual coldness and run from conference to conference and book to book and leader to leader "complaining" that we have lost our touch with God.

We blame God. If not in our carefully chosen words, in our attitudes. Most of all, we blame Him in our *refusal* of the state of oneness with Christ for which He prayed in the Garden before they crucified Him. "Father, I will that they also, whom thou hast given me, be *with* me where I am . . ."

"But your iniquities have separated between you and your God." God has not hidden His face. ". . . *Your sins have hid his face from you."* He *will* not hear our prayer for peace and a sense of oneness until He can hear our prayer for deliverance from those *sins* which have hid His face from us.

And He cannot hear our prayer for deliverance until we are willing to be delivered. Our part is to ask and then not be *afraid* to receive.

Fear not: for I have redeemed thee, I have called thee by thy name; thou art mine.

10

Behold, the Lord's hand is not shortened, that it cannot save . . . (Isaiah 59:1).

IN every other religion but Christianity, man is seeking God. Man is trying to earn his salvation. Trying to achieve his oneness with God as he understands Him. We have God's own word for it that we cannot earn our salvation, that we are saved by faith. We also have God's own word for it that His hand is not shortened. That He is *the* Saviour.

Some weeks after my book *Discoveries* was published, a young college professor, who had grown dissatisfied with the cold orthodoxy upon which he had been fed, wrote asking a question which I shall never forget: "What *is* the important thing to believe?"

I made an appointment to meet him in a city near the college town where he taught, but in the interim I asked one after another of God's older saints whom I met along the way—"What is the important thing?" I received some penetrating answers. And then I received the one I knew was *the* answer: "The important thing to believe is that *Jesus* saves!"

No-one else. Only Jesus.

". . . Thou shalt call His name Jesus: for He shall save His people from their sins."

The important thing is that we can begin with the One who Himself *is* our salvation. "Thou shalt call His name Jesus . . ." and this same Jesus who saves is not only the Saviour, He is also the Light which points out our sins.

There is no question but that His arm will reach all the way to where we are. There is no question about His power to save. There is no question about the penetrating power of His light. The only question is will we open our eyes and *look?*

. . . It is I; be not afraid.

11

JANUARY 5

For ye were sometimes darkness, but now are ye light in the Lord: walk as children of light (Ephesians 5:8).

GOD makes it very plain to us that we were not only *in* darkness—that we *were* darkness. But He makes it just as plain that since Christ indwells us, we actually *are light.*

Here the cutting edge of this "clear stone" truth cleaves right to the dark core of our unwillingness to *act* as though what God says is true. "Cuts right through" to the dark center of our refusal to *be* what God has said we *are* in Christ.

". . . but *now* are ye *light* in the Lord . . ."

We are beginning this year with the Lord of Light Himself.

"I am come a light into the world, that whosoever believeth on me should not abide in darkness."

Either Jesus Christ knew about Himself and spoke accurately of Himself or He did not. He has said He will never leave us nor forsake us. He has declared Himself to *be* the Light of the world. The diamond-clear words of Isaiah ring down through the ages, reaching us still diamond-clear: "Arise, shine; for thy light is come, and the glory of the Lord *is risen* upon thee!"

The glory . . . the very *character* . . . the very Light of God Himself *is risen* upon us and we sit in the corner and clutch at the darkness of our pet iniquities and complain "humbly" that *we* have lost our touch with God. My life is full of problems too. Just like yours. I also feel at times that I have lost my touch with God.

What we *feel* is beside the point.

Jesus is the Light of the world and He *has risen* in our lives and no amount of darkness can put Him out! This is fact:

. . . I am the light of the world . . . In him is no darkness at all.

12

JANUARY 6

Then thou shalt see, and flow together . . . (Isaiah 60:5a).

W HEN the light is turned on we can see.
When it is dark we stumble and sometimes we fall,
simply because we cannot see. We go this way and that,
not knowing which is the way. We seem to go a dozen directions
at once.

One direction, chosen in fear, only leads to more fear.

Another, chosen in confusion, leads to more confusion.

We are out of balance. Out of perspective. We are perplexed
and divided and acting as though we are several people instead
of one. We confuse ourselves and those around us. We *are*
confusion.

It is dark.

Our roads leading to nowhere are all dead end streets.

Isaiah still cries to us, cleaving the "clear stone" again: "Arise,
shine; for thy light is come, and the glory of the Lord is risen
upon thee . . . *Then* thou shalt see, and *flow together.*"

Perplexities and stumblings and personality quirks and character contradictions and wrong directions and wasted efforts all
"flow together" as we are brought into wholeness in Christ.

". . . The darkness is past, and the true light now shineth."

Balance is back, perspective is clear. We are no longer a
bundle of contradictions. We have been unified. The stray ends
are tied.

"I am come a light into the world . . ."

We can see now. And we can flow together.

Then thou shalt see, and flow together.

13

JANUARY 7

. . . the Lord shall be unto thee an everlasting light, and thy God thy glory (Isaiah 60:19b).

TAP this stone lightly in just the right place and it splits to expose a facet of diamond-hard truth which causes us to wince and close the Book or come again for further cleansing at the feet of the One who has promised that He Himself shall be unto us an *everlasting* light!

An everlasting light exposing us as we are all the way to the very depths of our beings. Even the prodigal son had to "come to" himself before he had sense enough to go home to his father. We need to "come to" ourselves. To see us as we *are*. We cannot begin to explore the deep places until we have allowed the Light of Calvary to shine into the shallow corners first. We may cry out sincerely for oneness with Christ, for power in our Christian lives. But "the Lord shall be unto thee an everlasting light" and we need to *look* by the light of the Lord. We cannot plead lack of light. The light is the Lord.

We need to look at the thin, wiry streak of criticism twisted through our natures. We need to look at the unlove we feel toward that particular Christian brother or sister. We need to look at the blunt self-defense we try to disguise under the cape of intercession for someone else's shortcomings. We need to look at all this and more in the light of the One who is our *everlasting* light. If we do, we don't dare plead blindness or lack of illumination.

He has promised to be our everlasting light, and "in Him is no darkness at all."

. . . I am the light of the world. . . . The darkness is past, and the true light now shineth.

14

... we wait for light, but behold obscurity; for brightness, but we walk in darkness. We grope for the wall like the blind, and we grope as if we had no eyes: we stumble at noon day as in the night; we are in desolate places as dead men (Isaiah 59: 9b, 10).

HOW can this be if Jesus Christ has come a light into the world?

He *has* come. Make no mistake about that. He *is* here. Now. The Bible is filled with reports of His Presence. With guarantees of His Presence. But, as with everything else within the depth and height and breadth of this greatest Book, the promise of the Light of His Presence is *not* ours until we take it by faith for ourselves. We *do* grope for the wall like the blind. We *do* grope as if we had no eyes. We *do* stumble at noon day as in the night. We are *waiting* for light as though Christ had not yet come.

He has come. And we can stop "beholding obscurity" the very instant we lay hold of the fact of His Presence *by faith*.

He is here right now.

If you are still beholding only obscurity, *realize* that He said He would never leave us and as you go on about your day's activities, you will begin to realize (when you least expect it) that the "darkness *is* past and the true light now shineth."

Even if you don't *feel* anything, go on about your day, *claiming* His Presence every time a shadow crosses your mind. "By faith are we saved" from beholding "obscurity." "By faith are we saved" from the unnecessary moods of darkness. *Take* His Presence and begin to practice it — by faith. As always, we have His Word for it:

I am come a light into the world, that whosoever believeth on me should not abide in darkness.

15

For as he thinketh in his heart, so is he . . . (Proverbs 23:7).

C LEAVE to this "clear stone" and dare to look at the source from which it sprang: The mind of God.

This is God's own analysis. It is not a psychological concept arrived at by any man. God quite simply tells us that we are *not* what we think we are. Quite the reverse. *We are what we think!*

It seemed strange to me at first that the writer of the book of Proverbs would use the verb "think" in connection with the noun "heart." We associate *feeling* with our hearts and *thinking* with our minds. But if we pay close attention, we soon discover that when the Holy Spirit speaks of the "heart" of man, He is including the mind and more. He means the central core of our beings.

Our *mind-hearts.*

The part of us which thinks, wills, chooses and loves. The part of us which will one day stand before God.

The part of us which *is* us: Our spirits.

Numerous in my collection of "pleasant stones" are the diamond-sharp verses which seem almost to attempt to shock us into allowing Christ to take captive our *thought lives.*

"For as he thinketh in his heart, so is he . . ."

How do we think in our hearts when we believe no-one is looking or listening?

How do we think? *What* do we think?

"O Lord, thou hast searched me, and known me." God *knows.*

We can only ask Him for courage to look at our own secret hearts and face what we see there! The analysis of God remains:

For as he thinketh in his heart, so is he . . .

And God said, Let us make man in our image, after our
likeness: and let them have dominion over the fish of the
sea, and over the fowl of the air, and over the cattle, and
over all the earth, and over every creeping thing that creep-
eth upon the earth. So God created man in his own image,
in the image of God created he him; male and female created
he them (Genesis 1:26, 27).

THERE is no such thing as a dark corner where anyone can
be completely alone.

For many years, before I became a Christian, I sought
an impossible state described by Lord Byron as "a life within
itself that breathes *without* mankind." Any human being seeking
a life completely shut off from mankind is simply illustrating
the disposition of sin. Any human being who lives as though
it's no-one's business but his own, is not only trying the impossible, but is stamping his foot and shaking his fist in God's
face as he shouts his *right* to live his own life!

There is no such thing as a cozy corner where you and I
can go to think our own thoughts as we want to think them
so that no-one will know. *We are what we think.* If we think
ourselves to be humble, gifted, charming people, we will go
right out of our "cozy corner" and act haughty and cold. If we
think critical thoughts of someone while we are in our "corner,"
we will leave our corner to find our would-be polite phrases
dripping acid.

Whether we like it or not we live in a world populated by other
people who see us as we *are.* So does God. But we can thank this
Creator God that *He* also sees us as we *can* be when our thoughts are
taken captive by the One who died to redeem our minds as well as
our souls.

. . . Be renewed in the spirit of your mind . . . casting down
imaginations, and every high thing that exalteth itself against
the knowledge of God, and bringing into captivity every
thought to the obedience of Christ.

17

O Lord, thou hast searched me, and known me. Thou knowest my downsitting and mine uprising, thou understandest my thought afar off. Thou compassest my path and my lying down, and art acquainted with all my ways (Psalm 139:1-3).

READ all of Psalm 139. And then read it again. And again. It is a study in depth psychology. It is a frightening study until we grasp the tremendous fact that God knows all of the unfathomable depths of our beings.

Our subconscious minds are like baskets. Into them has dropped everything we have ever heard, spoken or thought. And we cannot control them. But God knows all about subconscious minds as well as conscious minds. He created them in the first place. They are not too much for Him at all.

He knows.

That has come to be daily a greater relief to me.

He is "acquainted with all my ways" and still He loves me.

Each time something frightening floats to the surface of my subconscious mind and registers its ugly self on my consciousness, I deliberately remind myself that God is not shocked by the things I am just now seeing about me. "While we were yet sinners, Christ died for us." He is *unshockable* and *unshakable*, and He is, in the Person of the blessed Holy Spirit, *constantly* at work in the shadowy depths of our subconscious minds. This is His domain if we are Christians. Here we have no control. And even when consciously we feel out of touch with God, we can absolutely *rest* on the fact that *He* is *not* out of touch with us. He is there in the depths right now working.

We have His own word for the fact that He is there:

. . . If any man . . . open the door, I will come in . . . . I will never leave thee, nor forsake thee.

For there is not a word in my tongue, but, lo, O Lord, thou knowest it altogether. Thou hast beset me behind and before, and laid thine hand upon me. Such knowledge is too wonderful for me; it is high, I cannot attain unto it (Psalm 139:4-6).

SOMETIME ago I had the unique experience of conducting a Deeper Life Conference with teen-agers at Mound Keswick in Minnesota. Each young person was already a believer in Jesus Christ. We were all there to go deeper. Or *higher*, as my dear friend, Dr. Walter Wilson, once corrected me.

In going "higher" we went deeply into the fact that only God, through the Holy Spirit, *can* re-form our unconscious depths. We spoke of the shadows and darkness and filth lurking there. And one young lady stopped listening at that point and came to me later trembling with fear at what might be in her subconscious!

She had shut her ears just when the glory part came.

Without the indwelling Holy Spirit at work *in* our depths, there is reason for panic. Psychiatry can bring up the twisted ugliness and just bringing it up "for air" relieves some tension and lessens the immediate danger. But the best psychiatry can do is to leave the complexes and neuroses there squirming on the table. Only the blood of Jesus Christ *redeems*. And there are no depths too dark nor too far down for His blood to cleanse.

These depths are unfathomable to the human mind. But not to God. He is there right now working in the depths of you and here working in the depths of me.

What a glorious relief! I can just go on. By *faith*.

Such knowledge is too wonderful for me; it is high, I cannot attain unto it.

Whither shall I go from thy spirit? or whither shall I flee from thy presence? (Psalm 139:7).

UNTIL very recently I recoiled now and then at the thought that I could *not* get away from the Presence of God. Anyone who has lived away from Him as an adult will understand this. The down-pull in us draws us back to run here and there—wildly at times, in search of an old, familiar place where He won't haunt us by His nearness.

But He has said: "Lo, I am *with* you alway . . ."

And He is.

He is there at the close of every willful act against Him. Walking beside us as we try to walk *away* from a job He has asked us to do. He is there at the bottom of every empty bottle for every alcoholic who has received Him as Saviour, but who is still not following Him as Lord.

". . . if I make my bed in hell, behold, thou art there."

There are no "cozy corners" where we can get away from Him. And at last I am glad. Because if I could get away from Him, that would mean He had forsaken me too. And He does *not* break His promises. "I will *never* leave you nor forsake you" and in the moment between you and your pillow at night after you *have* forsaken Him, you will *know* that He never breaks His promises to us. You will know He never leaves us. You will know He is still there.

I know it too.

". . . When I awake, I am still with thee."

Never, never, never alone.

. . . I will never leave thee, nor forsake thee.

20

JANUARY 14

Let the words of my mouth, and the meditation of my heart, be acceptable in thy sight, O Lord, my strength and my redeemer (Psalm 19:14).

FOR a few years this verse seemed one of those less pungent ones to me. I had heard it repeated at numberless women's meetings where I spoke and like some other much-memorized verses, it had never done anything startling to me. But that is the way of our growth in Christ. Daily reading of the Bible, whether we get anything from it consciously or not, is a "must," because everything we read or hear drops down into our subconscious minds and then on the day when we need it, the Holy Spirit "explodes" it up into our consciousness with sharp, fresh meaning.

As I began to grasp the desperate necessity to bring my thought life into captivity to Christ, this verse from the Psalms leaped from the page and began its "diamond-cleavage" of several other verses far over in the New Testament! David wrote it. And David knew what *he* was capable of doing when for a brief time he did *not* keep his heart fixed on God. Therefore David cried—and I don't believe he *chanted* it—I believe he *cried*: "Let the words of my mouth, and the meditation of my heart, be acceptable in thy sight, O Lord, my strength and my Redeemer!" David knew that his *words* would indicate the condition of his *heart*. He knew he could not redeem his own thoughts. He had no strength to do it. And so he cried to the Lord, acknowledging his own need of a strong redeemer.

Do you *dare* pray this prayer right now? Do I?

Search me, O God, and know my heart: try me, and know my thoughts: And see if there be any wicked way in me, and lead me in the way everlasting.

21

. . . Those things which proceed out of the mouth come forth from the heart . . . (Matthew 15:18a).

THIS is one of the New Testament verses which the last verse of Psalm 19 "split" to expose new and hidden depths for me. Yesterday's "clear stone" (Psalm 19:14) is placed forever in my collection of diamond-hard stones that "cut right through."

We cannot *speak* or *pray* creatively unless the very *thoughts* of our hearts are clear with the clarity of Christ Himself. We may write and speak and pray aloud and do good works. We may even lead someone to Christ now and then, but *all* the words of our mouths cannot be acceptable to God *until* all the dark corners of our thoughts are thrown open to His cleansing Presence.

One verse cleaves another . . . and I know yesterday's "clear stone" is a true *clear* stone because Jesus Himself declared ". . . those things which proceed out of the mouth come forth *from the heart* . . ."

And He added that it is *they* which defile a man.

"Let . . . the meditation of my heart, be acceptable in thy sight . . ."

More, much more than what we *do*, it is what we *think* that defiles us. This in turn lights up another New Testament verse: ". . . Come out . . . and be ye separate . . ." I cannot live a separated life *unless* my every thought is in accord with what I see *inside* the Heart that broke on Calvary! Only then am I living a life separated from all that is against God.

God is Love. And if I cling to my right even to think unkind thoughts, I *am separated* from God on that point.

Jesus Christ declares that all sin begins in the thought life!

"For out of the heart proceed evil thoughts, murders, adulteries, fornications, thefts, false witness, blasphemies: These are the things which defile a man . . ."

Search me, O God . . . and see if there be any wicked way in me . . .

... out of the abundance of the heart the mouth speaketh.
... I say unto you, That every idle word that men shall
speak, they shall give account thereof in the day of judgment. For by thy words thou shalt be justified, and by thy
words thou shalt be condemned (Matthew 12:34b, 36, 37).

HERE the cleavage is complete.

The "diamond-hard" truth of this verse cuts completely
through the secret facets of every warning from God
about the necessity of a clean heart and a clean mind.

In words that seem purposely exaggerated so as to grab our
attention, Jesus declares that *so important* are the thoughts of
our hearts that our *words* will either *justify* or *condemn* us.

At first observation this seems fantastic.

Knowing the lethargy of the human mind, Jesus often shocks
us into attention. It seems to me He did this here. He also
phrases things to make us *think.* By saying our *words* will justify
or condemn us, He is urging us to go back to the truth *behind*
this statement: "A good man out of the good treasure of the
heart bringeth forth good things: and an evil man out of the
evil treasure bringeth forth evil things."

When we stand before Him we will stand *exposed* with our
hearts showing. What will God see? Exactly what He sees now.

Two days ago we asked if we *dare* pray this prayer. Now the
question—do we dare *not* to pray it?

Search me, O God ... and see if there be any wicked way
in me, and lead me in the way everlasting.
Let the words of my mouth, and the meditation of my
heart, be acceptable in thy sight, O Lord, my strength and
my redeemer.

> Hell is naked before him, and destruction hath no covering.
> He stretcheth out the north over the empty place, and hang-
> eth the earth upon nothing. He bindeth up the waters in
> his thick clouds; and the cloud is not rent under them. He
> holdeth back the face of his throne, and spreadeth his cloud
> upon it. He hath compassed the waters with bounds, until
> the day and night come to an end. The pillars of heaven
> tremble and are astonished at his reproof. He divideth the
> sea with his power, and by his understanding he smiteth
> through the proud. By his spirit he hath garnished the
> heavens; his hand hath formed the crooked serpent. Lo,
> these are parts of his ways: but how little a portion is
> heard of him? but the thunder of his power who can
> understand? (Job 26:6-14).

THESE are only "parts of his ways"!

Even in the face of the magnificent failure of these words to contain Him as He is, we tremble and hold back and refuse to act as though we believe that this God who "divideth the sea with his power" is powerful enough to change our minds.

If He is powerful enough to *create* the human mind, doesn't it make sense that He is also powerful enough to *transform* it?

Can we trust God with our minds?

Or do we need to remain victims of our wrong thought habits? We must decide once and for all that we do *not*. And once we have decided, then we must also choose. We must choose to *believe* once and for all, that the crucified and risen follower of a crucified and risen Lord need not remain a victim of anything. He has already become a victim *for* us on Calvary's Cross. We can be victors in all things. Even in our thoughts. We can be free, *if* we choose to be.

For Jesus Himself said: "If the Son therefore shall make you free, you shall be free indeed!"

Even *our* human nature is not too much for Him.

> Hell is naked before him, and destruction hath no covering.
> . . . my substance was not hid from thee, when I was made
> in secret, and curiously wrought in the lowest parts of the
> earth.

. . . If any man will come after me . . . (Luke 9:23).

I HAVE dedicated this book to one of God's great ladies, Anna Mow, who first impressed upon me the fact that every normal person is born with a "chooser." Most of us never use our "choosers" enough to develop their "muscles," but we all have them.

Jesus recognized this fact, of course. ". . . Without him was not anything made that was made." He was right there when all the component parts of the human mind including a "chooser" were conceived in the mind of God. "I and the Father are one." He knows about the necessity of our choosing. However, being one with the Holy Spirit also, Jesus was not ignoring the fact that we must be empowered by the Holy Spirit *in order* to choose *God's* way. We have all the power we need to choose the *Devil's* way. That comes "naturally." But still our "choosers" are to be in operation under the power of the Spirit according to the plan of God, and for a reason we cannot fathom, He *continues* to respect our free wills. That is why Jesus said: *"If any man will come after me . . ." We must choose!* Not only must we decide what it is that we must have changed in our thought lives, we must decide to *let* God change it. When we choose to be delivered, we are *given* the power to follow Him in the deliverance process whatever it costs. You and I *can* cast out those wrong thoughts at once in the Name and in the power of Jesus.

Again, we have the Lord's own word for that:

. . . I go unto my Father. And whatsoever ye shall ask in my name, that will I do, that the Father may be glorified in the Son.

I also will choose their delusions, and will bring their fears upon them; because when I called, none did answer; when I spake, they did not hear: but they did evil before mine eyes, and chose that in which I delighted not (Isaiah 66:4).

FOR many months after I became a Christian, I shuddered at passages like this in the Old Testament. They made God the Father seem so *unlike* Christ! Intellectually, I believed Christ and God were One. But my heart rebelled at passages which spoke of God's *bringing* fears upon us and *choosing* our delusions because we did evil before His eyes.

Everything in me *wanted* the Father to turn out to be what the Gospel of John said He was. I wanted the Father to be like Christ. I could trust everything I knew about Christ. And I could never, in the wildest reaches of even my writer's imagination, conceive of Jesus Christ *bringing* fears down upon someone. Nothing inside the Heart that broke on Calvary pointed to that. What was wrong? Wasn't this passage in Isaiah God's Word too? Wasn't it God Himself speaking? Yes. God Himself once more forcing me to *think*. To *use* the brain He gave me. This *was* the same God (One with Christ) merely clarifying Himself for me. The same God who created my mind in the way He knew would function best, was merely proving Himself to be a God of His Word. One whose moral laws were consistent with His laws of creation. If I *chose* to do evil before His eyes, certain fears and delusions *would be the inevitable consequences* of my choosing. God's part here is that He simply chose to create the mind in a certain way. If I choose to disobey His plan for me, specific fears and specific delusions will result. This no longer causes me to rebel. It causes me to rejoice. He is a dependable God and I can count on victory when I obey, just as surely as I can count on fears and delusions when I disobey.

I am he; I am the first, I also am the last.
. . . O God, my heart is fixed: I will sing and give praise.

To whom then will ye liken God? or what likeness will
ye compare unto him? To whom then will ye liken me . . .
saith the Holy One (Isaiah 40:18, 25a).

ONE day we will all know about going home.
One day we will all know about God. What He's really
like.

One day we will understand what it is He is doing.

For now, it is enough to know that "No man hath seen God
at any time; the only begotten Son which is in the bosom of
the Father, *he hath declared him.*"

"To whom then will ye liken God?"

"I and the Father are one."

This is the word of Jesus Christ "on the bosom of the Father,"
"Who being the brightness of his glory, and the express image
of his person, and upholding all things by the word of his power,
when he had by himself purged our sins, sat down on the right
hand of the Majesty on high."

We liken the Holy One of Israel to Christ. We dare to do
this on God's own authority. For God was in Christ on the
Cross of Calvary, as Jesus was, "by himself purging our sins."
God was in Christ reconciling us to Himself and giving us holy
authority to declare and to experience the fact that when we see
Christ, we see the Father also. It is well to remind ourselves
of this over and over again.

If ye had known me, ye should have known my Father also;
. . . he that hath seen me hath seen the Father . . . I and
the Father are one.

JANUARY 21

Hearken unto me, ye stouthearted, that are far from righteousness (Isaiah 46:12).

ALMOST every alma mater song in the world has the phrase "stouthearted" tucked or squeezed somewhere into its shakey rhyme scheme. A phrase designed to create a swelling in the chest and a "go get 'em" spirit among those who unite their "stouthearts" in song.

Now, don't misunderstand me. I loved three alma mater songs very much. As I remember, all three had something to do with what I fancied to be my "stoutheart"—and the "stouthearts" of my classmates. Actually, I remember the school song when I was in Lincoln Junior High back in Charleston, West Virginia, and it had its "stouthearted" phrase couched in words which urged us all to "have sand"! This, I assume, meant "grit." At any rate, a kind of synonym for a stoutheart, and it rhymed with "land," which it needed to do. We've all been taught that stoutheartedness is a characteristic much to be desired and sung about. And far be it from me to frown upon true courage.

But God warns sharply that we are to "hearken unto *Him*" if we have begun to *depend* upon our own stouthearts! Upon our own abilities. You are not alone if you have fallen into this pit too. I fell in with a thud as I began the writing of this very book. Two weeks of meditations went quite easily and then God had to cause me to "hearken unto him." My "stoutheart" was broken and melted, until I remembered that I couldn't write about the things of God even with my "stoutheart." *Especially* with my "stoutheart"! "Christ in me"—my only hope of *anything* became *everything* again. I remembered "it is not I, but Christ." We will go on sharing now. "Hearkening to him" . . . remembering that we are not our own. We have been bought with a price.

Hearken unto me, ye stouthearted, that are far from righteousness: I bring near my righteousness; it shall not be far off.

I have shewed thee new things from this time, even hidden things, and thou didst not know them. They are created now, and not from the beginning; even before the day when thou heardest them not; lest thou shouldst say, Behold, I knew them (Isaiah 48:6, 7).

THE self-conscious "stoutheart" will say even to God: "Why do I need to go through this humiliating experience? I've already learned that lesson thoroughly."

And God replies: "I have shewed thee new things . . . *created now* . . . even before the day when thou heardest them not: lest thou shouldest say, Behold, I (already) knew them."

God will go to all lengths to teach us what we need to know. Even to creating new things? Even to creating new wisdom? New need for lessons learned? Yes! At least that's what God tells us in this ice-sharp "clear stone" we are sharing today.

"They are created *now* . . ."

God *will* stay ahead of us. After all, He is God. He *is* before and after eternity. And He remains God, not to belittle us, but to give us cause to worship Him. How He loves us. How much more patient and how much less tolerant is God of us than we are of ourselves. Our first parents broke themselves over God's lovely command to them that they never try to "play God." That they remain in the glorious relationship of Father and children. They were swayed by their "stouthearts" and shook their fists at the sky over Eden shouting in effect: "Behold, *we* knew them!" God does not want to look again on us His redeemed ones, with our "stouthearts" broken and bleeding as do all human hearts until Christ heals them by His wounds. "A humble and a contrite heart God does not despise" . . . a humble and a contrite heart is a peaceful heart because it has hearkened unto God and has been made whole.

. . . Learn of me; for I am meek and lowly in heart: and ye shall find rest unto your souls.

29

> . . . I am the Lord thy God which teacheth thee to profit,
> which leadeth thee by the way that thou shouldest go
> (Isaiah 48:17b).

ACCORDING to Webster, the verb "profit" means "to improve, to become efficient" or "to benefit." Again and again in many parts of the Holy Bible, God reminds us that His whole idea for us is for our *gain*.

". . . I am the Lord thy God which teacheth thee to *profit* . . ." To improve. To become more efficient. To benefit.

Jesus Himself declares that He came that we might have a more abundant life. Nowhere does God indicate by word or action that His purpose is to hold us down. To force us into a strange pattern where we must "sit on the lid" and suffer Him to be God while we cringe and obey out of fear. Proper "fear" for God is proper respect for Him. Proper fear of God is simply sanity. It is simply being reasonable. After all, He *is* God. But over and over again He reminds us that He not only will lead us by the way that we should go, but that He does it because His way is the only way that really works to our benefit in the long run. If the teachings of Jesus Christ seem too strict, it is simply because we have strayed so far from what He intended us to be. "Without him [Jesus] was not anything made that was made." He was there in the beginning and He is teaching what He knows will work to our advantage throughout eternity — but also *now!* He commands what He commands, because He knows nothing else will work.

> I know the thoughts I think toward you, saith the Lord,
> thoughts of peace, and not of evil, to give you an EX-
> PECTED end.

O that thou hadst hearkened to my commandments! then had thy peace been as a river, and thy righteousness as the waves of the sea (Isaiah 48:18).

GOD will lead us in the way that we should go and in the way He knows is the only way along which we will benefit. "I am the Lord thy God which teacheth thee to *profit* . . ." God leads us as He does, not to be hard.

Not to prove His power over us.

Not to make our lives miserable. Not to frustrate us.

He leads as He leads because He *knows* us exactly as we are. Knows us as we are now, and what went before in your life and in mine. Knows us as we are now and what lies ahead too. God knows. And *only* God knows fully. And so He leads us as He leads not only from wisdom, but from love. If what He is asking you to do right now as you read these words seems too hard (as something He is asking of me as I write these words seems "too hard") by His grace, we can both remember *who He is*.

We can remember that the same Heart that reminds throughout the Old Testament that "I am the Lord thy God which teacheth thee to profit" is the very same Heart that ached in the human breast of the Lord Jesus as He looked out over Jerusalem just before they killed Him and sobbed:

". . . how often would I have gathered thy children together, as a hen doth gather her brood under her wings, and ye *would not!*"

"O that thou hadst hearkened to my commandments! then had thy peace been as a river . . ." But it is not too late. Even if you have fallen, it is *not* too late.

. . . him that cometh to me I will in no wise cast out. . . . Come unto me . . .

**Surely he hath borne our griefs, and carried our sorrows . . .
(Isaiah 53:4a).**

THIS precious "stone" rests as well in either my collection of "clear stones" or "purple stones" or "red stones." Surely it contains all anyone could ever need for comfort in time of sorrow. I have put the "purple stones" in that collection. None of us escapes trouble, and my own heart longed to have ready a treasure-pile of "purple stones," little reassurances from God's own Word, when those times should come. As they will for us all. Surely, this "stone" could also be among the "red stones" . . . verses concerning His very Life become ours.

But somehow it seems necessary that we look at it in its diamond-sharp "clear stone" nature first. After all, words of comfort are just words of comfort unless they are backed up by *action*. This verse "cuts right through!"

"Surely he hath (already) borne our griefs, and carried our sorrows . . ."

God has backed up every beautiful phrase of comfort from Genesis to Revelation in this great action He took *in* Christ on the Cross two thousand years ago. Perhaps as you sit there reading this, your very heart is numb with grief. So numb that what I have written makes little or no impression. That's all right. God knows that too. And it does not change the fact that He *has* already borne your sorrow. And because He is alive right now and not at all limited by time as we know it, He is right now *still bearing your sorrow* and is right now *still carrying your grief!*

If you can do no more than just *look* at Him now, that's enough.

Look unto me, and be ye saved . . . Surely he hath borne our griefs and carried our sorrows . . .

. . . yet we did esteem him stricken, smitten of God, and afflicted (Isaiah 53:4b).

SURELY he hath borne our griefs, and carried our sorrows: yet we did esteem him stricken, smitten of God, and afflicted."

Tap this magnificent verse lightly and watch it cleave to expose a facet many never see. One I missed for a long, long time. Sometimes men and women have clung to life because they have been able to cling to the first part of this verse about God's having already borne our griefs and carried our sorrows, but then some turn away at that point.

I did. My heart leaped up with adoration and rested in relief that Christ on the Cross of Calvary had already taken my grief and my sorrow as well as my sin into His great Heart. I rejoiced that He had smothered them to death there in His Love. I knew it had broken His Heart but I also knew there was no other way for me and so I just accepted the gift of what He had done and tried to give thanks. But still there was unrest so deep down in my own heart that I seldom permitted it to reach the surface. And that unrest came when I read the end of Isaiah 53:4!

". . . yet we did esteem him stricken, *smitten of God*, and afflicted."

I *wanted* God and Christ to be one and the same. That's why I finally became a Christian. I wanted it to be true when Jesus said "I and the Father are one." Then how could God smite the Christ who had saved me?

"Rejoice and again I say rejoice," because cleave this "pleasant clear stone" to its heart and you see as I have seen at last, that God actually *smote Himself* for our sin!

"Surely he hath borne our griefs, and carried our sorrows . . ." but just as surely He afflicted *Himself*, as the Lord God "laid on him (*self*) the iniquity of us all."

. . . God was in Christ, reconciling the world unto himself . . .

> . . . he was wounded for our transgressions, he was bruised for our iniquities: the chastisement of our peace was upon him; and with his stripes we are healed (Isaiah 53:5).

WHEN our wounds are laid up against His wounds we are healed. Those of us who have tried this close, personal relationship with the living Christ know this is true. Those of us who have watched Him stand and wait until our anger dies down or until our selfish weeping is through, *know* that Jesus Christ *was* wounded for *our* iniquities. The same patience and love that held Him to the Cross keeps Him waiting now, while we run our little self-fevered courses of rebellion.

This kind of selfless waiting is only possible with Christ.

Only Christ is sinless.

And so we know that it was for *our* sin that He was bruised. We also know that our sin *still* bruises that tender Heart of love.

We know that it was "chastisement" to this pure, sinless, Son of God to hang there in such shame for our sins. But it was not the chastisement of an angry Father that put Him there. Such distortion of the Heart of the One who gave His only begotten Son is blasphemy!

God did not create sin. Sin is simply the ugly, diseased consequence of wrong action on the part of man. And wonder of Holy wonders, God holds *Himself* responsible for it! God was *in* Christ on Calvary reconciling us to Himself. He did it of His own choosing. He wanted us to be peaceful. He knew there could be no peace as long as sin separated us from Him.

That's why the chastisement of our sin was upon Him.

He was making "peace by the blood of His Cross."

> . . . with his stripes we are healed.

He was oppressed, and he was afflicted, yet he opened not his mouth: he is brought as a lamb to the slaughter, and as a sheep before her shearers is dumb, so he openeth not his mouth (Isaiah 53:7).

ONE of the most majestic things about Jesus was the way He stood before Pilate and said nothing.

He didn't sulk.

He didn't jut out His chin in defiance.

He didn't bite His lip to keep from talking.

He simply stood there when He was accused and "answered nothing."

"He was oppressed, and he was afflicted, yet he opened not his mouth . . ." His silence was so majestic and so cutting that it shattered the poise of all those about Him and caused them to scream and tear their clothing like mad people in their fury at His calm. But His poise held. He was *being* held by the Father. And as their fury rose, His silence rose. And His silence in the face of affliction should have proven to them that *He* would rise too no matter what they did to cut Him down!

"He was oppressed and he was afflicted . . . and he answered to him never a word; insomuch that the governor *marvelled greatly.*"

His silence was so God-like that the governor marveled at it. His silence was so God-like that Pilate tried to maneuver a way out of any part in His crucifixion!

His silence was so deep, all who beheld it must have known that kind of silence is possible *only* with God. Can we know it *now* as we stand before our "shearers"? Yes. We can be silent too. The same Christ who was silent then has come to dwell within us. We can *learn* to be willing to be misunderstood. Even by those we love. "Christ in me" . . . my only hope of silence in the midst of anything.

. . . nevertheless . . . not I, but Christ liveth in me.

35

Enlarge the place of thy tent, and let them stretch forth the curtains of thine habitations: spare not, lengthen thy cords, and strengthen thy stakes (Isaiah 54:2).

IF you have never *suffered* the true meaning of this verse, it is not completely yours. I did not use that word "suffered" here without some thought before I used it. All of God's written-down Word to us in the Holy Bible must be *taken* by faith for our individual use. But some passages only come by the *use* of a faith that holds through suffering.

"Enlarge the place of thy tent" is clearly understood by anyone who has opened the door at three A.M. to a disheveled, self-pitying alcoholic. Anyone who is still "sitting up" with the same "visitor" pouring black coffee down him or her at nine A.M. the next morning, listening for the fourth time to "how God has failed by not knocking the bottle out of his or her hand the night before," knows also that it involves suffering to "let them stretch forth the curtains of thy habitations." Not alone alcoholics. So with anyone who blesses your life by causing you to suffer this verse into the very fibre of your being! So with the cheating husband and the critical friend and the child who is annoyed when your money is all gone. So with the neurotic daughter of the neurotic mother who calls and repeats *her* side of the story, already well-memorized from mother's version.

And in it all God is speaking to us gently, clearly . . .

. . . Spare not, lengthen thy cords, and strengthen thy stakes; for thou shalt break forth on the right hand and on the left . . . fear not; for thou shalt not be ashamed: neither be thou confounded; . . . spare not . . . spare not.

The meek will he guide in judgment: and the meek will he teach his way (Psalm 25:9).

IT is well for us to pray for guidance. God has promised that He will give us wisdom if we but ask Him for it. And one of the most precious things about this lovely promise is that He takes time to add that He will not belittle us for asking.

"If any of you lack wisdom, let him ask of God, that giveth to all men liberally, and upbraideth not; and it shall be given him."

So, it is well to ask believing that God will keep His promises and more. *But,* the danger in attempting to twirl through life using only a dozen or so texts shows itself a flashing signal light here. It is true James writes that God "giveth to all men liberally." But here in Psalm 25, verse 9, is the "diamond-clear stone" which lays open to our clouded vision God's *qualification* for "giving liberally" of His own wisdom:

"The *meek* will he guide in judgment: and the *meek* will he teach his way."

As I understand the spiritual meaning of the word "meekness" it really means "teachableness." Docility. Willingness to learn. If you are praying for guidance concerning a change of position, a personal relationship, a new purchase — if you are praying for God's wisdom in any situation, perhaps it would be well to stop right here and check up on *your meekness.* Are you teachable?

Are you really willing to do what God directs? Or are you doing what I have done so often, seeking God's guidance as to what He thinks is the best way for *you* to get *your* way in the whole thing?

If any of you lack wisdom, (simply) let him ask of God . . . (remembering that) the MEEK will he guide in judgment: and the MEEK will he teach HIS way.

... learn of me; for I am meek and lowly in heart ...
(Matthew 11:29).

JESUS always took plenty of time to point things out to us in a way we can all understand. At times I have rebelled at the simplicity of His teachings. The part of me that wants to cry out as did old Augustine, "Save me, Lord, but not yet." still wishes now and then that I could plead confusion, or wonder just what He meant. But on the basic issues of daily obedience, the Lord Jesus leaves no room for the use of this satanic loophole.

He simply says what He means in the fewest possible words.

And tucked within the many-faceted depths of the last three verses of the eleventh chapter of Matthew, is a gleaming "clear stone." We most often think of His gracious invitation to "Come unto me." Or we think with joy that with Him the "burden is light." But tap those "clear stones" lightly in just the right place and bend closer to look into the secret of how to acquire that "rest" and that "light burden."

"... Learn of me; for I am meek and lowly in heart ..."

The only reason Jesus gives for telling us to learn of Him is that He is meek and lowly in heart. Oh, so wisely, He placed the sharp edge of the open secret within the framework of His open invitation to rest when you're weary for any reason. We are all weary at times. Jesus knew this would catch the eye of us all. It catches the heart forever of those who let His words "cut" right through to the cause of our weariness: pride, arrogance, self-satisfaction ... worse yet, self-pity. He wants to give rest to everyone in the world. But the way to enter into that rest is by the way of meekness. The really meek person does not have to be proven right. He is willing to be made right.

The MEEK will he guide in judgment: and the MEEK will he teach his way.

I am crucified with Christ . . . (Galatians 2:20).

WHEREVER I have written or spoken of this verse, amazing things have happened to at least some who read or listened. I had decided not to include it among our "pleasant stones," but just last night, as I finished writing the month of January, a dear friend, one who has just recently come all the way into the Christian life, surprised us by asking my friend Ellen and me to explain Galatians 2:20. I began to think about it again.

No-one can explain it.

But *anyone* can experience it. No-one can explain it and yet, in His time, the Holy Spirit puts within all sincere hearts an overwhelming desire to grasp its true meaning. Do we dare to be literal about it? Do we dare believe that the part of us which causes our trouble — our disposition toward sin — do we dare believe *that was* crucified with Christ? We not only dare, we *must!* This one facet of this crowded verse is perhaps more cutting than any diamond in our entire collection. This same dear friend, had answered her own question without realizing it, as she answered one of her old friends not long ago. When she refused to take part in an "other life" amusement, her friend said, "Aw, drop dead!" Lucy replied, "That's just what I've done!"

If we believe Christ did a *completed* work on Calvary, we must believe also that He included us in it!

But we must not only claim to believe it, we must *dare* to act as though we do. The next time you want to strike back, remind yourself that a dead man or a dead woman *cannot* strike back. And if Christ is to be trusted, we *were* crucified with Him on the Cross, and there is nothing left to do but claim it. Again, we have the Lord's own word for it:

. . . It is finished . . .

... **nevertheless I live** ... (Galatians 2:20).

HERE another sharp edge of our sharpest "clear stone" cuts through to reality. "I am crucified with Christ: nevertheless *I* live."

A contradiction?

No. A spiritual truth that must be *revealed* by the Holy Spirit Himself. One which cannot be grasped with the mind, nor set down in words. Certain things can be said *about* this truth, but perhaps even they will only be known intellectually *after* the truth itself has been revealed by the Spirit. Here is an excellent example of what Paul meant when he wrote that "the natural man receiveth not the things of the Spirit of God: for they are foolishness unto him: neither can he know them, because they are spiritually discerned." I mention this here for *you* particularly, if you are a new Christian. Don't be discouraged if these pages make no sense to you. Just go on. And trust God to reveal them in *His* time. When it is just right for *you* to know them. If you have not received Christ, you are still holding shut the door. Open it, and He will come in and with Him, light. The "nevertheless I live" rings glad bells in your heart, however, if you have begun to experience His life within you. You know now that He did come to bring abundant life, not to squelch you. As you watch Him untangle you and those around you, you know this in a way I could never express. You realize that eternal life is so much more than an endless life. It is a totally *new quality* of life right here — now. You look in His face with nothing between you and Him, and your heart sings: "This is living — because He is life!" And His heart answers yours: "Yes, my beloved . . . I am . . . life."

And this is life eternal, that they might know thee the only true God, and Jesus Christ whom thou hast sent.

FEBRUARY 3

. . . yet not I, but Christ liveth in me . . . (Galatians 2:20).

WE have just declared that Christians are those who are really *living*. And here Paul's "clear stone" flashes so brightly that we almost turn away in confusion. ". . . nevertheless I live; *yet not I* . . ."

What does this mean? In my own experience I have found that it means not the *I* with whom those around me had to contend for those years before my conversion to Jesus Christ. I believe it means "not (the false) I." Nevertheless my *true* self (the one God intended and created in the first place) really *lives*. My *false*, phony self — the self my unregenerate heart "created" and intended — is no longer the dominant factor. *She* was crucified when Jesus died. Therefore my *true self* lives.

And this true self is *able* to live for the first time because she is *enabled* to do it. Christ lives in me. Right in my mortal being. He didn't until I received Him there. But He does now. And how could anyone — *even I* — remain the same when my entire central being is kept constantly in contact with the sinless Son of God? How could even I remain the same when I have fallen under His influence?

This cannot be captured in words. They grow more stubborn as they go stumbling by, and I can only understand Paul's relief when the Spirit directed him simply to say: ". . . Christ in me, the hope of glory!"

. . . nevertheless . . . not I, but CHRIST liveth in me . . .

FEBRUARY 4

. . . and the life which I now live in the flesh I live by the faith of the Son of God, who loved me, and gave himself for me (Galatians 2:20).

IT is no wonder to me that so much has been written on this verse. It is no wonder to me that after having tried it once in my book EARLY WILL I SEEK THEE, I drew back at trying again. And yet God longs to have us all make *use* of it. It is not a goal too high for any one of us to reach. It is not a goal at all. It is a simple statement of fact. It is the *proof* of the victorious life. Not merely a challenge to live it!

And yet as mere mortals we need to know *how*.

If I accept the earth-shaking fact that I have already been crucified with Christ, that my old self need not trouble me again, that Christ Himself has come to live within me, I have come a long way in grasping this verse, but there must be more. At least that is not enough for me. To a certain extent I can lay hold of this grand pattern of God *after* He has revealed it to my spirit, but I am powerless to *act upon it*. And here, in the closing lines of the verse, Paul shares with us the fact that *he* had to have more too. Paul knew what it was to be totally without Christ. So quickly and lovingly he includes the "diamond-white" secret for us: ". . . and the (this) life which I now live in the flesh I (must) live (not by my own faith, that is impossible!) by the faith *of* the (same) Son of God, who loved me, and gave himself for me." Christ gave Himself to the Cross to free us of our sins. But it seems to me that here God is reminding us that He gave Himself *for our daily living, too. Christ is giving Himself to us right now.* And of course, right along with Him comes His faith. He has laid down His *entire* life for our *use*. Try to take it in. Oh, *try* to take it in.

Greater love hath no man than this, that a man lay down his life for his friends.

42

FEBRUARY 5

. . . It is finished . . . (John 19:30).

WHAT did Jesus mean when He said that? He meant so much more than we will know until we are with Him forever, and He meant so much more than we could express, if we could know. But concerning our co-crucifixion with Him on Calvary, concerning the true meaning of "I am crucified with Christ," I must share with you on this page *two* dazzling "clear stones" which God gave me to light up my dark mind during the first almost fearful days when I was trying to lay hold of real freedom. I came upon them in two most unexpected places. I had just read Dr. F. J. Huegel's great book FOREVER TRIUMPHANT, in which he described the power released on Calvary at the moment of Christ's death as a kind of radium to kill the cancer of sin in us. I strained to understand this. Desperately I needed to get hold of it. And then, riding alone on a train from Oregon to Chicago, the great truth of God's glorious power to *kill* grasped me.

"See now that I, even I, am he, and there is no god with me: *I kill, and I make alive* . . ." (Deuteronomy 32:39).

My heart leaped up with joy. Suddenly I *knew* what I had read so often, that resurrection life *can* only come out of death. Tears of relief forced me to stop reading, but I asked God for one more assurance. Several hours later, just before I went to sleep in my pullman room that night, suddenly these words were "tapped lightly" by the Holy Spirit and *another* "clear stone" revealed itself to convince me forever.

"The Lord killeth, and maketh alive: he bringeth down to the grave, and bringeth up . . . he bringeth low, and lifteth up" (I Samuel 2:6, 7).

My false self *has* been crucified with Christ.

That's why Jesus could cry with such certainty when He died:

. . . It is finished . . .

43

... let us therefore cast off the works of darkness, and let us put on the armour of light (Romans 13:12b).

THE redemption of Jesus Christ is as complete as "complete." When a thing is complete it is as final as when a thing is perfect. There are no degrees of completion or perfection. A perfect October apple is just as complete and as perfect in May when it is in bloom, as in October when it is harvested. We grow, but *complete* growth has already been provided for us.

We learn more and still more about how to take advantage of the work of Calvary, about how to make *use* of the life Christ laid down for us to use. But Calvary was complete, and the life has already been laid down.

I believe stressing the importance of choosing is merely being realistic. All the electrical power we now use was available and just as potent during all the ages before man learned how to harness it. So, we definitely must, by faith, make a direct move to make use of this complete redemption by casting off the works of darkness. God has all the power available to break a habit, but you will never know that power unless you choose to "cast off" that habit under the power of God. You are not doing it in your power. You are *choosing* to take what God so freely offers. We must "cast off the works of darkness."

And once again Paul warns us in the same sentence: ". . . let us therefore cast off the works of darkness, and (then) let us *put on the armour of light.*"

Casting off the works of darkness is all right to a degree. But when they are cast off, we are only *vulnerable* to *more* danger *until* we have *put on* the armour of light. As one friend of mine wrote in a letter, we are not to carry the helmet under our arm.

Put on the whole armour.

Now the God of hope fill you with all joy and peace in
believing . . . (Romans 15:13).

THIS (now) unmistakable "clear stone" would have been
dropped once into my basket of "purple stones" for comfort, or at least into the basket of "green stones" for
rejoicing that there is such a God of hope.

It could still fit in either place.

But I tapped it once lightly as my friend Ellen read it aloud,
and it fell open to expose two little words I hadn't even
noticed before! Words which "cut right through" to the "how"
of experiencing this joy and peace.

Perhaps you have read through some of Paul's "letter closings" or "salutations" with as much haste as I. Now and then
a phrase will strike into our very hearts or minds, but I confess skipping them too often. But God directed their writing,
and we only rob ourselves when we read them hastily. Here
in this one is a gleaming facet of secret instruction which exposes the way to receive this peace and joy.

"The God of hope fill you with all joy and peace *in believing!*"

In believing.

And blessedly Paul, again within the framework of the same
sentence, reminds and reassures us that he too knows we can't
manage this kind of believing on our own. "The God of
hope fill you with all joy and peace in believing, that ye may
abound in hope, *through the power of the Holy Ghost.*"

He will give us the power to believe.

. . . ye shall receive POWER, after that the Holy Ghost is
come upon you . . .

Ho, every one that thirsteth, come ye to the waters . . .
(Isaiah 55:1).

EVERY *one* that thirsteth . . . come.

Sometimes in the most impossible places my heart wants *me* to fall down and weep with thanksgiving that Christ died for everyone "that thirsteth"! Those urges to true worship come when I am suddenly impressed all over again that He loves the whole wide world because He *is* love and not because we are lovely.

Or lovable.

Those urges come when I am struck with the wonder that He loved me too. That He loves me now. Knowing me as He does. Having known me as He knew me all those years before I belonged to Him.

Those urges to kiss His feet come most strongly when I know in my heart that His love is universal and wide, stretching out like the arms of the Cross or it would never have included me too.

I once read of a three-year-old girl who complained because Jesus loved everybody in the world. She wanted Him to love her "best." And in reality, He did.

In reality He loves me "best." In reality He loves *you* "best" of anyone. Because God *is* love. He can love us all "best." His love is wide with no charmed circles. And yet His love is *so* wide that we are each in a charmed circle of our own with Him whose we are, because He bought us with His own life.

And this love has been shed abroad in our hearts, causing us to *want* Him to call "*every one* that thirsteth."

There is no other requirement but thirst. If we thirst, we are invited to come. Invited by Jesus Himself.

. . . If any man thirst, let him come unto me, and drink.

. . . and he that hath no money; come ye, buy, and eat . . .
(Isaiah 55:1).

THERE is no other requirement but *thirst*.
There is also no other requirement but *poverty*.
And there is no other requirement but *hunger*.

"Ho, *every one* that thirsteth, come ye to the waters . . ."
"Ho, *every one* . . . that hath no money; come ye, buy . . ."
Here are extended arms too low for anyone to crawl under
and too high for any to soar above! They are open arms, flung
wide at the dictate of a heart that is forever incomplete until
we come home to be one with Him as He and the Father
are one.

". . . he that hath no money; come . . . buy wine and milk
without money and without price."

This would seem to be another one of those contradictions.
And surely it is. This invitation is utterly contradictory to any
human reasoning. Even the highest form of human love has
its price. On God's love the only price is that we bring our
needs. God only wants us to be thirsty so He can give us
living water to drink. God only wants us to be poor so He
can show us that Christ has already bought us with His own
blood because He loves us so much. God only wants us to
be hungry so He can feed us on the bread of life.

And Jesus said unto them, I am the bread of life: he that
cometh to me shall never hunger; and he that believeth on
me shall never thirst.

Mine eyes are ever toward the LORD; for he shall pluck my feet out of the net (Psalm 25:15).

WHEN God invites every one to come, as surely He does through the open arms of His Son, Jesus Christ, He does not invite us to attend a meeting or to read a book or to observe a rite. He does not even invite us to embrace a religion.

He invites us clearly and plainly to enter into a relationship with a Person.

"Come unto *me* . . ."

"Look unto *me* . . ."

God invites us to come to Him in time of trouble and find out for ourselves that His *is* a shepherd heart. Throughout the Old Testament we find God's people calling on Him in times of trouble and heartbreak and loss. And God replied: "Comfort ye, my people . . . I am the Lord . . . that is my name." God knows we all get our feet tangled up in the "nets" of trouble and snap judgments and failure. He knows the "nets" of sorrow and heartache and sudden tragedy snarl around our feet, and He knows we would surely fall without Him to set us free. Certainly, it is completely true that God *is* a deliverer. That we *can* depend upon Him to get us out of our predicaments. *But,* there is a subtle trap here also. We are too prone to depend upon the *fact* of His deliverance, rather than upon God Himself. I am coming to believe that He does not even want us to depend upon His promises to deliver us, but upon *Himself.* That is why David wrote about the Lord first in this verse and *then* about the net. Our tendency is to look at our feet tangled up in the net and try to quote Scripture verses that suit our special trouble. But David, the man after God's own heart, says: "Mine eyes are ever toward the *Lord;* for he shall pluck my feet out of the net." Toward the Lord — not the net.

Looking unto Jesus, the author and finisher of our faith . . .

Be not wise in thine own eyes: fear the LORD, and depart
from evil (Proverbs 3:7).

THE reason we are not to look at the net and the reason
for our "tangle," is that what gets our attention gets *us*.
In and out of my reading and study and prayer comes
the constant reminder from God that all sin begins in the
thought life and that my every thought must be brought into
captivity to Christ. Here is the reminder once more in the
three-word admonition in this Proverb to "depart from evil."

In Proverbs 4:15 we find still another one:

"Avoid it, pass not by it, turn from it, and pass away."
Still another Proverb in chapter 6: "Can a man take fire into
his bosom, and his clothes not be burned?"

Can you and I hold critical thoughts, lustful thoughts,
thoughts of revenge, can we cling to thoughts of self-pity and
self-defense, and not be burned? God tells us over and over
again that we are to "depart from evil." I am just as capable
as you of nursing my self-inflicted wound, of feeling sorry for
myself. I am just as likely as you are to *rebel* at "turning
away" from a sinful idea which attracts me. God does not
ask us if we *want* to "depart from evil." He simply tells us to
"avoid it, pass not by it" — in other words, why make it harder
for ourselves? If an alcoholic stands outside a bar and sniffs
the blend of gin and vermouth that used to make up his
favorite dry martinis, he is only asking for trouble.

If God has told you to break up a relationship and you
spend your evenings alone, outwardly obeying, but savoring
and reliving old memories, you are still holding your own
thoughts captive in a deadly vise, and God warns you that
this is the hard way! I know you cannot cancel memory. But
you can invite God *into it*. When the person or the thing
comes to mind, give it to Christ at once. Then "turn away."

Can one go upon hot coals, and his feet not be burned?
Look unto me and be ye saved.

The LORD by wisdom hath founded the earth; by understanding hath he established the heavens. By his knowledge
the depths are broken up, and the clouds drop down the dew
(Proverbs 3:19, 20).

A S we have already said, God created our minds a certain way. "The Lord by wisdom hath founded the earth;
by understanding hath he established the heavens."

By the same wisdom and by the same understanding did
God create *us*.

By the same wisdom and by the same understanding does
He long to "establish" us. To give us the "feel" of the Rock
beneath our feet. To lift us up onto ever higher ground.

By this same knowledge does the Holy Spirit "break up our
depths" when we give Him freedom to work there. God knows
about your old thought patterns, and He knows about mine.
In the realm of our subconscious minds, as well as in our
conscious minds, God is at work, through the Holy Spirit
"breaking up our depths" in order to free us from the old
tyrannies. He has full knowledge of what He's doing there
too. And by the same knowledge that causes the clouds to
drop dew, He causes new refreshing to fall upon our spirits
because He also knows how much we need refreshing even
when our "depths are being broken up" by the gentle, capable hand that created us. God knows of the pain of the
"maimed" new life. He understands the grief that lingers
when that certain phase — or person — is gone forever. God
alone truly understands the pain of emptiness because He
Himself created living creatures to fill the *first void* "in the
beginning."

"The LORD by wisdom hath founded the earth . . ." We
can rely upon Him for complete understanding because "by
understanding hath he established" it all. We are not too
much for Him!

In the beginning, God . . .

The way of the wicked is as darkness: they know not at what they stumble (Proverbs 4:19).

HAVE you passed this proverb by, almost as though it is nothing more than a warning to the wicked? Read it again? It is among the most cutting of all the "clear stones." And it has directly to do with us as followers of Jesus Christ; with those of us who have been *given* His righteousness. It is a double-edged warning which most of us never notice. At least our behavior indicates that we don't notice it. Because how many times have *you* condemned someone who is *not* a Christian, simply because he or she did not act in a Christian manner? Here is an illustration: A zealous, generous Christian man once testified that he was so tough on the men who worked for him because of their swearing that he heard one of them say, "Don't *say* that around Mr. .... He'll give you h——! He's a Christian!" This dear, misguided brother was *pleased* about that. He felt unconsciously superior. As I understand it, he believed somehow that unconverted men should *not* swear! *He* was a Christian. *His* sins had been forgiven by the blood of Jesus Christ. He had been given a *new* nature. Of course, he didn't swear anymore.

But his attitude said: "These men shouldn't do it, either." And why wouldn't they do it? They were *not* Christians. God reminds us over and over that darkness is *not* light. How foolish to be surprised at a sinner who acts like a sinner. Does God not remind us that "the path of the just is as the shining light"? We *should* be able to see! But doesn't God also warn us that we are to remember in our lack of love for sinners that "the way of the wicked is as darkness"?

My son, attend to my words; incline thine ear unto my sayings.
For who maketh thee to differ from another? and what hast thou that thou didst not receive?

Judge not, that ye be not judged . . . And why beholdest thou the mote that is in thy brother's eye, but considerest not the beam that is in thine own eye? (Matthew 7:1, 3).

HAVE you ever thought of the occasional seeming exaggeration in speech which Jesus used when He was teaching on earth? Now and then He seems to stab us with such an extreme analogy or simile that we just have to notice it!

The camel going through the eye of the needle is, to me, not as sharp an illustration of this teaching pattern as the verses quoted at the top of this page. It is as though Jesus stopped at nothing to impress upon us the seriousness of the sin of judging others. I have heard it said that we cannot sit in the judge's seat and the witness box at the same time.

Jesus made a fantastic statement to capture our attention in these verses.

"And why beholdest thou the mote that is in thy brother's eye, but considerest not the *beam* that is in thine own eye?" Some of the current translations use the word "plank" instead of "beam." No matter. It is evident that Jesus was trying to shock us into attention. Because whoever heard of anyone having an eye big enough to contain a plank or a beam? But Jesus didn't stop with this strong warning about condemnation. He went on to the Cross to prove that in *His* heart was no condemnation. He hung there asking for forgiveness for those who were enjoying His death! He used this striking expression to show God's loathing of condemnation, and then did what He did on Calvary to illustrate His point.

For God sent not his Son into the world to condemn the world; but that the world through him might be saved.

Because strait is the gate, and narrow is the way, which
leadeth unto life, and few there be that find it (Matthew
7:14).

SOME of us seem to take these very words of Jesus and
use them as grounds for judging. Use them to twist His
original meaning to *our* advantage. Shame breaks upon us
when we are willing to let this "clear stone" split to show our
sin of judging one another, glibly using Christ's own words in
the process.

Jesus stated a fact when He remarked that the gate into
the victorious life is strait and the way into oneness with Himself is narrow. The highway of holy obedience *is* blessedly
narrow. I'm glad that it is. Otherwise, knowing myself, I'd
stray in this direction and that and lose my way. It is joyfully narrow. It holds no dark corners and no bypaths to explore. It is just wide enough for us always to be able to see
Jesus up ahead, walking it first. It is wonderfully simple because it is wonderfully narrow. Jesus was simply stating a
fact.

And we twist that fact to make us somehow seem *superior*
because we have not entered into the "wide gate" or because
we no longer walk the "broad way." What a relief and what
shame come at once when we realize over and over again
that the Lord Jesus knows our *hearts!* He knew we'd twist
this statement to our own advantage. And so *before* He said
what He said about the "narrow way" with few upon it, He
took care to *command* us not to judge one another. The follower of Jesus Christ is the last person on earth who should
feel exclusive. ". . . narrow *is* the way, and few there be that
find it." This is true. But these few have not found it by
their own superior efforts. And the number is not few because of the merit of the "few." The number is few because
these follow a Master who —

. . . took a towel . . . and began to wash the disciples' feet . . .

But he said, Nay; lest while ye gather up the tares, ye root up also the wheat with them (Matthew 13:29).

JESUS had just told the parable of the wheat and the tares. And His disciples in those days wanted to leap up and do just what His disciples now are still doing. They wanted to plunge right in and pull out the "tares" themselves. Perhaps I am guilty of indulging in the very point I am warning against — judging. If I am, God forgive me and show me. But as I have gone from church to church and from denomination to denomination I have been reminded of this warning of Jesus to His disciples the day they wanted to flex their muscles and "get in there and fight" and help the Lord do the work which the Father Himself gave over completely to Christ. The Father has turned all judgment over to our Saviour. Could it be that we haven't taken the Father seriously in this act of His?

Once more Jesus is warning us because He knows what is in man. "Don't uproot anything now — you might tear out some of my precious wheat while you're at it." So often my heart has bled because one "doctrinally correct" brother whom I love is flexing his "judging" muscles against another brother whom I also love. And in the process, almost invariably, I learn of one or two non-Christians who jump quickly to use the "doctrinally correct" brother's fighting spirit as an excuse *not* to become a Christian. I jumped at it myself once many years ago as I laughingly turned the page on a newspaper account of one group blasting the marginal beliefs of another in the same denomination. My remark went something like this, "How do those Christians expect me to agree with them when they can't even agree with each other?"

. . . NAY; lest while ye gather up the tares, ye root up also the wheat with them.

And into whatsoever city or town ye shall enter, enquire
who in it is worthy; and there abide till ye go thence. And
when ye come into an house, salute it. And if the house be
worthy, let your peace come upon it: but if it be not worthy,
let your peace return to you. And whosoever shall not
receive you, nor hear your words, when ye depart out of that
house or city, shake off the dust of your feet (Matthew
10:11-14).

WHAT Jesus is saying here strikes me as being very
gentle, and deep with the true humor of heaven.
Many of us take it as instructions to flaunt our "su-
periority" again because *we* have the truth and those who "do
not receive us" are not "worthy" of our presence, and so we
toss our heads and shake the dust from our feet and flounce
on. I believe Jesus might have smiled as He said, "And if
the house be not worthy, let your peace return to you." After
all, if you and I give our peace to anyone and that person
refuses it — even if he or she throws it back in our faces —
our peace is *returning* to us, isn't it? It seems to me Jesus
is simply reminding us that the Christian just can't lose. The
truly humble Christian cannot even be insulted. We are just
to "shake it off" and go on in the name of Jesus.

". . . when they persecute you in this city, flee ye into
another . . ." Just go on.

Just go on.

Nothing changes Jesus Christ. You and I can always just
"let our peace return to us" and go on. The "diamond-clear"
truth here is that if we do *not* offer peace, but ill will, toward
those who do not receive us well, then we cannot get peace
back in return.

. . . Let your PEACE return to you . . .

Fear them not therefore: for there is nothing covered, that shall not be revealed; and hid, that shall not be known (Matthew 10:26).

THIS "clear stone" verse splits into many hidden meanings. Some of which most of us might not grasp. But one "depth" lights up to me as I read what Christ spoke before and after this verse, and so I have put it in our collection of "clear stones" because it is to me, at least, an unexpected meaning. And it does "cut right through" much of the cause for hurt feelings among us.

When someone criticizes us or otherwise cuts us with a remark or an action, it seems to me Jesus is saying: "Fear them not: . . . for there is nothing covered that shall not be revealed." In other words, if we are being accused unjustly, God will take care of revealing it. We must let the full light of Calvary fall upon ourselves in the matter, of course, and let the Holy Spirit show us who is right and who is wrong in the particular situation. Perhaps there are degrees of right and wrong on both sides. We must face this too. But the beginning of our victory in the situation, whether we are right or wrong, is to remember that "nothing is covered" with God. Not even your aching heart. He cares very much about the whole thing which is causing you pain right now. Hear Jesus say: "Are not two sparrows sold for a farthing? and one of them shall not fall on the ground without your Father."

Not only will the Father *know* when the sparrow falls; Jesus says the sparrow will not fall without the *Father*. He'll *be there*. So He is there in this thing with you right now. Caring with all His tender heart.

. . . I will never leave thee nor forsake thee.

Fear ye not therefore, ye are of more value than many
sparrows (Matthew 10:31).

WHEN my parents built the home in which they now
live, my father indulged his extreme love of windows.
As a consequence, our living room is almost entirely
picture windows. The effect is lovely and brings the outside
"in" and mother's indoor plants grow as though they knew
the outside was "in" and even on a dark day, it is a cheerful,
light room. But there is a tragic aspect. The songbirds who
grow fat and glossy eating the splendid assortment of special
songbird seeds my daddy buys by the sack, don't understand
about picture windows. And now and then, as one bright-
backed cardinal takes a sharp swoop from an oak bough
toward what he thinks is another oak bough, I hear a thud
and outside on the ground, the soft breast turned up, a red-
bird with a broken back has illustrated the words of Christ:
". . . one of them shall not fall on the ground without your
Father . . ." I know as I stand there breathing a little prayer
of thanksgiving that He is there with the quiet bird, that the
very hairs of our heads *are* numbered.

If only we could get hold of the life-changing fact that
there are no little things with God! Your seemingly small
trouble is of eternal importance to Him this moment. He has
some lovely lesson in it for you. A lesson, which if well
learned now, will affect you eternally. If you and I refuse to
learn it now, He still cares. The next time we "fall to the
ground" He will still be there.

Fear ye not therefore . . . It is I . . . ye are of more value
than many sparrows.

**Think not that I am come to send peace on earth: I came
not to send peace, but a sword (Matthew 10:34).**

WHAT a strange thing for the Prince of Peace to declare! But tap this "clear stone" lightly under the direction of the Holy Spirit and we find that He did not come to send peace, He came *as* peace. He came declaring that He *is* our peace, and that outside of Him there is none. No peace anywhere. For anyone.

"Think not that I am come to send peace on earth . . ."

". . . On earth peace, good will toward men."

These do not contradict themselves except to the heart still shut away in darkness. "I came not to send peace, but a sword." And then Jesus goes on to explain that He will set a man against his father, a daughter against her mother. But this is the scalpel act which must come before true peace can come. If Christ came merely saying: "Now, dear children, let us all get along with each other and act peaceful, no matter how much selfishness and sin remain in our hearts . . . let's spoil our mothers and pamper our fathers and lavish gifts upon our children to show we are good sports, even if we disagree about God and His claims upon our lives . . ." — if Christ came sending this kind of "psychological" peace, He would be a fiend.

Being God, He knows that there *is* no eternal peace outside of obedience to God. And so He came, not to get us all to agree with each other by agreeing with us Himself. He came to declare the heart of God and the claims of God and to show *true* caring and *true* compassion toward us by making it very clear that there can be no compromise between us and Himself for the sake of the family. If we remain true to Him, then we can trust Him to handle the family. He did not come to reconcile us to each other, or Himself to *us*.

. . . God was in Christ reconciling the world unto himself . . .

And he that taketh not his cross, and followeth after me, is not worthy of me (Matthew 10:38).

I have known many new Christians who immediately get set to "do battle" with their friends and family who may not approve of their new walk with Christ. I was guilty of some of this myself in the early days of my Christian life. It is quite natural. That's *just* what it is, in fact.

It is "natural."

It is in part, at least, our flaming egos wanting to be proven right. I do not say it is all this. Much of it is because we are so dazzled by the new light we have, we can't wait for our loved ones to see it too. We haven't found out yet that *only* the Holy Spirit can convince people that Christ died for their sins. We sincerely want them to see what we see, but it *is* still our flaming "natural" egos which cause us to obey Christ's instructions often in the wrong spirit.

". . . I am come to set a man at variance against his father, and the daughter against her mother . . ." But He didn't say we were to throw scenes and be sarcastic and use harsh words. We are merely to be willing to be *misunderstood* by them, *if* need be, and refuse to compromise. But we are to do it in the same spirit in which Christ carried His Cross.

". . . he that taketh not his cross, and followeth after *me*, is not worthy of me." If we follow after *Him*, we follow in His footsteps. And the Lord Jesus treads softly when He is near the hearts of those who do not yet know Him.

. . . he that taketh not his OWN cross, and followeth after ME, is not worthy of me.

. . . Woman, where are those thine accusers? . . . (John 8:10b).

JESUS warns us carefully that His presence in our lives will oftentimes bring a sword between us and our loved ones who do not yet know Him. But the little sharp "clear stone" we look at now flashes to my mind as I think on what Jesus must have meant when He said we were to be willing to take up *our* crosses and follow *Him*. In the same spirit in which He carried His Cross in the midst of persecution and jeers and ridicule.

Perhaps your mother or your father or your brother or sister or friend or husband is not a follower of Jesus Christ. Perhaps you are an exuberant *new* follower. Perhaps you have known Him for a long, long time and are still living among those who do not. Perhaps they give you a "rough time," as we say. Jesus warned us about this, but He also showed us by His personal behavior, even on His way to the Cross, that we are *not* to fight back. We are not to adjust our "martyr's crowns" and act superior. We are not to argue. We are not to accuse. We are not to lecture. We are not to condemn. Let this truth shine to the depths of our beings: The Lord Jesus treads *softly* when He is near the hearts of those who do not yet know Him! He drove the religiosos from the temple, and He spoke harshly to the Pharisees of His day, but He didn't even *look* at the sinful woman the religious people wanted to stone, for fear of embarrassing her. He is always gentle with sinners. He Himself experienced the pain of sin when He took our sins into His own heart on Calvary. He is always tender with those still in darkness. Not soft, but gentle. He never compromises His holiness, but He remembers the pain of sin. He who was sinless, bore the pain of the sin of the entire world in His own heart on Calvary, and He will never forget it. Therefore it would be impossible for the Lord Jesus to be harsh with sinners still in darkness.

For he hath made him to be sin for us, who knew no sin . . .
. . . Woman, neither do I condemn thee: go, and sin no more.

There cometh a woman of Samaria to draw water: Jesus saith unto her, Give me to drink (John 4:7).

JESUS was not only always gentle with those who were still locked up in the prison of themselves; He actually had true *empathy* with them. Webster defines the noun *empathy* as the "imaginative projection of one's own consciousness into another being." My favorite newspaper columnist, Mr. Sidney J. Harris of the *Chicago Daily News*, defines it even more clearly: "Sympathy is feeling 'for' someone else; *empathy* is feeling 'with' him."

Jesus Christ is the master of empathy. He made complete identification with us, and no-one can doubt that He felt "with" those He met, when He was on earth. No-one who knows Him now doubts that He still feels and suffers with us. He didn't just sympathize with man in his lost condition, He *became* Man. He was still God, but perfectly human too! One striking illustration of His ability to feel *with* someone else was His behavior at the well with the immoral, socially inferior Samaritan woman. Jesus was very tired. He had gone there to rest. But He was never *too* tired, even while carrying a Cross up a hill, to feel "with" those around Him. And to prove that He knew exactly how that outcast, guilty woman felt, He, the Son of God, put Himself in the position of helping her hold up her head a little. He used the same word "woman" in addressing her as He used in speaking to His own mother from the Cross! Jesus was human as well as divine, and He knew from His own experience that it does something for us to have someone say, "Thank you." We want to feel needed.

Jesus won this woman to Himself because He *was* the Messiah, but also because He was willing to ask *her* to do Him a favor.

Woman . . . give me to drink . . .

That they all may be one; as thou, Father, art in me, and I
in thee, that they also may be one in us: that the world may
believe that thou hast sent me (John 17:21).

NO "clear stone" in our collection has struck into my mind
and heart with more sharpness than this one. I am
further "cut" by it when I remember that it came from
the lips of the Saviour just a few hours before they killed
Him. It was spoken by His human lips, but it sprang from
His heart which was the heart of God.

Jesus praying there that night for us to be *one!*

Jesus praying like that about us because He knew us so
well. Knew how our marginal differences would divide us.

The very Son of God prayed and then repeated His prayer
to the Father that we might be one as they were one. His
Saviour heart wanted us to be together. His shepherd heart
wanted us to be together. He knew He prayed in the Father's
will because the Father heart wanted us to be together. And
the sharp edge goes into our hearts right here: *One of the
very issues which have so divided us was the reason Jesus
gave for His prayer that we would be united in love.*

". . . that the world may believe that thou hast sent me
. . ." We fight over the Divinity of Christ . . . whether or
not the Father sent Him, and He pleaded that we would *not*
do this very thing. If I did not believe Jesus Christ was sent
by the Father, that He and He alone is the *one divine Son of
God,* I would not be a Christian at all. This was what convinced me. I wanted God to turn out to be Jesus Christ.
And He did. But Jesus, knowing us, anticipated our taking
this central and most blessed truth and making it a battle-
field to divide us. Oh, the amazing wisdom of God to us-ward!
Jesus saw that our unity with each other would *prove* His
divinity to the world.

I in them, and thou in me, that they may be made perfect
in ONE; . . . that the world may BELIEVE that thou hast
sent me . . .

Pilate saith unto him, What is truth? And when he had said this, he went out again unto the Jews, and saith unto them, I find in him no fault at all (John 18:38).

PERHAPS you are not convinced, as you "share my pleasant stones," that Jesus Christ *is* the only Son of God. That the only way to the Father is by faith in this same Jesus. No doubt, most who read this will be His . . . but some of you have written to me after reading one or more of my other books, and I know you are still searching. You stimulate me and force me to learn more of what He is really like, and I *do* thank you from my heart. Believe me, I don't condemn you for not believing. I am the last one who should do that. My heart aches over your indecision because I can feel it *with you*. This "stone" is surely for non-believers. But those of you who are His own, may well examine it, too. We are guilty of doing as did Pilate when we disobey.

Many persons quite sincerely ask, as did Pilate, "What *is* truth?" But before they are willing to enter into a personal relationship with the One who *is* Truth, they "go out again" and say in effect: "Well, I looked into Christianity, and I found Jesus a very admirable person, but I am not convinced that He is God." "Pilate saith unto him, What is truth? And when he had said this, (with no more knowledge of Jesus) he went out . . . and saith unto them, I find in him no fault at all."

Many persons inquire, find no fault in Him, but go out again, still searching. Unless we take His word for it that He *is* "the way, the *truth* and the life," we not only go out again unfulfilled; we fall into Pilate's fatal trap, as the years go on. We listen to the crowd roar, and fearing what they will say about us, we follow Pilate. The "clear stone" cuts deeply in the first verse of the next chapter: (John 19:1).

Then Pilate therefore took Jesus, and scourged him.

Jesus saith unto him, If I will that he tarry till I come, what is that to thee? follow thou me (John 21:22).

PETER was afraid John would get something he missed. He doubted the love of Jesus for a moment, as he learns from the Master Himself about his own (Peter's) death, and wants to be sure John gets no less. Jesus' "diamond-sharp" answer is our "stone" for contemplation this time.

"If I will that he (John) tarry till I come, what is that to thee (Peter)? Follow thou me." Peter's predicament is so human and so understandable. Jesus understood it, too. That's why He went straight to the only point that would help Peter: *Complete and uncomplaining obedience to Himself.*

How often have you attempted to inquire of the Lord about some Christian brother or sister whose lot seems to be better than yours? How often have we carefully told the Lord everything that is wrong in the attitudes and conducts of our brothers and sisters? And how often have we heard the Lord Jesus gently, but firmly reply, as He did to Peter: "What is that to thee? follow thou me."

Once in particular did He prompt *me* with this verse. In my prayer, I was explaining in colorful terms, the shortcomings of a Christian brother. Then came the word: "What is that to thee? follow thou me!" And more yet: "If you see his failings, it is *only* because I have *given* you the insight to see them. Your part is to turn your criticism to *true* intercession." There was still more to come: "And even after you have prayed in love for this brother, he may still go on behaving in the same way. But your only concern is to see to it that you *increase* your own value to me to help make up for his defects!"

The Lord Jesus is not being hard here.

He is showing His *need* for us, and He is showing His love.

If I will that he tarry till I come, what is that to thee? follow thou me. . . . The fields . . . are white already to harvest . . . but the labourers are few.

I have blotted out, as a thick cloud, thy transgressions, and, as a cloud, thy sins: return unto me; for I have redeemed thee (Isaiah 44:22).

THIS "clear stone" must be shared because it "cuts right through" the thick coating of "false guilt" inside which so many sincere Christians gasp for spiritual air. I have spoken to such persons who have neither the insight nor the courage to take what has already been done for them. The blood of Calvary does not avail for you, according to what *you* think about the blackness of your sin!

The blood of Calvary covers *everything*, not because the sin isn't "too bad," but because of whose blood it is.

One woman was practically an invalid; she had slept until noon for years and had taken expensive mineral baths all over the country. Then my friend Ellen helped her "bury" the guilt of a teen-aged sin which still tormented her. *Christ had forgiven her but she would not forgive herself.* In one sense she was making Calvary "much ado about nothing." Suddenly she saw it, accepted what He had already done for her, forgave herself, and now she is a radiant, healthy, active Christian, to whom others come for help.

If some past sin still haunts you, don't do another thing until you have accepted His forgiveness. If you've asked, He has already forgiven you. Perhaps you asked years ago, as did our friend. And all this time you have been hurting His cause because you refuse to forgive yourself and to take what He gave His life to make possible.

No more discussion is really required. We must simply take God's word for it, and He says:

I have BLOTTED OUT, as a thick cloud, thy transgressions, and, as a cloud, thy sins: RETURN UNTO ME; for I have (long ago) redeemed thee.

How oft did they provoke him in the wilderness, and grieve
him in the desert!
Yea, they turned back and tempted God, and limited the
Holy One of Israel (Psalm 78:40, 41).

I F you and I are holding onto old guilts and pretending to
ourselves and others that we are just so "low" that we feel
God can't forgive us for "*this* one," we had better stop
provoking Him in the "wilderness" of our own towering egos,
and we had better stop grieving Him in the "desert" of our
sandy hearts.

We are ego-centered if we refuse His forgiveness because
we cling to something *we* did which was "so dreadful" *He* can't
cope with it. And we know the pain of the dry and sandy
heart in which there is no oasis-pool of concern for anyone
but ourselves. We don't mean to turn in upon ourselves. But
when we carry unnecessary guilt, we *do*. We are so painfully
aware of *us* that we lose our awareness of those around us.

Calvary is complete.

We "limit the Holy One of Israel" when we clutch our
old thought patterns and run from psychiatrist to minister to
doctor, when *He* says to us:

I have blotted out . . . thy transgressions, and . . . thy
sins: RETURN UNTO ME; for I have redeemed thee . . .
I have called thee by thy name; thou art mine.

Wherefore seeing we also are compassed about with so great a cloud of witnesses, let us lay aside every weight, and the sin which doth so easily beset us, and let us run with patience the race that is set before us. Looking unto Jesus the author and finisher of our faith . . . (Hebrews 12:1, 2).

SEEING that there are two thousand years of "witnesses" to prove that the indwelling life of Christ *works* even in the "tight places," we really have no excuse at all not to *let* it work for us, too. This is the last "clear stone" we will share together for now, and I have chosen it purposely as the last. It too, "cuts right through" to leave no question marks as to what we are to do in order to know the peace and the continuous victory of the "life hid with Christ in God."

Quite simply God lets us know that He knows about all those particular "besetting sins" of ours, and quite simply He tells us to lay them aside. *All of them.* Every sin is a weight, holding us earth-bound. We are already seated in heavenly places in Christ Jesus, and again we "limit the Holy One" if we do *not* choose to lay aside the weights so that we *can* run! We are also told that we must "run with patience the race that is set before us." These are not idle words. If you see someone is getting ahead of you, just keep running — *with patience.* No need to flare at that person. Impatience is simply lack of love. We are to run with patience. If someone else is ahead, that's all right. It doesn't change Jesus Christ. And if we have "laid aside every weight" and if we are running, that is our part. The rest is up to God.

And God will take care of the end of the race, providing we are looking unto Jesus!

If our eyes are fixed on Him, we don't know who is winning the race anyway. We are just on our way toward Him. And nothing ever changes Him.

Jesus Christ the same yesterday, and to day, and for ever.

RED STONES

"Red stones" throughout the ages have gathered their share of strange legends as men have searched for the truth and grabbed at the ever-crumbling foundations of superstition and mythology. Red gems, such as the ruby and the garnet or carbuncle have long been the symbols of love and divine power over temptation and danger.

Christ, the cornerstone of all truth, has set us free from the need to clutch at such pathetic "remedies" for coping with life. But to me, certain verses of Scripture fall easily into my collection of "red stones," as certain others fell into the basket of "clear stones."

Onto my heap of "red stones" I want to place the verses which speak of God's love, of His passion, His death, His resurrection life, and the wonder of His indwelling. Here I want to add also the "pleasant stones" which have proven to me that God's power over temptation is NOT limited by MY "beloved temptations"!

The possessor of a flawless ruby or carbuncle was once thought to be free from danger because the ruby was believed to have its own radiance which it LOST at the approach of a foe, thereby warning its owner in time. But Christ has come! We can depend upon OUR "red stones" to INCREASE in radiance because He prayed that the Father would send the Spirit of Truth to live IN us and to teach us what we need to know — always in time to avoid spiritual disaster.

Now, share my "pleasant red stones."

> In the year that king Uzziah died I saw also the Lord
> sitting upon a throne, high and lifted up, and his train
> filled the temple (Isaiah 6:1).

I well remember the first time I learned that "In the year that king Uzziah died" meant more than merely an historical date. Uzziah was one of the great kings of Judah. He made great improvement in Judah's military strength; he developed their agricultural resources; he strengthened the very walls of Jerusalem. Uzziah *was* a great king. And when he died of leprosy, his people were shattered emotionally. To them, tragedy lay all around everywhere. Their king was dead and of an outcaste's disease! But, our God is a Redeemer, and He used even this tragic death, to shock His prophet Isaiah into *seeing* Him as He is — high and lifted up.

Isaiah was a godly man before Uzziah's death. But so great a human being was Uzziah, that even Isaiah could not see God clearly. So when Uzziah *died*, Isaiah began to *see*.

Who has to die before you can begin to see God as He is — high and lifted up? Not merely as Someone available to help you out of your difficulty with as little inconvenience to you as possible, but "the Lord sitting upon a throne, high and lifted up" and His train filling the entire temple of the universe! *Who* has to die before we *can* or *will* see?

Perhaps no-one physically. Or perhaps someone *will* die. At any rate, God will *use* the tragedy which shocks us to give us a better look at Himself, if you and I will only *look*. But no-one needs to die, if we will but let God move into the center of our lives and allow Him to place that other person or those persons where *He* wants them to be. No-one but the living God, who wants to live His holy life right *in* us, has a right to the throne of our lives. It isn't fair to *anyone* to keep Him off the throne. Least of all is it fair to the mere human being whom we force to sit there.

> . . . Holy, holy, holy, is the Lord of hosts: the whole earth
> is full of HIS glory.

In the year that king Uzziah died I saw ... the Lord sitting
upon a throne ... Then said I, Woe is me! for I am undone;
because I am a man of unclean lips, and I dwell in the midst
of a people of unclean lips: for mine eyes have seen the
King, the LORD of hosts (Isaiah 6:1a, 5).

WHEN King Uzziah died, then the prophet Isaiah began to see God as He really is. And when he began to see God, he also began to see himself too — as *he* really was! ". . . I am a man of unclean lips." When God opens our eyes, He opens them so we can see in both directions. We can see God as He is, and we can also see ourselves as we are. One-directional vision is not enough. In fact, we cannot see ourselves as we really are, in need of the Saviour, *until* we see God as He is, in His uncompromising holiness. It is not only unscriptural, it is *futile* for a Christian to point a condemning finger at someone who is not a Christian. For a Christian to attempt to "break someone of a habit" is ridiculous. Only the Holy Spirit, by lighting up the face of Jesus Christ, can convince a man or woman of unclean lips. Only the Holy Spirit can convince a Christian that, even with the "correct doctrine," he also may be a man of unclean lips dwelling in the midst of a people of unclean lips. Oh, my brothers and my sisters, let *us* look at God as He was in Christ, "high and lifted up" on the Cross, with our sin breaking His pure heart as He prays for us and pours out His blood that we may no longer be "undone"! Our part is not to point accusing fingers at those for whom "Uzziah has not yet died." Christ *has* died for them, and if we but look at Him, we will draw back our fingers and hide our own faces in our hands as we cry:

Woe is me! . . . mine eyes have seen the KING, the LORD
of hosts.

Then flew one of the seraphims unto me, having a live coal
in his hand, which he had taken with the tongs from off the
altar (Isaiah 6:6).

PERHAPS you are asking why these particular verses are
included in our collection of "red stones" which remind
us of the love and the indwelling life of God. God has
worked out this wonderful arrangement whereby He *can* come
and live His holy life, right *in us;* but first we need cleansing.

He is a holy God, and we are a people of unclean lips.
We have all "sinned and come short of the glory of God."
We must be fit for Him to dwell in us before He can come
in. Before we can experience His life within us, we must have
our sins washed away. He has made this possible and He has
the "seraphims" ready to keep us fit.

Perhaps the "seraphim" God has ready to fly unto *you* right
now doesn't look much like your idea of a seraphim. This
messenger may look like your mother-in-law or your boss.
But our God is a *Redeemer* and the "seraphim" will fly unto
you with a live coal from off the altar, and God will do His
part if we are willing to do ours. We are to receive the
"seraphims" *as they are.*

Perhaps the "live coal" is a stinging blast of criticism or a
slap of lofty condescension. God is *in* it and we are to accept
it from Him as a sign that He wants to change us so much
right there on that point that nothing "unclean" will rise up
within us no matter how many "seraphims" fly at us.

The "seraphim" flying at you right now may look like that
one person whom you just "can't take." Trust God's timing.
See your need to be able to love — even that particular "seraphim." For woe are we if we can't. We are simply "undone."
Thank God for showing us this new need. All we need to come
to Him is — need.

Him that cometh to me I will in no wise cast out . . .

Then flew one of the seraphims unto me, having a live coal in his hand, which he had taken with the tongs from off the altar. And he laid it upon my mouth, and said, Lo, this hath touched thy lips; and thine iniquity is taken away, and thy sin purged (Isaiah 6:6, 7).

THE "seraphim" did not do the cleansing. The Lord *used* the "seraphim" to handle the live coal from off the altar. We are cleansed by the holy fire of God's love.

"For God *so loved* the world," and then He gave.

What Jesus Christ did on Calvary was more than enough to cleanse even our lips. To purge even our sins. To take away even our iniquity.

Those of us who have seen God in the face of Jesus Christ know something of the depth of that sin. Only God could bear to know it all the way down! And it broke even His heart. But those of us who have seen Christ have at least seen *some* of our deep need for cleansing. And when we really see it and become honest with ourselves and before God, we welcome the onflying "seraphims" holding the cleansing fire toward our lips.

We welcome them and hold up our mouths to be touched and weep softly so as not to miss one word which God is saying to us through this often painful ordeal. Tenderly, surely, God speaks through this difficult person, through this seemingly unbearable time: "While you were yet sinners, I died for you . . ."

. . . this hath touched thy lips; and thine iniquity is taken away, and thy sin purged.

*Also I heard the voice of the Lord, saying, Whom shall
I send, and who will go for us? Then said I, Here am I;
send me (Isaiah 6:8).*

MANY people wonder and fret and act "put upon" by
God Himself, because they are "ready" for service
and God does not open any doors. We say we are
"dying to do this or that."

Let's face it. God has *already died* to be able to use us.
We *never* need to pray, "O Lord, please use me." This is
totally unnecessary in the light of what Christ has already
completed on Calvary.

Please do not misunderstand. Perhaps God does not *seem*
to be using you now, but later on you will see that He has
all along been using you in a way you didn't even suspect.
Or He is making you ready to be used.

Please do not jump to the conclusion that I am saying
you are not good enough to be used. No-one is. But it
doesn't take much of a man to be a useful Christian, it
just takes *all* of him. And sometimes even our desire to be
used must be purged away under the "live coal" of in-
activity. *We* do not *know* when we are ready. Only God
knows that. And since He has already died to be able to use
us, don't you think He will call us out at just the right time?

He will not only call us out, He will send us well supplied
with all we need. After all, hasn't He promised to fill us with
Himself? Could we need anything else if we are actually filled
with the very life of God Himself?

"Then said I, Lord, how long? And he answered, Until
the cities be wasted without inhabitant, and the houses without man, and the land be utterly desolate." When we are
really empty of ourselves and our beloved plans and schemes
"for His glory," then He will send us out. Filled with Himself.

*If any man hear my voice, and open the door, I will come
in . . . go ye.*

> And I will pray the Father, and he shall give you another Comforter, that he may abide with you forever; . . . I will not leave you comfortless: I will come to you (John 14:16, 18).

OUR "red stone" collection of verses speaks to me of the very life of God. For in His life we find His love and His wisdom and His redeeming power. All we need is *in Him.*

And wonder of wonders, Jesus Himself promised in our radiant "red stone" above that He will not leave us comfortless. Not in time of sorrow, but also not in time of need for our work *or* our peace of mind. He said He would pray the Father for another Comforter who would abide with us forever. This is a great relief. But to me, it is an even greater relief that Jesus added almost immediately that He Himself would come to us.

He died to cleanse us of our sins. To make us a fit place for Him *to* come. And then, when we receive Him in His fulness, He comes. No two ways about it. No questions asked. No theology to understand. No dues to pay. No written invitation needed. He just comes because He said He would. And although I have read and reread this, as you have, I love to write it again: *He comes and fills us with Himself!* He is enough. He doesn't rule out the other things we need. He *includes* them. "By Him all things consist." By Him all things hold together. All we need for anything.

Our part is to discover the riches *in* Christ Jesus. We don't need to struggle to put them there. They are there. "In the beginning was the Word, and the Word was with God, and the Word *was* God." All that God is, Christ is, and all that we can possibly contain of Him has come to live His very life within us in the person of the Holy Spirit. There is no end to the wonder. There is no end to the love. There is no end to the resources. No end to the joy.

> . . . the water that I shall give him shall be IN him a well of water springing up into everlasting life.

Who hath directed the Spirit of the LORD, or being his counsellor hath taught him? With whom took he counsel, and who instructed him, and taught him in the path of judgment, and taught him knowledge, and shewed to him the way of understanding? (Isaiah 40:13, 14).

LOOK who it is who has come to live within us. "I will pray the Father, and he shall give you another Comforter, that he may abide with you forever; even the *Spirit of truth;* . . . I will come to you. . . . At that day ye shall know that I am in my Father, and ye in me, and *I in you.*"

"That day" can be *today.*

We must *know* that God Himself has come to live within us.

And glowing with its own inner radiance which no danger can put out, our "red stone" for this time reminds us once more what God is like.

It isn't that He was just there in the beginning. He *is* the beginning. "I am Alpha and Omega, the first and the last." We cannot really grasp this with our minds. But we can be willing to let this *grasp* our hearts. No-one has taught God. He *is* all knowledge and learning and wisdom and judgment.

And Jesus Christ has been made unto us *wisdom!* I revel in His simplicity. He does everything possible to simplify things for us. He simply states that He *is* the beginning and the end. And if we are open to the Holy Spirit's showing us something of what the character of this Jesus Christ is really like, we will find ourselves not even wondering about things at the beginning, nor fretting about things at the end. He *is* both. He will be there at the end, and He was there in the beginning. He tells us to relax in Him.

I am he that liveth, and was dead; and, behold, I am alive for evermore . . . and have the keys of hell and of death . . . I am the first and the last.

How beautiful upon the mountains are the feet of him
that bringeth good tidings, that publisheth peace. . . . I
will make the place of my feet glorious (Isaiah 52:7a and
60:13b).

NO-ONE can leave behind the footprints of Christ, unless
Christ be *in him.* No matter how many mountains our
feet cross, no matter how beautifully we couch the "good
tidings" nor how magnificently we "publish peace," we can
leave behind only the footprints of our "busy selves," unless
Christ is dwelling fully within us.

This "red stone" has many facets. One or two are these:
Our feet *can* be "beautiful upon the mountains," and the
"mountains" can be reached and crossed from a sick bed. I
never cross the Rocky Mountains by train or plane that I do
not think of my dear friend, Mother McOuat, leaving the truly
"beautiful" prints upon the "mountains" she crosses as she
brings the good tidings and publishes the peace from her bed
in California! Her feet *are* beautiful upon the mountains.
I am at last learning why hers are and some others are not. I
am at last learning why some who are out traveling across real
mountains spreading the good tidings leave beautiful footprints
behind and why others who use the same means and the same
words do not. Here is the secret. ". . . beautiful upon the
mountains *are* the feet of him that bringeth good tidings . . ."
But God adds: ". . . I will make the place of *my* feet glorious."
"I myself will come."

Christ in me is my only hope of leaving behind beautiful
prints upon the mountains. Christ *in* me assures this. Christ *in*
you assures it. For He has said that He will make the place of
His feet glorious. If He is doing His own "walking" in us,
beautiful will be our feet upon any mountain.

I will put my Spirit within you, and cause you to walk in
my statutes . . . ye in me and I in you.

There hath no temptation taken you but such as is common to man: but God is faithful, who will not suffer you to be tempted above that ye are able; but will with the temptation also make a way to escape, that ye may be able to bear it (I Corinthians 10:13).

PERHAPS you know this "red stone" verse from memory. But have you ever dared to believe that for the sincere follower of Jesus Christ there *is no such thing as too much* temptation? The first bright facet of this "stone" to catch anyone's eye is the fact that God reminds us that we are not "special cases." Our temptations vary with our backgrounds and environments, but if we are completely honest, no temptation has taken us which is not common to many, many other people. So, at the outset, God gently but firmly reminds us that we are not "special cases" causing Him to bring out little-used grace just for us.

However, I am perfectly willing to admit that this fact, realistic as it most certainly is, would not be enough to keep me free from the danger of succumbing to my pet temptations! Had Paul stopped with the factual reminder that basically we're all alike, it would not have been enough for most of us In fact, to be reminded in the midst of battling our biggest temptations that we are just like a lot of other people, usually makes us more apt to yield to the temptation.

There is something in us which doesn't want to be thrown into a barrel with all the rest of human nature. God *knows* this. And so Paul goes on, under the guidance of the Holy Spirit, to add that *God* is faithful. This is my authority for declaring to myself and to you that for followers of Jesus Christ there is no such thing as *too much* temptation! The reason is very simple, and it holds good for us all. There is no such thing as too much temptation because:

GOD IS FAITHFUL, by whom ye were called unto the fellowship of his Son Jesus Christ our Lord.

God is faithful, by whom ye were called unto the fellowship of his Son Jesus Christ our Lord (I Corinthians 1:9).

I dare to say that there is no such thing as too much temptation for the follower of Jesus Christ, only because I know that God is faithful. This "red stone," deep with the very life of God, "came alive" to me one morning on a train as I was riding *away* from my dear friend Ellen Riley, who led me to Christ. I ride away from her often, but that morning I was warned by our doctor that I could expect a long distance call at any moment. Ellen was very, very ill. But God had sent me out on His business, and so I had to leave her with Him. Giving back a loved one to God is a tremendous experience. It tears us in deep places of our souls which we didn't know existed before! But God is faithful, and He has *promised* to "make . . . all our borders of pleasant stones," no matter what temptation and heartache rage within those "borders." That morning, riding on a train from Chicago to South Bend, Indiana, God laid another "pleasant stone," and my borders were strengthened. He gave me this "red stone."

I was tempted far beyond my own strength that day. Tempted to give in to the luxury of self-pity. After all, my book THE BURDEN IS LIGHT, telling the story of how Ellen had reached me for Christ, had just come out. Others were asking, "Why would God let Ellen get so ill now of all times?" I was tempted also to ask "why." I was tempted to break the engagement on which the Lord had sent me. I was *so* tempted to be afraid. But that difficult morning I dared to believe for the *first time* that for me, that day and forever, there never again need be "too much" temptation. I knew in a deeper way that God *is* faithful. And that *I had been called into fellowship* with the One who Himself did the calling to a whole sinful world from the Cross.

. . . God is faithful, who will not suffer you to be tempted above that ye are able; but will with the temptation also make a way to escape, that ye may be able to bear it.

What time I am afraid, I will trust in thee. (Psalm 56:3).

THERE is no greater temptation than the temptation to fear. But God is faithful. And we have been called into fellowship with Jesus. John, the beloved disciple, late in his life on earth, gave us a three word characterization of Jesus, His Lord and Saviour and Friend, whom he *knew* to be God. John told us that "God *is* love." And this same John tells us also that ". . . perfect love casteth out fear . . ."

What a relief it is that the temptation to fear has also already been experienced by Jesus when He walked the earth as God, but having also been made *perfectly human.* He was tempted to be afraid too! And he did what we are to do. What time He was afraid, He trusted in His Father.

"What time I am afraid, I will trust in thee."

We can do this if we want to. When we really *want* to trust, the indwelling Christ has all the power available for us to do it. He hasn't changed since He walked this earth, trusting in the Father to escape the human temptation to be afraid. Jesus Christ is just the same today as He was yesterday and He will be just the same forever. *He is living in us* if we have received Him, and He knows *how* to trust the Father during the times *we* are afraid.

Christ in me is my only hope of not being afraid again.

"God was in Christ . . ." They are one. Christ is God. "God is love. . . ." And "perfect love casteth out fear."

"Fear not . . . it is I."

This is the voice of God speaking to us. But it is also the voice of the Son of God who became the Son of Man, and who *experienced* the temptation to fear. It is not some remote deity, commanding us to do something He has not Himself tried.

> For we have not an high priest which cannot be touched with the feeling of our infirmities; but was in all points tempted like as we are, yet without sin.

Hear my cry, O God; attend unto my prayer. From the end of the earth will I cry unto thee, when my heart is overwhelmed: lead me to the rock that is higher than I (Psalm 61:1, 2).

WHY is this among my "red stone" verses? Turn back and reread the description of "red stones" at the beginning of this section. Do you recall the legend about the ruby? In olden times, the ruby was considered a safeguard against impending danger. It was supposed to *lose* its brilliance when danger came near. *You and I still need safeguards against danger.* And temptations are our *warnings* that it is at hand.

The "red stones" in our collection of verses from God's Word go far beyond the old superstition about the ruby. Christ has come and *in us*, if we have received Him, He is living His life. Our "red stones" are true safeguards, because they speak of His life within us, and we must be constantly reminded that *He was and is without sin!* If He is being permitted to "be Himself" in us, there is no such thing as too much temptation for His followers. But we must be *willing* to be delivered. We must truly cry out to be free, when our hearts are overwhelmed with temptation to give in to *anything*. The "rock that is higher than I" is available. It is perfectly defended on all sides. It is impregnable. God wants, not only to lead us to the "rock that is higher than" our earth-pulls, He wants to *keep* us there.

No temptation ever swamps us unless we are willing to be swamped. When our hearts are overwhelmed with grief, with longing, with lust, with greed, with worry, with anxiety, with fear — the "rock" is there. It is high enough. And the Lord *is* a God with a shepherd heart. He wants to lead us there. To safety. If we are willing to be led.

Search me, O God, and know my heart: try me, and know my thoughts: and see if there be any wicked way in me, and lead me in the way everlasting . . . to the rock that is higher than I.

God hath spoken once; twice have I heard this; that power
belongeth unto God (Psalm 62:11).

THIS rare "pleasant stone" could rest as easily and as cor-
rectly in any of our baskets of "pleasant stones" which
we are sharing during these days of learning together.
Surely it "cuts right through" as our diamonds did. Power does
belong to God. Surely it holds all the *hope* there is for mere
human beings, and so could fit nicely into our collection of
"blue stones" which we will look at next. From every syllable
of every word there rings the song of praise and victory, and
so it would go well with our "green stones," the stones of rejoicing. Within God's power is all the strength we need in
time of trouble and sorrow, and so it would be right in place
with our "purple stones" too.

But we've put it here among the "red" ones because to me,
His power is so completely a part of His resurrection *life*. Christ
got up and walked out of that dark sealed tomb by the *power
of God*. By ". . . the spirit of him that raised up Jesus . . . and
will also raise us up by his power . . ." The very life of God
active within us is our *only way* out of temptation, and so I
have placed this verse about power belonging to God here,
among our "red stones" which offer us "a way to escape" out
of temptation. God does not promise that we won't *be* tempted.
Christ was. But He does promise a "way to escape" falling
into temptation's trap. Power does belong unto God. God said
so once, and then He said it again.

". . . twice have I heard this . . ." Power belongs to God
and if God is living in us, it also belongs to us. It is still
God's power, but it is ours to *use*. Just as Christ Himself is
ours to use. He has given Himself for us — to use. We don't
need God's power to choose to sin. We were born with power
to do that. But the power to choose to obey God "belongeth
to God." We *do* need that. And it is ours in Christ.

I can do all things through Christ which strengtheneth me.

But we have this treasure in earthen vessels, that the excellency of the power may be of God, and not of us (II Corinthians 4:7).

POWER does belong unto God. The power that is powerful enough to give us victory over all temptation *has* to belong only to God. Only God could be the source of power like that!

And it is good that we have this "treasure" in earthen vessels; otherwise the "excellency of the power" would seem to be of *us* and not of God. The power is the very life of the indwelling Christ. God Himself, come to live in our mortal bodies. The whole idea is too high for me. I cannot take it in. But I can be possessed by the One who can not only understand it, but whose idea it has been from before the beginning.

Thank God, the power *is* in earthen vessels such as our mortal bodies. Those of us who have lived as adults *not* knowing the Presence within us, devoid of all access to this power over temptation, understand the quiet desperation that is choking the hearts of those who walk the streets of the world *without* this power. Nothing works right without it. It may seem to for a time. I was even quite happy during certain periods of my life before Christ came in. But I had no power over myself. No power to resist temptation. The alcoholic will understand this. But the powerless life is not restricted to the alcoholic without Christ. It is the desperate lot of *every* "earthen vessel" walking around in the dark — empty of God.

But when Christ comes into that "earthen vessel" the quiet desperation goes out, leaving behind deep gratitude that things are as they are. If the power were of us, we would break ourselves over it. I am glad that I know at last that without Him I *can* do nothing. But He has said:

My grace is sufficient for thee: for my strength is made perfect in weakness . . .

83

In the midst of life we are constantly handed over to death
for Jesus' sake, so that the life of Jesus may yet be evidenced
through our mortal flesh (II Corinthians 4:11, 12, Berkeley).

I N the midst of life we are constantly handed over to death
for Jesus' sake," so that His life may *show through us.*
God's own life right in our mortal flesh. "Always bearing
about in the body the dying of the Lord Jesus," so that His
life may show through *our* daily lives.

None of this is for worship services only. It is for right
now. Just before you begin to do what it is that you must
do — now. On this date. "In the midst of life."

In the midst perhaps of a strong, nerve-tearing temptation.

Right in the midst of *your* present circumstance, you may
be "constantly handed over to death for Jesus' sake," so that
His life will be evident in your life. Right while this difficult
thing is going on. He has already died to give us the *power* to
bear about in our body the "dying." If this sounds gruesome
and too hard to you, ask the Holy Spirit for a better look
at the *inside* of the heart that broke on Calvary. If He had
fought the Cross — if He had rebelled as perhaps you are
rebelling now, He could not have saved you. He could not
have saved me. But He just died and blessed His murderers
as they killed Him. And by that act, the power that is of God
can flow into you now, as *His life* flows into you. Power for
your "dying" to this rebellion, this temptation to say, "This is
too much!"

There is no such thing as too much temptation for the crucified and risen follower of the crucified and risen Jesus. All
the power required to resist it is right there in your "earthen
vessel," and it is the power of God. You are free just as soon
as you agree to begin to *partake* of His death and His resurrection. We are free when we die. Then He can raise us
up. And fill us with *His power.* And we can shout:

From henceforth let no man trouble me; for I bear in my
body the marks of the Lord Jesus.

Thou tellest my wanderings: put thou my tears into thy
bottle: are they not in thy book? (Psalm 56:8).

W E have purposely repeated the fact that there *is* no
such thing as too much temptation to the sincere disciple of Jesus Christ. He *is* a deliverer out of all things.
If we choose to be delivered. And here is the secret. Most of us
plead with God to set us free, but we really are asking to be set
free to "take the thing or leave it." We want to be able to do a
bit of "social criticizing." As the alcoholic who prays for God
to make him able to do a bit of "social drinking." We want
to remain a part of a wrong relationship — or at least retain
our memories alive and tormenting. Broken human relationships, or radically changed human relationships, bring heartache only understood by those who have been broken this
way. Broken by new obedience to God or by death of the
loved one. Either way, the heart breaks and the tears flow
and the "couches" of our lives are "watered" by the torrent
of grief or darkness or aloneness seeming to spring from the
very source of hell itself. The temptation may be to sink into
self-pity or to make a telephone call and start it all over
again. The temptation may be to buy a bottle or to curse
God. No matter. *He knows about it.*

Right here, as your heart cries for God to handle even
your weeping — *right here* is the moment for "choosing."
"Jesus wept." He knows about weeping. And *if we choose*
to give even our tears to Him, the miracle is under way. He
will handle the timing of it. You may yield either to the
temptation *or* to God. So may I. But *we choose.* By His
power we *can* choose to recognize that this is no new thing,
this weeping. God knew we would weep. Our tears *are* "in
his book." We are in His hands. He has wept too. He is one
with you in it. He knows.

Who in the days of his flesh . . . offered up prayers and
supplications with strong crying and tears . . .

Thou hast ascended on high, thou hast led captivity captive:
thou hast received gifts for men: yea, for the rebellious
also, that the LORD God might dwell among them.
(Psalm 68:18).

WE can choose to be kept *from* yielding to any temptation which plagues us. *But*, if we choose to *yield* to the temptation, one thing inevitably results — we become *rebellious!* If we yield to the temptation to self-pity, we rebel against the fact that the world does not treat us as nicely as we think we should be treated. If we yield to grief, we rebel against God Himself for "taking our loved one." If we yield to the temptation to drink again or overeat or criticize or "blow our tops," this also leads to rebellion against God, because of course, He always knows about *everything*.

But wonder of wonders, He has *already* taken all of these "captivities" captive! He has already opened the doors to all of these prisons into which we lock ourselves. He Himself *is* the door and it is open forever. We can come out if we *choose* to come out. And when you see your rebellion, your tears may overflow "his bottle" as did mine when this "red stone" verse came alive. ". . . that the Lord God might dwell among them." I wept when I saw for the first time that He did what He did on Calvary so that *He* could be one with *me*. My life before Christ literally demonstrated the meaning of the word "rebel." And since He has redeemed me, I have over and over again rebelled at obeying Him. But the tears flow freely now when I do rebel, and the times of rebellion grow fewer. I *see* now and have no more alibis left. He has already led *my* "captivity captive." I need not yield to the temptation. I will not be smothered if I do not give in to it. I will not be thwarted. I will be freed. By a Saviour Who did what He did because He wanted to "dwell among" one even as rebellious as I. It is real freedom to see this. We know then some of what Jesus meant when He said:

If the Son therefore shall make you free, you shall be
free indeed.

MARCH 18

> God setteth the solitary in families: he bringeth out those
> which are bound with chains: but the rebellious dwell in a
> dry land (Psalm 68:6).

GOD has already taken your particular "captivity captive."
You may walk out of your prison, whatever it is. You
and I need never yield again to *that* temptation. And
it *is* the glorious truth that He did this "for the rebellious also."

I share your shame when I admit (as you may) that even
though He has redeemed me, I still rebel at times *before* I
finally obey Him. I argue with Him and with any human
being near by that "I must be fulfilled." That somewhere
someone is missing the point in all this. I *say* it is I. What I
mean is that in *my* special case, God must have somehow
neglected to put *into* the person of His Son, Jesus Christ, that
special something which *I* need to fulfill *me*. The facts are
that only He knows what will fulfill our true selves. The
"selves" He created in the beginning. We allow sin to create
"familiar *false* selves." And when we rebel, we are not allowing for the fact that He is working His way *down* through the
layers of sin and phony virtues and selfishness to reach our
true selves and set us free.

Perhaps your special rebellion is that you are alone. Perhaps you are a widow or an unmarried woman who thinks
God should have sent you a mate. Perhaps you are a lone
man—and rebellious also. Perhaps you are a young person
without a family to care for you. Whatever the circumstance,
it is causing you to rebel. But listen, He *is* faithful, isn't He?
We can depend upon Him to fulfill our *every* longing according to what He knows to be the very *choicest* way. *But not as
long as we are rebelling.* Do believe right now that out of all
this, He has some lovely eternal lesson to teach you. Drop your
rebellion. Tell Him you *do* trust Him to know best. And remember . . . remind yourself over and over that:

> God setteth the solitary in families: he bringeth out those
> which are bound with chains: but the rebellious dwell in a
> dry land.

87

Because he hath set his love upon me, therefore will I deliver him: I will set him on high, because he hath known my name (Psalm 91:14).

WE would never need to pray for humility, if we would permit the Holy Spirit to show us into the depths of this "red stone." Because in its depths we find the nature of the depths of the heart of God Himself. It is impossible to *give* love unless you can also *receive* it. And in one sense this is true of God also.

Since God *is* love, He needs love in return. If we are far from Him at this moment, our glimpse into the depths of this "red stone" will cause us to want to turn the page, throw the book aside, or fall on our knees and "return." The human heart *cannot* remain hard and icy when it is laid up against a heart like the one Jesus showed us on Calvary. The very thought of God's heart *needing* our love in response to His, melts the most thoroughly frozen human heart.

When I read in the book of Proverbs that His "delights were with the sons of men," my heart began to melt. In fact, I read it on the very morning of the day He took me as His own. To think that Christ *wanted* to be with me! I could not take it in. The Holy Spirit had to reveal it to me. And here, in this amazing "red stone" verse, we hear God again declaring that He wants our love first of all.

God will deliver you from your temptation freely and willingly *if* you will love Him. If you will begin, even in a very small way, to *respond* to His loving advances toward you. He wants to be intimate with us. He longs to be familiar to us. He says He will set us "on high," out of danger, *because* we know His *name.* He wants His name to be the most familiar one of all to us. The only responsibility we ever have is to *belong* to Christ. And to listen to Him as He says over and over again to us:

Fear not; for I have redeemed thee; I have called thee by thy name, thou art mine.

Hear me, O LORD; for thy lovingkindness is good: turn
unto me according to the multitude of thy tender mercies.
(Psalm 69:16).

WHEN God begins to move within a human life, even in
the midst of the rebellion and the natural fears of
leaving the old and embarking upon the new, all
around us (if no human being is "pushing") is the strangely
certain feeling that a great kindness is drawing near. And the
nearer that kindness comes, the more we are drawn toward the
One who *is* all kindness. I felt this during the days just before
I let my last defenses shatter. I *knew* this kindness even *before*
I knew Christ as my own Saviour. Of course, He was already
the Saviour. And the same loving-kindness which held Him
to the Cross, was holding my attention in those last trembling
bitter-sweet moments before He invaded my life with His own.

I know this "loving-kindness." And I know that it *is* good.
So do you, if He is your *personal* Saviour.

And it is with an overwhelming sense of relief that I look
into the depths of this "red stone" and see more of His heart.
See more of His intention toward us. Here, He gives us per-
mission to ask Him to "turn unto" us *according* to this very
same "lovingkindness." We are to seek comfort and help and
forgiveness and strength and wisdom — *not* according to our
merits, but according to *His* loving-kindness. According to the
"multitude of thy tender mercies." Not even according to my
need. But according to His mercy.

And this God came down here to live among men so that
He would have the *added* entrée into our hearts of *identification* with us in our every need. If you have suffered a certain
heartache, you are more merciful to another who is suffering
that same pain. God's mercy was not *increased* when Jesus
came to earth, it was *illustrated!* Illustrated in a way we can
understand. Jesus knows.

Not by works of righteousness which we have done, but
according to his mercy he saved us . . .

Now . . . when Jesus knew that his hour was come that he should depart out of this world unto the Father, having loved his own which were in the world, he loved them unto the end. And supper being ended . . . (John 13:1, 2).

JESUS waited until *after* supper.

Because being God, He understands *us* fully. He told them things when He was here on earth, only as they could receive them. He had the poise and the strength to wait. He never blurted out more than the wondering disciples could cope with. Even on the day when He "knew that his hour was come," He still waited until after supper. He is not only merciful, He *is all mercy.*

And He is all love.

". . . having loved his own which were in the world, he loved them unto the end." He loves *us* exactly the same way. And He still knows just how much we can take. Long before I became a follower of Jesus Christ, I would sit Sunday night after Sunday night and listen to a marvelous negro choir, and my heart longed most intently when they sang, "He Knows Just How Much We Can Bear!" I was "bearing" it all alone in those days. And I was being broken by it. And I longed to be "simple enough" to *believe* that someone else *knew* about me. My life was so much too much for me most of the time that it seemed as though it would be "just like heaven" if someone else really understood about it.

Now I know that He knew all along and was just waiting for me to be ready to give my burden to Him. Now, I also know that "having loved his own," He will love me to the end. He will love you to the end. And He Himself *is* the end.

Let it go, whatever it is that is "too much" for you right now. Let it go over onto the shoulders of the Son of God, who will never rush you into any action you cannot bear. He knows all about you. No matter what is up ahead, He will wait for you, "until after supper."

Let not your heart be troubled: ye believe in God, believe also in me.

Jesus knowing that the Father had given all things into
his hands, and that he was come from God, and went to God;
he riseth from supper, and laid aside his garments; and took
a towel, and girded himself (John 13:3, 4).

ONE look into the bright depths of this "red stone" will
show us a way to glorify our drudgery. It is not by a
psychological trick, but by "knowing" as Jesus knew the
night He "took a towel and girded himself" and began to
wash His disciples' feet.

He did it all to the glory of His Father.

If we wash dishes and iron clothes and type letters and
repair automobiles and sell merchandise *all* to the glory of
God, our daily drudgery is "deified" and we are surrounded
with glory, simply as a *result* of our making a sacrament of
the dreariest thing. But we can't do this unless we *do know*.

And what is it that we must know?

Just what Jesus knew when He took the towel. We must
know *who He is*. "Jesus knowing that the Father had given
all things into his hands, and that he was come from God,
and went to God . . ." Jesus *knew* He had come from God
and was going to God. That was enough. He was freed from
the usual humiliation of menial tasks. How could He have
an inferiority complex *knowing* that He is the Son of God?
What does that have to do with us? Just this: If we *know*
who He is, and that He lives *in us* and that we are His own,
we are also free. The Son Himself has made us free. Because of
who He is. We must simply *know* it. We must be conscious of
it at all times. Dr. Verkuyl in his excellent Berkeley translation
of this passage uses the word, "conscious." ". . . Jesus, *conscious*
that the Father placed everything into His hands and that He
came from God and was going to God, rose from the table,
put away his robe and, taking a towel, girded Himself." We
must develop the consciousness of who it is who has come to
live within us.

I myself will come to you.

After that he poureth water into a bason, and began to wash the disciples' feet . . . (John 13:5a).

HERE is a "red stone" which could well go among our "clear stones" because it does "cut right through." Whose feet did Jesus wash? He washed the feet of His disciples. His *twelve* disciples.

Because this took place *before* Judas ran outside to do what he did to his Master. Judas was there too. Jesus, the sinless Son of God, stooped down and lovingly washed the dirt from the feet of the man who had *already* sold Him for a few dollars! This didn't bother Jesus at all. At least, not in the way it would bother us. "He loved them unto the end." Judas too. Even though He knew, all the time He was on His knees before Judas, all that was in Judas' heart! What must Jesus have thought as He knelt there doing this lowly thing for His disciple who would betray Him with a kiss in just a few hours from that moment? What would we think? My opinion is that *we* wouldn't be there washing the feet of someone whom we *knew* had sold us for a few pieces of money. We might if we didn't know about what was going to happen, but Jesus *knew*. Things don't happen *only* in sequence for Him as they do for us. He knew. And still He knelt before Judas and with the same hands which Judas' treachery had condemned to be nailed to the Cross, He lovingly and carefully "washed the disciples' feet." You see, Jesus not only knew what Judas had done and would do a little later on that evening, He also knew that it was *not* Judas alone who condemned Him to His Cross. It was *sin* in Judas and in us. It was our *need* that condemned Him to die. And since it was His love for Judas and for us which held Him to the Cross, He *could* show the same love to the disciple who had sold Him for thirty pieces of silver. We can "sell" Him right now, but He has already paid a much bigger price than we will get.

God commendeth his love toward us, in that, while we were yet sinners, Christ died for us.

92

He then having received the sop went immediately out: and it was night (John 13:30).

JUDAS had been exposed to the heart of God. He had lived and talked and eaten with Jesus. He had watched Him heal. He had never seen Him lose His patience. He knew His compassion had no end. Judas had experienced the love of the One he was about to betray with a mocking symbol of "love."

Judas had been exposed to the Lord's love. He had been affected by it as is anyone who is *ever* exposed to it. He would not have killed himself for what he did, if he had been utterly untouched by the love of Christ. And since Judas had been exposed to His love, he had also been exposed to His *light*. Because Jesus *is* "the light of the world."

I shudder when I attempt to imagine the violent turmoil in the heart of Judas as those gentle fingers handed him the bite of bread at their last supper. Even in letting him know He knew the evil intention of Judas' heart, the Lord handed him something to *eat*. He didn't point his finger at Judas. He gave him bread. Not knowing what else to do, Judas apparently ate the little piece of bread. And then, driven by the fury of fear and guilt and evil which raged within him, he ran from the room.

"*And it was night.*"

It was dark out there without Jesus. It is always darker to those who consciously betray Him; who have been touched by His love and who have seen by His light. We are more aware of the darkness once we have known light. Turn off a bright light and you see *nothing*. The contrast is so great and the darkness so sudden, panic can come. But the Heart of love will follow you and He, Himself, will be waiting for you to "return." It is night out there away from Jesus.

. . . Return unto me, for I have redeemed thee . . . I am the light of the world . . .

A new commandment I give unto you, That ye love one
another; as I have loved you, that ye also love one
another (John 13:34).

JUST after Judas ran from the room the night before they
killed Jesus, the Lord began to talk about His *new* commandment of love.

I'm glad that John, "the disciple whom Jesus loved," tells
us about this. John must have been very sensitive to the love
of God, because he was the one who wrote so simply and so
clearly, as an old man, that "God is love."

How like the Lord Jesus to begin talking about love almost
the minute Judas ran from the room! If He could speak of
love at the very moment of His betrayal by one of His own
disciples, do you think for an instant that He would refuse
to "shed abroad in our hearts" this same kind of forgiving love
— *if* we make room for it? Far from refusing, He commands
that we love with the kind of love only possible to God.

Often it is harder to love a Christian brother or sister who
"rubs us the wrong way" than it is an outsider of whom we
don't expect so much. Perhaps for this reason He spoke particularly of love that last night when His own human creations
were about to murder Him because one of His *own* had betrayed Him. "A new commandment I give unto you, That
ye love one another; as I have loved you, that ye also love
one another" (John 13:34).

He said we were to have for each other the *kind* of love
He has for us. He told them of His love that night, but He
also washed their feet and dried them with His own hands.
"I have given you an example, that ye should do as I have
done to you." Then He went out and died to make it possible
for us *to* do it.

If I then, your Lord and Master, have washed your feet;
ye also ought to wash one another's feet.

By this shall all men know that ye are my disciples, if ye have love one to another (John 13:35).

JESUS didn't specify a long list of "things" we are to believe in order for the world to know that we are His followers. He didn't command that we believe much about *Him* at all! He wanted us to believe *Him* and to *love one another.* He knew these two things go together, like His love and His light. We write long articles and open our prayers a certain way, and shout that we are Christians because we believe this and this and this; and if people don't agree with us at once, our tempers flare and we climb higher on our spiritual pedestals and shout more loudly all the way "down" to where those who don't agree are still *wondering* about the heart that broke on Calvary as they *wander* around outside in the darkness without Him! They "wonder" what it has done for *our* spirits and *our* hearts and when they don't see any family resemblance in us to the Saviour we shout about, they continue to "wander" in the same darkness outside without Him. And His heart continues to break with longing for them whom He loves so much. And whom He wants for His own.

Jesus didn't say we had to "fight the good fight" for Him so that people will know that we are His disciples. He said: "By *this* shall all men know that ye are my disciples, *if ye have love one to another.*" He didn't tell us to write articles tearing down the reputations of those with whom we disagree. He *commanded* that we love one another in the same way that He loves us. He will give us discernment because He is *light,* but we are to let our points of *agreement* get our attention, not our points of *differences.*

If ye know these things, happy are ye if ye do them.

And Jesus going up to Jerusalem took the twelve disciples apart in the way, and said unto them, Behold, we go up to Jerusalem; and the Son of man shall be betrayed unto the chief priests and unto the scribes, and they shall condemn him to death, and shall deliver him to the Gentiles to mock, and to scourge, and to crucify him: and the third day he shall rise again. Then came to him the mother of Zebedee's children with her sons, worshipping him, and desiring a certain thing of him (Matthew 20:17-20).

ZEBEDEE'S children" were Jesus' disciples, John and James. Of course, they were right there when Jesus "took the twelve disciples apart . . . and said unto them, Behold, we go up to Jerusalem." He told them as plainly as He could that He was going to be crucified. That first He would be mocked and scourged. John and James couldn't have missed hearing what He said. John was even His *beloved* disciple. And yet they sent their mother to Him immediately after He had told them about His horrible death up ahead, to ask Him if they could have the choice seats in His Kingdom.

They even came with her. "Then came to him the mother of Zebedee's children *with her sons*, worshipping him, and desiring a certain thing of him."

Of all Jesus' disciples I seem to love dear John the best. And I can never read this passage without tears getting in my way. Even John, "the disciple whom Jesus loved" couldn't yet understand what was up ahead. What was *at hand*. The Lord of Glory was there in person telling them how He was to suffer and die and they sent mama to "worship him" in order to get something *they* wanted for *themselves*.

John and his brother James missed the point entirely. But Jesus took even this flagrant bit of self-seeking and "turned it to a testimony." He redeemed even this utter selfishness by using it to hand them *and us* the key to the Kingdom:

Whosoever will be great among you, let him be your minister (servant); And whosoever will be chief among you, let him be your (bond) servant: Even as the Son of man came not to be ministered unto, but to minister, and to give his life a ransom for many.

And he took with him Peter and the two sons of Zebedee, and began to be sorrowful and very heavy. Then saith he unto them, My soul is exceeding sorrowful, even unto death: tarry ye here, and watch with me. (Matthew 26:37, 38).

THE same two sons of Zebedee who sought favoritism in the Kingdom and the one whom Jesus knew in just a few hours would deny that he had ever met Him. James and John and Peter were the three the Lord chose to go with Him — to watch with Him there in the dark of the Garden of Gethsemane.

We can rejoice in this. Knowing what He knew about these three, He still chose them because He needed them to be with Him. He will still choose us too. We'll never understand why if we try to find some merit in ourselves. He chooses us because He *loves* us. He chose Peter and James and John because He loved them too. Knowing full well that they would fall asleep right at the moment He lay struggling on the ground in the dust and the little sharp rocks and the blood and the tears.

What a relief it is to know, to begin to remember that Jesus knows about all our past failures, and He knows about all the times still to come when He will "find us asleep."

But He still calls us to go with Him as He walks among the violence and the blood and the tears in the shadows of the world, seeking those who are not yet His own. He still pleads with us: "My soul is exceeding sorrowful, even unto death; . . . the Son of man is come to seek and to save that which was lost . . . it is not the will of your Father which is in heaven, that one of these little ones should perish . . . could ye not watch with me one hour?"

Perhaps He has chosen *you* to "watch with him" over someone who has driven you to the breaking point! He chose John and James and Peter too. If we fall asleep, we can always wake up and go on with Him.

Ye have not chosen me, but I have chosen you . . .

97

Then cometh he to his disciples, and saith unto them, . . . behold, the hour is at hand, and the Son of man is betrayed into the hands of sinners (Matthew 26:45).

HERE is a "red stone" reflecting the deepest recesses of the great heart of Jesus Christ. His decision was made. He came to do His Father's will and He would do it "even unto death."

Even unto the death of the Cross.

He made His decision and then came back to His sleeping disciples and said quite simply and peacefully that His time had come. He used the present tense in the little verb "is." "The Son of man *is* betrayed into the hands of sinners."

The betrayal had already occurred. So had the dark mystery of His conflict in the garden among the shadowy olive trees in the place called Gethsemane. His torment of soul was ended. He was ready to drink the cup. Knowing all that was in it. He had already tasted it and had overcome His loathing of it and was ready now to drink it. All of it. Jesus was strong and poised and gentle and waiting to die.

And the facet of this "red stone" verse which cuts *me* to the heart is that He was dying for the very ones who were going to murder Him. "The Son of man is betrayed into the hands of *sinners*."

"Christ Jesus came into the world to save *sinners*."

He came to save His murderers.

Somehow the divine poignancy of His simply telling them that He was already betrayed into the very hands of those He had come to call to Himself, melts me.

There is no spirit of revenge.

Listen to Him say *after* the agony under the olive trees in the hideous shadows of that garden:

> The Son of man is betrayed into the hands of sinners . . . I came not to call the righteous, but sinners . . . him that cometh to me, I will in no wise cast out.

But he (Peter) denied before them all, saying, I know not
what thou sayest . . . And again he denied with an oath,
I do not know the man . . . Then began he to curse and to
swear, saying, I know not the man . . . And he . . . wept
bitterly (Matthew 26:70, 72, 74a, 75b).

I am sure this passage belongs among our "red stones" because it shows the effect of the Lord's love upon a hard
heart. Peter denied; then he swore and cursed; and then
"he went out and wept bitterly."

Those of us who have in any way denied the Lord Jesus
know something of this kind of weeping.

It is the bitterest weeping of all.

It is the kind of weeping I have seen come upon men and
women who have loved Christ for many years, but who have
fallen into the devil's own trap of condemning a *non*-believer
for "swearing and cursing." When we as Christians do this
— when we expect someone who does *not* know Christ, to act
as though he or she *does* know Him, then we are belittling
His Cross and the very blood He poured out there to save
us. When we begin to see our own hardness, we weep.

What is in a man will come out under pressure.

Have you never let fly something under pressure which hor-
rified you? It came from something sinful within you or it
could not have come out. Peter swore because he was under
tremendous pressure, but He would not have done it had
there not been something sinful in him at the time. *What was
still in Peter came out. But* when the Holy Spirit came to
dwell *within* him at Pentecost, when Peter gave himself fully
to be possessed by the Spirit of God, the same process took
place when he spoke. What was *in* him came out. Only
then God's own life was in Peter and instead of swearing and
oaths, there came from the same lips these words:

. . . As he which hath called you is holy, so be ye holy
in all manner of conversation; because it is written, Be
ye holy; for I am holy.

MARCH 31

And sitting down they watched him there (Matthew 27:36).

IT is almost inconceivable to think that people like us sat down around the foot of the Cross of Jesus Christ and just "watched him there." But that's what some of them did.

How must they have looked to Jesus as He watched their ugly, amused, fiendish, upturned faces — watched them through the blood running down into His own eyes. What must He have seen in *their* eyes?

I carry around in my purse a picture of myself taken when I was only twenty-six years old and successful and "happy." It is a casual snapshot and it is a smiling picture, but cover up the mouth and the look in the eyes will force your attention to the foot of the Cross of Christ and those *other* eyes which "watched Him there." The look in my eyes holds nothing of a smile in it. *It is utterly selfish.* It is utterly sinful.

It couldn't have been any other way because I was one of the sinners Jesus came to call. And when the picture was taken I hadn't even heard His voice. This verse is included among our "red stones" because it reminds me that the worse they treated Him that day as they sat there and watched Him die, the *more love* He poured down upon them. Why? Because He could tell by the look in their eyes how much they *needed* His love. *He knew they didn't know what they were doing.* That they were in the prison of sin. Jesus knew this. And He also knew He had been anointed "to proclaim liberty to the captives, and the opening of the prison to them that are bound . . ." That's why He could say as He poured down His love on those who watched Him there:

Father, forgive them; for they know not what they do.

April 1

He saved others; himself he cannot save. If he be the King of Israel, let him now come down from the cross, and we will believe him (Matthew 27:42).

HIMSELF he cannot save . . ." Himself He *could* not afford to save! If He had saved Himself, He could not have saved us. If His prayer that the cup might pass from Him had been answered in the affirmative, our prayers could never be answered at all!

All His earthly life, Jesus had walked long, weary miles, pouring His humanity out to those who needed a shepherd. Healing, teaching, admonishing, showing His love. Now, some of the same lost sheep to whom He had been giving of His strength and love were there beneath the Cross jeering at Him! In His deep love and concern for their eternal lives, "Jesus (had) stood and cried, saying, If any man thirst, let him come unto me, and drink." Now, those to whom He cried, jeered at Him, ". . . let him come down from the cross, and (then) we will believe him."

Does this sound familiar to you? "If God will just do this thing which I want so much, *then* I'll believe Him."

He did not die to give us what *we* want. He died to give us eternal life. An exchange of lives. His for ours. An exchange of cries . . . His cry for ours! We cry for Him to do this and that and *then* we will begin to "believe." We will "condescend" to believe in the Son of God on *our* terms. This blessed Son of God, now alive forever, knew that *sin* prompts a cry like ours. And so when He died, He cried in response to *our* cry: "It is finished!" It *is* finished.

And, behold, the veil of the temple was rent in twain . . . and the earth did quake, and the rocks rent; and the graves were opened . . . and they that were with him, watching Jesus, . . . feared greatly, saying, Truly this was the Son of God.

101

So they went, and made the sepulchre sure, sealing the stone, and setting a watch (Matthew 27:66).

THEY carefully selected a huge boulder. Rolled it against the open tomb, sealed it, and placed a hand-picked guard of soldiers to watch the grave of Jesus. They "made the sepulchre sure." They made sure, to their own satisfaction, that the body of Jesus would never be seen again. Jesus had said He would rise again and the chief priests and Pharisees urged Pilate to take all possible precautions to see that His disciples didn't steal His body and then spread the story that He had risen. So, they "made the sepulchre sure." Completely sure, they thought.

But, glory to God in the very highest, the *only* thing that was really sure was that Jesus was going to get up under the power of God and walk out of that sealed tomb! He didn't roll the stone away in order to get out. He didn't need to. The stone was not even rolled away until ". . . the end of the sabbath, as it began to dawn toward the first day of the week . . ." The guards were still there, the stone was still in place, but Jesus was gone. The stone was merely rolled back so that when His disciples came they could see *inside* and know that He had told them the truth.

They "made the sepulchre sure" against themselves only. Jesus Christ Himself could not have been "sealed in" by a mere stone, because He Himself *is* Eternal Life.

I am he that liveth, and was dead; and, behold, I am alive for evermore . . .

In the end of the sabbath, as it began to dawn toward the first day of the week, came Mary Magdalene and the other Mary to see the sepulchre. And, behold, there was a great earthquake: for the angel of the Lord descended from heaven, and came and rolled back the stone from the door, and sat upon it. His countenance was like lightning, and his raiment white as snow: and for fear of him the keepers did shake, and became as dead men. And the angel answered and said unto the women, Fear not ye: for I know that ye seek Jesus, which was crucified. He is not here: for he is risen, as he said, Come, see the place where the Lord lay. And go quickly, and tell . . . (Matthew 28:1-7a).

GO quickly and tell" that no amount of careful sealing with a stone could keep back the Son of God! *He created the stone.*

". . . Go quickly and tell" that "He is not here: for He is risen, as he said . . ."

". . . Go quickly and tell" that Jesus did just what He said He would do. He got up and walked out of that dark, sealed tomb, and to help them adjust to the idea, to give them assurance that God *was* in total command of the whole amazing event, the Father sent an angel down out of heaven to explain things to the poor, dazzled, earth-bound disciples. ". . . For the angel of the Lord descended from heaven, and came and rolled back the stone from the door, and sat upon it." The angel of the Lord *sat* upon the stone that was supposed to have held the Lord Jesus Christ a prisoner of death forever!

The great stone became a resting place for God's messenger who came to announce the resurrection. The tomb was empty. The One, whose enemies will someday be a footstool for His nail-scarred feet, was no longer there. He was risen as He said.

. . . Go quickly, and tell . . . the Lord is risen indeed!

And as they went to tell his disciples, behold, Jesus met
them, saying, All hail (Matthew 28:9a).

GO quickly, and tell . . . And they departed quickly from
the sepulchre with fear and great joy; and did run to
bring his disciples word. And as they went to tell his
disciples, behold, *Jesus* met them, saying, O joy!" The literal
translation of the words we know most familiarly as "All hail"
is really "O joy!"

My own heart leaped up when I first learned this. After
three days and nights of a darkness we cannot comprehend,
after having completely and forever overthrown death and having broken the power of sin over His creations, Jesus Himself,
was overflowing with His own joy.

In His great heart of love was sheer *joy* that He had been
able to do what He had done to conquer the ghastly killer,
sin, in His dear ones.

How can we comprehend love like His?

How can we bear it? It is too sweet to bear consciously
and keep on sinning. This is one way He broke the power of
sin for us. Let His love become real to you. Realize that
"salvation *is* equal to the fall"! *Know* that what Christ did
can fill *you* with joy too, *if* you begin to take part in it.

Jesus, going up to His grief-stricken, harried disciples that
first morning, could say nothing but, "O joy!" His heart was
singing too. He had made a way out of futility for those He
had created. And now He would be with them forever.

He couldn't say anything but, "O joy!" His joy is complete
somehow when He is *with us*.

Father, I will that they also, whom thou hast given me,
be with me where I am . . .

*These things have I spoken unto you, that my joy might
remain in you, and that your joy might be full (John 15:11).*

WHAT else could Jesus have said to His heartbroken
friends that first morning after the victory on the
dark little hill but "O joy!" "God was in Christ"
there on the Cross "reconciling the world unto himself." And
when two are reconciled, they can then be together. Side by
side. *In* love. *In* one another. "Abide in me, and I in you."

"These things have I spoken unto you, that my *joy* might
remain in you, and that your *joy* might be full . . . That they
all may be one; as thou, Father, ·art in me, and I in thee, that
they also may be one in us . . ."

God created us to belong to Himself. Nothing less than
actually being *with us* can ever satisfy God. But He is a holy
God and so He did what He did on Calvary to make it possible for us to be with Him. To make us "holy as He is holy."

To cover us with His robe of righteousness.

To cover us with His love.

To cover us with Himself.

That *His* joy might be in us. There is no other way that
our joy can be full. God knew this because He created us.
Oswald Chambers says, "Joy is God in your blood." This Jesus
Christ shed His own blood that He might be *in* us. That our
joy might be full. God was in the blood of Jesus Christ on
Calvary. God was also in the blood of Jesus Christ that glorious first resurrection morning when He met His disciples
and said all He could say at the moment: "O joy"!

He knew what He had done. He knew that, from that moment on, the way had been cleared for Him to be with those
He loves forever.

*I will not leave you comfortless: I will come to you . . .
if it were not so, I would have told you . . .*

Then when Jesus came, he found that he [Lazarus] had lain in the grave four days already. Now Bethany was nigh unto Jerusalem . . . (John 11:17, 18a).

DEAR Rufus Mosely used to say, "Jesus never conducted funerals. He only conducted resurrections!"

This is true.

There is no account in the Bible anywhere of Jesus having preached at a funeral. No Christian ever needs his or her funeral preached. Where Christ is, there are *only* resurrections.

And the key to this tremendous fact is in the first phrase of John 11:18 quoted above as a part of this "red stone." It would seem to be merely factual. To locate Bethany.

It is.

"Now Bethany was nigh unto *Jerusalem* . . ."

At a garden grave in Jerusalem, just a few days after Jesus raised Lazarus from His grave in Bethany, He demonstrated *how* He did it! How it was Lazarus was raised from the the dead. It was hard for them to understand or grasp then. You see they stood weeping at the grave of Lazarus on the *other* side of Jerusalem.

Jesus has now "gone up to Jerusalem." Calvary is complete. He is out of His *own* tomb. He has demonstrated resurrection.

The grave by which you stand weeping now, or by which you have stood weeping in the past, is located even *nearer* to Jerusalem. But more important, it is on *this* side of it.

True to God's great and flawless timing, it was exactly the right time for Jesus to do what He did at Bethany that day. He *knew* that "Bethany was nigh unto Jerusalem" and He knew what He would do at Jerusalem just a little later on.

He has already done it now. His own tomb is empty. We can rejoice through our tears that our Bethany is located on the resurrection side of the Cross. Nigh unto the *new* Jerusalem.

. . . Said I not unto thee, that, if thou wouldest believe, thou shouldest see the glory of God?

APRIL 7

Jesus said unto her, I am the resurrection, and the life: he that believeth in me, though he were dead, yet shall he live: And whosoever liveth and believeth in me shall never die. Believest thou this? (John 11:25, 26).

WHEN Jesus walks up to a grave, resurrection inevitably results. "Whosoever liveth and believeth in me shall *never* die." Fantastic? Yes. To us, from where we live here on earth. Almost meaningless at the moment a human heart collapses with grief at the sight of the still, lifeless face of a physically dead loved one.

But Jesus said that whosoever believes in Him shall never die. We have His word for that. And the moment our hearts *collapse* with grief they have also collapsed, for that moment, with unbelief.

Didn't Jesus weep? Yes. "Jesus wept . . . [and] Jesus therefore again groaning in himself cometh to the grave" of the friend whose earthly body and human personality and companionship He had loved so much. He wept and groaned with grief. But some of that grief must have been the grief that has been on the heart of God since "the Lamb was slain before the foundation of the world." God knew that a Cross of pain would be set up because of our disobedience, and His grief was and is intense. It was human grief, but it was godly sorrow too. The sorrow that proved itself on Calvary.

Jesus *was* eternal life at the grave of His friend Lazarus. But He made this life accessible to all of us the moment He stood outside His own empty tomb. Your loved one *has not died.* The resurrection covers even your grief. According to Jesus Himself who is the resurrection, ". . . Though he were *dead,* yet shall he live."

. . . Believest thou this? . . .

APRIL 8

And he that was dead came forth . . . (John 11:44a).

A ND when he [Jesus] thus had spoken, he cried with a
loud voice, Lazarus, come forth."
Why doesn't the Lord Jesus still do this? Why is it
that our loved ones cannot be brought back from the grave
to be with us as Lazarus was again with his sisters, Mary
and Martha? Wouldn't it glorify God now as it did then?
Wouldn't our non-believing friends be likely to become Christians just as did the friends of the little family at Bethany
when the one who had been dead in his grave four days
once more sat at the dinner table rejoicing with them all?

Why does that chair at our table have to remain empty?

Doesn't God love our loved ones as much as Jesus loved
Lazarus?

Yes. This has nothing whatever to do with God's love for
us or our loved ones, as I see it. God could still bring our
loved one back. His power has not lessened. But He has
done something even greater now. "God was in Christ" on
the Cross. God was in Christ when He walked out of the
open tomb victorious over death so that the words of Jesus
to Martha could be forever true for each one of us. When He
raised Lazarus from the dead, that was only one resurrection.
One man. Now, since Jesus Himself broke out of the grave,
all have access to eternal life. Physical death is but an inci-
dent along the way.

Your loved one and mine have graduated into another field
of service. Their questions have become exclamations of joy
because they know *all* of what the Lord is "up to" at last!
Life goes on for them. With Him. And it is of the utmost
urgency that we remember that "His mercy endureth forever."

. . . If it were not so, I would have told you . . .

ETERNAL life is *eternal* life.

It is the very life of God Himself. " .. . I am the resurrection *and the life* . . . I am the way, the truth *and the life* . . ." Jesus did not say He would show us a better *way* of life. He is *not* a "way-shower" as the modern cult would have us believe.

He Himself, *is* the way.

He Himself, *is* the life.

That's why we can know that when Jesus walks up to a man or woman dead in sin, life inevitably results. *If* that person *believes* in Jesus as eternal life itself. Where He is, death cannot remain. Things and people spring to life around Jesus. It's inevitable.

Any man or woman who *believes* in Jesus Christ simply *cannot* die. ". . . Whosoever believeth in him shall not perish, but have everlasting life." God's life. And He is eternal. He goes on. So do we, if we have received His life into ours. We can no more stop than God can stop! Eternal life *is* everlasting life. It lasts *forever.* Therefore, seeing all things as He does, and knowing *all* that was in His own heart when He created us and knowing *all* that He did for us when He redeemed us on the Cross, God would *know* it to be an inferior thing for Him to raise a few people from their graves now. He Himself came up from His. The gift of eternal life *has been given.* Believers in Jesus Christ just don't die.

God continues working out His purpose among our loved ones who have actually never even been *in* those graves we decorate. God would be retrogressing if He raised *some* now. He has done much *more* than that. He has given us Himself, and He *is* eternal life. We already *know* this if —

. . . we trust in the living God, who is the Saviour of all men, specially of those that believe.

Then he said unto them, O fools, and slow of heart to believe. . . . Ought not Christ to have suffered these things . . . ? (Luke 24:25a, 26a).

JESUS had risen from His grave when He spoke these words. And He spoke them to some disciples of His, whom He joined as they were walking along the road to Emmaus. He had already told them that He would be killed and that He would rise again after the third day and here He was risen and walking with them, but they didn't recognize Him at all! I believe the reason for this is that they weren't really expecting to see Him again. They did not really *believe* what He told them.

These disciples were so like most of us, however. They were gabbling on about what had *happened to* Jesus of Nazareth, "but him they saw not." Quite plausibly, in the face of things as He knew them to be, Jesus said to them, "O . . . slow of heart to believe . . ." And just as plausibly, He added: ". . . Ought not Christ to have suffered these things?" If only they would look at Him and find out what He's really like! If only we would look at Him and find out His true motives. Jesus Himself, *after* the Cross, after the resurrection, asked: "Ought not Christ to have suffered these things?" He might have pressed His point: "Doesn't it make sense to you that I, *being* love, would 'endure the Cross,' for the 'joy that was set before Me,' in knowing by doing it, I could set my loved ones free? I created you. I knew when sin twisted my creations all out of shape. My heart broke on Calvary to set you free from this disease to which you have all fallen victim. Look at Me, *as I really am.*" "Ought not Christ to have suffered these things . . .? O . . . slow of heart to believe . . ." Look at Him as He really is. He is love.

Looking unto Jesus the author and finisher of our faith; who for the joy that was set before him endured the cross . . . that whosoever believeth in him should . . . have everlasting life.

The messages I relate to you all, I do not tell just from
Myself; the Father, who dwells in Me carries on His activities (John 14:10, Berkeley).

W HEN we look "unto Jesus," we also look unto the
Father. Father and Son are two and yet they are
inseparable. We should not try to *understand* this
with our intellects. We cannot. We should permit the third
person of this glorious Godhead, the Holy Spirit, simply to
do what Jesus promised He would do — make it clear to us.
The Holy Spirit, if you allow Him, will cause you to realize
everything needful for your victorious life. A little over seven
years ago, as I write these pages, I knew *nothing* of the
things of God. I have not been academically trained in them
during these seven years. And yet, this dear Holy Spirit has
caused me to realize truths which continue to revolutionize
my life. My part is simply to stay open to Him.

And one of the truths He has recently made clear to me is
that when I realize Christ's presence within me, I also realize
the presence of the *Father* in me too. Dr. Walter Wilson put
this into words once as I walked beside him at Winona Lake,
Indiana. It arrested my attention, but it was *not* real to me,
until I asked the Holy Spirit to make it real. Now, I thrill
to the *fact* of our "red stone" verse at the top of this page.
If Christ dwells in me, then so does the Father, and He "carries on His activities." Ask the Holy Spirit right now to make
real to you the indwelling presence of the Father too. And
then trust Him to do it at exactly the right time.

On that day you will recognize that I am in my Father,
and you in me and I in you.

APRIL 12

And I will pray the Father, and he shall give you another
Comforter, that he may abide with you for ever; Even the
Spirit of truth; whom the world cannot receive, because it
seeth him not, neither knoweth him: but ye know him; for
he dwelleth with you, and shall be in you. I will not leave
you comfortless: I will come to you. . . . At that day ye
shall know that I am in my Father, and ye in me, and I
in you (John 14:16, 17, 18, 20).

THIS glorious "red stone" contains all there is to realize
about the plan of the Christian life. Live with it, let it
become the base-stone for all your thinking and you
will find your actions have changed.

In these lines Jesus assures us that we will never be left
destitute. "I will not leave you comfortless . . ." But more
than that, He assures us that *within us* as Christians, dwells
the "fulness of the Godhead bodily"!

I cannot explain this theologically. But I have experienced
it. Not in cataclysmic bursts of power usually. More likely
the realization comes when I least expect it, while stamping
a letter, or brushing my hair, or waiting for a train.

Now that I have received Christ as my Saviour, I know
that when I take a step, the whole Trinity moves with me.
Can I explain this? No. But I can experience it. And even
when I am *not* experiencing it, I can *know* it.

Jesus said He would pray the Father to send the Holy
Spirit to be within us forever. Then He said He Himself would
come. And once more He assures us that He and the Father
and the Spirit are one. When I receive Christ's life within me,
the whole Trinity comes too.

. . . It pleased the Father that in him should all fulness
dwell.

Return to sobermindedness as you should, and quit sinning. For I say to your shame, some have no sense of divine Presence (I Corinthians 15:34, Berkeley).

THIS may seem a strange "red stone," but don't pass it by because Paul sounds cross. I have found that much of what I used to pass by quickly because I thought Paul was being irritable, was actually because I was irritable.

I now see that Paul was simply completely sure of what he wrote. "Return to sobermindedness as you should, and quit sinning" sounds as though he were whipping us up to a burst of self-effort. He wasn't. Read the remainder of this "red stone" verse and remember that our "red stones" tell also of the power of the indwelling presence of God to enable us to withstand temptation. Paul, of all people, knew that when he was weak, then he was strong. He would *never* have recommended self-effort in order to stop sinning. In this verse, he simply *reminds* the wayward Corinthians (and us too) that *as long as* anyone has a sense of the divine Presence, the power of sin is broken! We must cultivate the sense of the constant, minute by minute presence of God with us and within us. This is a habit *we* can consciously form. He is always there. Our part is to remember it. And when we do, we find the *only* power by which we can "quit sinning." When we are born of God, some of God's own life is put within us. This is the *only* safeguard. *Consciously* in His presence, we just *can't* keep on sinning.

. . . having been born of God, we cannot practice sinning.

APRIL 14

*In God's presence I have such confidence through Christ,
not because we possess self-sufficiency to form personal
judgments; but because our sufficiency is God-given (II
Corinthians 3:4, 5, Berkeley).*

ONE of the great heart-cries of men and women everywhere and under all circumstances is for "confidence."
Sometimes it seems that the whole world trembles from
fear. When we can't find any other explanation for someone's
difficulty, we say "insecurity." And it's usually right.

Some "insecurity" shows itself in cringing and shyness. Some
in egotism and boasting. Mine was the latter. Yours may show
itself in timidity or withdrawal. No matter. Neither of us
needs to continue in a state of "no confidence."

Paul sings out joyfully in our "red stone" verse above .that
"In God's presence" he has "confidence through Christ."

We can sing out in confidence too.

Through Christ.

If only there were adequate words to express to you how
my own life has been changed because of the *realization* that
I *cannot get out* of His presence. If we could see Him with
our eyes, or feel His strong hand holding ours, or actually hear
His voice with our ears, we'd have supreme confidence for
anything. But look at us cringing or boasting, showing everyone around us that we dread life and fear it, even though we
call ourselves Christians. "For I say to your shame, some have
no sense of divine Presence." Paul is right. We must listen
to him. "In God's presence I have such confidence through
Christ. . . . I can do all things through Christ . . ." *And no-one
can get out of His presence.* We have His own word for it:

. . . Lo, I am with you alway . . .

When Israel went out of Egypt, the house of Jacob from a people of strange language; Judah was his sanctuary, and Israel his dominion (Psalm 114:1, 2).

WE long to hear God's voice and yet when we hear it, we so seldom recognize it as His. The physical sound of it may vary, but when we know Him, we can recognize that it is God who speaks — *if* we want to. Too often, hearing Him means obedience, and we prefer to remain deaf. But God does speak through human voices and for the next four days of sharing among my "red stones" I want to share with you a rare experience when I heard God's own voice in the voice of my very dear friend, Rosalind Rinker, early one morning when I was speaking in Seattle, Washington. In her morning devotions, Psalm 114 "came alive" to her and she phoned me to tell me she "had a word from the Lord for me." And then she began to share what we will share in these four pages. Psalm 114 had been a blur to me before. Now, it fairly shouts victory. I shall be forever grateful to her.°

The first two verses which make up our "red stone" above, simply say this: any temptation has a touch of "Egypt" in it. In us all is at least a shred of longing to go back to "Egypt" even though we "enjoyed" it in slavery. God leads us ever farther away, *if we obey.* And the memories dim. Now and then, however, we look back. But all along the way, "Judah was his sanctuary and Israel his dominion." We are His chosen people. ". . . I have chosen you . . ." And just as surely as "Judah was his sanctuary," so are we. No matter about our conflicts over the things we've left behind, God dwells *in* us. We can just keep walking. We need not *feel* His presence. He is there. We can just go on.

. . . for he hath said, I will never leave thee nor forsake thee.

° It is suggested that you read Psalm 114 each of these four days.

The sea saw it, and fled: Jordan was driven back. The mountains skipped like rams, and the little hills like lambs (Psalm 114:3, 4).

WHEN Christ dwells in us, His chosen ones, ("Judah was his sanctuary," v. 2), we have within us all the power we need to overcome any obstacle. Power resolutely to turn attention toward Canaan and *not* to look back longingly toward Egypt.

I cannot remind myself too often that "what gets our attention gets us." And we don't need any outside power to choose to look at the things of our old life. We were all born with this power. But when we choose to leave "Egypt" behind and go on with God, we need His power *every minute* to look to Him. This is a joyful thing instead of a desperate thing. It keeps us constantly dependent upon Him and this increases our union with Him and therefore our joy and our strength. When we partake of the life of God within us, it shows too. Others around us see it. The very things which draw us away from God "see" it. The obstacles "see" it. The sorrows. The heartbreaks. The fleshly desires. And they are "driven back."

"The sea saw it, and fled: Jordan was driven back."

Even that ocean of trouble out there in front of you will flee, if you begin right now to partake of the life of God within you. Every "Jordan" will be driven back by the same hands into which the nails were driven for your sake. For my sake. That "mountain" of fear will skip away. The nagging "little hills" of annoyance will trot off like lambs! Think back to when you tried it on all those other painful occasions. He has never failed any one of us yet. He is still living within you now. Act on it. And watch the sea and the Jordan and the mountains and the hills.

I will go (on) in the strength of the Lord God.

What ailed thee, O thou sea, that thou fleddest? thou Jordan, that thou wast driven back? Ye mountains, that ye skipped like rams; and ye little hills, like lambs? (Psalm 114:5, 6).

WHAT ailed thee, O thou sea . . .?" Here I see the humor of God. Here I begin to understand why every real saint of God *has* a kind of humor that is not even understandable to those outside of Christ. Here is humor based on God Himself. More deeply rooted than the mountains which have just skipped out of the way like rams! Humor based on a certainty that is deeper than the very sea itself! Holy laughter that laughs at Jordans to cross and hills to tunnel through!

Humor that springs from the *absolute certainty* of God's love.

Humor that does not wash away in tears shed at a fresh grave or from sheer annoyance over a trifle.

Humor that is eternal because God is eternal.

"What ails thee . . .?" asks the Holy Spirit through the psalmist of any and *all* our seemingly uncrossable obstacles *after* we have remembered Who it is Who lives within us. What ails thee, O wounded pride . . . what ails *thee*, O sleepless nights? . . . what ails *thee*, O ruined career? . . . what ails *thee*, O bitter heart?

Fled away, driven back, skipped off! Gone.

God lives within us. Draw on Him. And watch the enemies vanish like April snowflakes. Just go on "out of Egypt." God is *in* you as you go.

> . . . for ye are the temple of the living God; as God hath said, I will dwell in them, and walk in them; and I will be their God, and they shall be my people.

Tremble, thou earth, at the presence of the Lord, at the presence of the God of Jacob; which turned the rock into a standing water, the flint into a fountain of waters (Psalm 114:7, 8).

WHEN we set our feet down on the solid earth after a stormy plane trip, we feel completely secure again. We speak of the good, sure feeling of "old terra firma" again. We think of the earth beneath our feet as steadiness and safety.

But here is the Word of God, saying: "Tremble, thou earth, at the presence of the Lord, at the presence of the God of Jacob; . . ." Here is the Word of God reminding us that the One who dwells within us is mighty enough to cause the very earth to shake. The strongest earthly security trembles at the presence of the God who has come to live within us.

Why? Not only did He create the earth in the first place, but He can change and re-create as He wills. If you, His child, need "water" and there is only "rock" near-by, God, who created both "water" and "rock," can turn the "rock" to "standing water" for *you*. For me.

Whatever constitutes "Egypt" for you, He can lead you out of it. Whatever overflows you with its waves and billows, He can cause it to flee. He can drive back *your* "Jordan" and turn the "flint" into a veritable "fountain of waters." He is *our* God as well as the God of Jacob. He didn't make miracles for Jacob because Jacob was a lovely character. He made them because He loved Jacob. And He loves us too. Faithfully. Forever.

God is faithful, by whom ye were called unto the fellowship of His Son Jesus Christ our Lord.

. . . I have declared unto them thy name, and will declare it; that the love wherewith thou hast loved me may be in them, and I in them (John 17:26).

WHEN Jesus had spoken these words, he went forth with his disciples over the brook Cedron, where was a garden, into the which he entered . . ."
This "red stone" contains facets of truth so deep we can perhaps not penetrate them fully in this life. Jesus finished His high priestly prayer with the words above on the night before they killed Him, and they still hung glowing in the night air among the leaves above their heads as they walked toward the Garden of Gethsemane. And they still hang glowing above our heads now that He has fulfilled and is still fulfilling them.

". . . I have declared unto them thy name . . ." Jesus came to declare the Father to us. "No man hath seen God at any time; the only begotten Son, which is in the bosom of the Father, *he hath declared him.*"

". . . and will declare . . ." Jesus Christ is still declaring the name of the Father to us, His disciples of today. And He is doing it for the same reason He did it then: ". . . that the love wherewith thou hast loved me, may be in them, and I in them." Above everything, Jesus wanted and still wants us to know, to experience, the *love* of the Father just exactly as He experiences it. He knows the Father's heart. And knowing it, He also knows that if only He can show us what it is really like there, we will be forever finished with fear and anxiety and dread. The very last line of His prayer on the night before the crucifixion is the key to our being able to experience the Father's love for us.

He said He had already declared this love and would continue to declare it, even to us. He does this by His indwelling presence within us. ". . . that the love wherewith thou hast loved me may be in them, *and I in them.*" He is love. And —

There is no fear in love; but perfect love casteth out fear . . .

... for God is love. ... God is love ... (I John 4:8b, 16b).

"JOHN, the disciple whom Jesus loved . . ."
"Now, there was leaning on Jesus' bosom one of his disciples, whom Jesus loved."
"John, the beloved, . . . lying on Jesus' breast . . ."
John, filled with the Spirit of this Jesus Christ, began to experience in his last days the very essence of the Gospel.

John, who had heard the human heart of Jesus beat with love, finally realized that he had also heard God's heart beat, not only *with* love, but *because* of it. And when he saw this, as an old man, dear John wrote, not once, but *twice* — "God *is* love. . . . God is love."

God doesn't merely have a heart of love. He *is* love.

We do not fear His wrath if we know about His love, because knowing His love, we understand at last that His wrath is *not* against sinners, but against the *sin* that has crippled their lives. Hannah Whitall Smith wrote in her last years, as the realization of God's love broke on her in an intensity almost too great to bear: "When His enemies are scattered, ours are also!"

God is not weak, He is tender. He is not angry, He is kind even in His justice. Especially in His justice.

Actually, my heart sings that the justice of God is beyond our understanding. Where would any of us be if God were a just God, as we understand and mete out justice? If I depended upon His justice, as *I* know justice, I'd be cast into outer darkness forever. But, as John's old love-filled heart poured forth, not once but twice . . . I can depend upon God's love — because

... God is love. ... God is love ...

But love ye your enemies, and do good, and lend, hoping
for nothing again; and your reward shall be great, and ye
shall be the children of the Highest: for he is kind unto
the unthankful and to the evil (Luke 6:35).

FOR he is kind unto the unthankful and to the evil." What
a startling statement! But Jesus made it and He should
know all that can be known about the heart of the Highest. He came from Him and was going back to Him. He
came to let us know what that great heart is really like. When
we look closely at it, through this "red stone" verse above,
what we find there is too amazing and we pass on quickly,
not really believing it.

"For he is kind unto the unthankful and to the evil."

The inherited disposition of sin in us *prevents* our even
noticing this startling observation. The disposition of sin in
us somehow *wants* God to "get even" with those who are "unthankful and evil." And we are implicated in that desired
"getting even" because it seems to us that if God will only
punish those who are less thankful and more evil than we are,
it will somehow "help our cause." But here are the gleaming
facets of this exceedingly precious and rare "red stone" and
if we dare to look deeply into them under the light of the
Holy Spirit, we may find ourselves sitting in amazement
among the splinters of our shattered ideas of God's vengeance.
Vengeance does belong to the Lord, but only He knows its
direction and purpose. We are not to call it down upon the
head of any man or woman, no matter how unthankful and
no matter how evil. Jesus says we are to love them and treat
them well and *then* we will "be the children of the highest;
for he is kind unto the unthankful and to the evil."

. . . God is love. . . . God is love . . .

Surely he hath borne our griefs, and carried our sorrows: yet we did esteem him stricken, smitten of God, and afflicted. . . . and the LORD hath laid on him the iniquity of us all. (Isaiah 53:4, 6b).

HERE is one of those gleaming New Testament truths from the Old. Most of the Old Testament teaching leaves us with the impression that if we are good to God, He will be good to us. Or, that He loves us in direct proportion to how much we are obeying Him. But now and then, the prophetic beam swings for a bright instant onto the very face of Jesus Christ as in this "red stone" verse. And we see into the very heart of the Highest Himself.

". . . and the Lord hath laid on him the iniquity of us all." Does this mean that the Father, the Highest, forced Jesus to bear our griefs and carry our sorrows in order to pacify the Father's desire to be avenged?

No!

"God was *in* Christ, reconciling the world unto himself . . ." not "getting even," but taking the blow of sin *for us*. We do "esteem him stricken, smitten of God, and afflicted . . ." but we see God smiting Himself and laying on Himself "the iniquity of us all." Jesus and the Father are one. He and only He could say that the Father is "kind to the unthankful and to the evil." Only Jesus Christ knew. It has all turned out to be a love story, but we don't know it because we don't know about the true state of the Father's heart.

. . . God is love. . . . God is love . . .

Or despisest thou the riches of his goodness and forbearance and longsuffering; not knowing that the goodness
of God leadeth thee to repentance? (Romans 2:4).

BECAUSE we are ignorant of the Father's heart, most
of us don't act as though we believe it *is* a love story.
God is not a "grandmother God," musty with sentiment and stiff with old laws packed away in the dark corners
of antiquity. We act as though He is a dual-natured God with
one trunk full of ancient laws we can never keep and another
full of lace handkerchiefs with which to dry our eyes and blow
our noses when we feel sorry that we broke the laws He knew
we would break all along! God is not "soft." But He is kind.
He is not a God of compromise, but He is a God of forgiveness.

He does not pat us on the head and say, "There, there, my
child, I know you didn't mean to do that ghastly thing; I will
forgive you because I am a softhearted God." NO. He stands
before us in the person of the Crucified One and cries: "Come
unto me." God forgives freely, oh, so freely! But it is not an
easy forgiveness. It cost Him His Son. And this shows me
more about His love than sentiment could ever show. No-one
can grasp "the riches of his goodness and forbearance and
longsuffering" until that one has fallen in true repentance at
His feet, knowing there is no other way out. Being glad
there is none! His "goodness leadeth thee to repentance."
Rejoice. Because there is no forgiveness without repentance.
And it is His love that leads us to repentance.

God does not drive us to our knees with a big stick. No-one
is brought to true repentance any other way except by the
goodness and the longsuffering and the forbearance of God.

I gave her space to repent . . . , and she repented not. . . .
Repent ye. . . . God is love . . .

APRIL 24

. . . repent ye, and believe the gospel (Mark 1:15b).

JESUS said this. ". . . Jesus came into Galilee, preaching the gospel of the kingdom of God. And saying, The time is fulfilled, and the kingdom of God is at hand: *repent ye, and believe the gospel.*"

The kingdom of God is at hand and anyone can enter into it who will "repent . . . and believe the gospel." The gospel of Jesus Christ tells us that a way has been made for us to find peace with God. But it is a way that leads into a new life. A life which invades us from outside ourselves. A life which has its origin in the kingdom of God. In God Himself. It is not an improved human life. It is an entirely new life. ". . . old things are passed away; behold, all things are become new. And all things are of God, who hath reconciled us to himself by Jesus Christ."

"All things are of God . . ." This is why everyone must repent before entering upon the new life. True repentance comes slowly to some. Perhaps I should say a sense of the need for forgiveness comes slowly. We can be so twisted that we seem almost unaware of sin. I was. But God knew this, and by His love, He brought me to repentance.

But Jesus did not stop by preaching, "repent ye." He knew that being willing to turn around and go an entirely new direction is not possible *until* we "believe the gospel." And so He said, "Repent ye and believe the gospel." When we believe the gospel, we believe Christ. And when we believe in Christ, He becomes our Saviour from the old ways. Only then *can* "all things be made new." Being sorry isn't enough. Being repentant is.

. . . and godly sorrow worketh repentance to salvation.

124

Come unto me, all ye that labour and are heavy laden, and I will give you rest (Matthew 11:28).

THIS is among our "red stones" showing the love of God as it leads to true repentance, because I believe it is impossible for anyone to "come unto" Jesus Christ without repenting. Now, it is possible to learn things *about* Christianity and still go on in the old life, but He said we were to "learn of" *Him.* And when we begin to learn what He is really like, we begin to know in our hearts that He did what He did on the Cross because He Himself was personally *assuming full responsibility* for our individual dispositions of sin. This melts us.

This kind of love leads to repentance.

Sorrow and shame for our selfishness usually go along with repentance and may precede it. But the alcoholic who is merely "sorry and ashamed," will go right out and get drunk again, as a rule. He is filled with sorrow but it is *human* sorrow. And only "*godly* sorrow worketh *repentance* to *salvation.*" Someone very dear to us kicked me once when he was very drunk. When he sobered up his heart was broken with sorrow and shame because of what he had done. But it did not lead to repentance and he got drunk again. It was human sorrow only. But "godly sorrow" which alone leads to true repentance (which alone leads to salvation), shows us in one ugly, blinding flash that we have *really kicked God!* "Against thee and thee only have I sinned . . . ," sobbed David and I know what he meant! And knowing that, I now know *why* it has all turned out to be a love story. Because I now know in my own experience that "God is love." Jesus Christ proved it to me.

Greater love hath no man than this, that a man lay down his life . . .

125

And account that the longsuffering of our Lord is salvation
. . . (II Peter 3:15a).

LOOK closely at that small "red stone" above.
Many have told me they have never really seen it before. This was true with me. I had experienced His
salvation for four years before I saw that what I was experiencing *was* the *longsuffering* of the Lord Jesus Christ.

Peter, who experienced this longsuffering of Jesus when He
was still on this earth, could write this. And so the Holy
Spirit directed Peter to remind us that what we too often
think of as a patent "process" is, in reality, the Lord Himself
being willing to suffer endlessly for us!

He suffers *for* us and *over* us.

He never runs out of patience. We never get on His
nerves. He never stops loving. He always welcomes back.
And even when we leave Him for a time, He never leaves us.
This is His longsuffering. And it saves us, and keeps us saved.

". . . the longsuffering of our Lord *is* salvation."

If we have seen this, we *know* the Gospel is a love story.
Within us begins to stir a longing to obey a God who can
love like this. We stop deciding who is "saved" and who is
not. We see beyond the "process" to the heart of God that
prompts longsuffering of a quality that can save a human
race! We are melted by the heart that broke over our sin
on a Cross on a dark hilltop and we can only fall before Him
and worship when we *try* that heart and find it still breaking
— for love of us. I can only bow my rebellious heart to His
and give thanks.

. . . God is love. . . . God is love . . .

And to know the love of Christ, which passeth knowledge,
that ye might be filled with all the fulness of God
(Ephesians 3:19).

H ERE seems to be proof of some of what we have been
saying as we have examined these "red stones" which
speak of the love of God. Most of us do not act as
though it has all turned out to be a love story. And I believe the reason is in this verse from Paul's letter to the
church at Ephesus. Paul said, "For this cause I bow my
knees unto the Father of our Lord Jesus Christ." He was not
praying for the filling of his spiritual children with the fulness of God. Paul knew that those Ephesian Christians, like
us, *would not* be filled until they really *knew* the love of
Christ. Like us, they didn't quite trust themselves to God's
mercy. But Paul, knowing them and knowing Christ, knew
that when they once got a glimpse of the *love* of God through
Christ, they would then be filled.

". . . to know the love of Christ . . . that ye might be
filled . . ."

Let Jesus Christ love you all He wants to at this moment.

Expose yourself to His love. He will love you into loving
Him. "We love him, [only] because he first loved us." Let
Him love you all He wants to and then you'll be willing to
let Him fill you with Himself. Most of us would be glad to
be "filled with God," if God could just come in and "fill up"
the places left over from our own self-occupation. But He is
a holy God and He must have a holy place to dwell. And
He must have all of it. If you feel you simply *cannot* give
Him everything, at least you can begin to expose yourself to
His love. Once you do, He will woo you night and day,
and at last you'll know, as I believe I am beginning "to know
the love of Christ, which passeth knowledge . . ."

For I am persuaded, that neither death, nor life, nor
angels, nor principalities, nor powers, nor things present,
nor things to come, nor height, nor depth, nor any other
creature, shall be able to separate us from the love of God,
which is in Christ Jesus our Lord.

For God so loved the world, that he gave his only begotten
Son, that whosoever believeth in him should not perish, but
have everlasting life (John 3:16).

FOR several years I wrote and directed a dramatic Christian radio program, which originated in Chicago. One cold, snowy winter night a man came to the studio where the broadcast was produced to tell me that two weeks ago one of the actors had misread John 3:16. This was his complaint:

"Whoever read it said, 'whosoever believeth *on* him should not perish'; and *my* Bible says, 'whosoever believeth *in* him . . . ?'"

After he was gone, I thought, "The whole world is sitting on an atomic bomb pile and that poor man traveled all the way from northern Wisconsin to correct us on a preposition!"

I was grateful for his interest. No doubt when I wrote the script in the first place, I made the error. *My* Bible also said: "Whosoever believeth *in*," but this true story has no value to us whatever unless it startles us afresh with the tremendous content of John 3:16.

So much has been written about it by many more learned than I, but I have experienced it and what we will share is very simple. Actually, John 3:16, which has been called "the twenty-five most important words in history," *is* very simple.

As we look at it among our collection of "red stones" that show God's love, I would only call your attention to God's motive for "giving." You know it, but look again. His motive is love. True, ". . . there is no remission of sins except by the shedding of blood" and we are redeemed by the blood of Jesus Christ; *but* even before the blood was poured out, love was in operation in the divine heart. Giving *always* comes out of love. Love cannot sit by itself and *not* give.

For God so loved the world . . . that he gave . . .

As many as I love, I rebuke and chasten . . . (Revelation 8:19).

T HIS may seem a hard saying. But the glorified Jesus Christ said it, and if we really look deep into the gleaming heart of this "red stone" we see great joy there for all of us.

I don't believe it means only that God's love for you can be measured by the amount of suffering in your life, as so many seem to think. This is relevant, but more thrilling and more meaningful to me is the fact that *He only punishes by love!*

God never punishes by any means but love.

If only we could ask Peter about *this* personally!

"Simon, Simon . . . I have prayed for thee, that thy faith fail not." Yet in spite of the fact that the Lord was praying for him, Peter swore violently and denied Jesus three times. I'd like to ask Peter about the rebuke and chastening of the Lord Jesus. Peter would know. Because ". . . while he [Peter] yet spake, the cock crew. And the Lord turned, and looked upon Peter. . . . And Peter went out and wept bitterly." In the Lord's look was disappointment, yes, but also love. Otherwise Peter would not have wept. If the Lord had spoken harshly to him, Peter might have sworn again. He had been known to argue with Jesus. But the Lord "punished" him in the only way that heals. With love.

. . . God is love. . . . God is love . . .

Jesus saw Nathanael coming to him, and saith to him, Behold an Israelite indeed, in whom is no guile! Nathanael saith unto him, Whence knowest thou me? Jesus answered and said unto him, Before that Philip called thee, when thou wast under the fig tree, I saw thee (John 1:47, 48).

IT would be impossible to love as God loves us without His being constantly *aware* of us. Dr. Albert Day says we can think of our moment of most intense concentration upon the one we love above all others in the world, multiply this by infinity, and still not realize how acutely God is aware of each one of us every minute of our lives!

Jesus Christ is *never indifferent*.

"Nathanael saith unto him, Whence knowest thou me?" Jesus told him He knew about him while he was just standing under a certain fig tree. And what Jesus knew about Nathanael was true. He knows and cares and is *aware* every minute of each one of us. We reject this because we can't imagine one person being able to concentrate on more than one object at a time. But this is God. He can do it. He is never, never indifferent. We could ask Peter about this too. And he could answer with the same bitter weeping, because even in the midst of the tragic trial for His own life, "the Lord turned, and *looked upon Peter* . . ."

He is *never* unaware of us. Never indifferent. We *cannot* "leave Him cold." We can *leave Him,* but He never forgets about us. And Peter and you and I and any other disciple who comes to love Him, only do so because we have come to know *His love first*.

Herein is love, not that we loved God, but that he loved us, and sent his Son to be the propitiation for our sins.

BLUE STONES

An Hebraic tradition states that the original Ten Command-
ments were inscribed upon a blue sapphire. Whether this is
true or not, those of us who have tried to keep the Ten Com-
mandments have found that we need the very life of God
within us to do it. For that reason and one other we have
gathered our "blue stone" verses into a pile beside those
"red stones" we have just shared during the months of March
and April. Our "red stone" verses told of this life of God
within us. Of the love of God. And anyone who has attempted
to live victoriously with no sense of the life of God within or
with a distorted conception of His love, knows such an attempt
is doomed to failure. So, in the months of March and April
we have exposed ourselves to His love and to the power over
temptation which comes ONLY *from a cultivated sense that*
He DOES *live within us!*

These "blue stones" placed beside the "red stones," then,
are verses to increase our faith. Hope verses. Promise verses.
All directly contingent upon His love and His Presence within.
Promises mean very little if we don't know the promiser. If
these verses seem out of your reach, look again at the "red
stones" and open yourself to His love and His indwelling
Presence.

Actually, rubies and sapphires are physically the same.
Rubies are called red sapphires and sapphires are called blue
rubies. So, our verses are also essentially related. The "red
stones" reassure us as to God's character. The "blue stones"
can show us how to lay hold of His very life. Wonderful to
me is the fact that rubies and sapphires are among the most
precious stones, but both are merely a form of crystallized
alumina or common clay. We can be still more certain, re-
membering this, that even our "earthen vessel" can be fit for
the Master's use.

Now share my "pleasant blue stones."

And David was greatly distressed; for the people spake of stoning him, because the soul of all the people was grieved, every man for his sons and for his daughters: but David encouraged himself in the Lord his God (I Samuel 30:6).

FAITH and hope and love are essentials of every day. "Faith, hope, love, these three." But on some days, when we are "greatly distressed" and in danger of "stoning" of one kind or another, *hope* becomes an acute necessity! On those days, "we are saved by hope." On those days we can rejoice that we have been "begotten . . . again unto a lively hope . . ."

The word "begotten" is the key word here. We have been "born again" *unto* living hope. The very life of God Himself has been put within us when we receive Christ as our Saviour. David, on the day he "was greatly distressed . . . encouraged himself in the Lord his God." Not in a theory *about* Him.

We can do this too.

We have easier access to God now, in fact. He is within us. And the "stonings," instead of discouraging us, *can*, if we are willing, actually *encourage* us. How? By allowing them to remind us who it is who has come to live within us.

None of us is immune to being "greatly distressed." David was "greatly distressed." But he did exactly what we can do. "David encouraged himself *in the Lord*, his God." This implies a personal relationship. If you are His, then He is yours.

. . . Christ in you, the hope of glory . . .

MAY 2

Stand in awe, and sin not: commune with your own heart upon your bed, and be still (Psalm 4:4).

WE cannot "encourage ourselves in the Lord our God" *unless* we are in fellowship with Him. Hope springs from oneness with God. Faith springs from oneness with God.

If you are having trouble "whipping up faith," perhaps a moment of self-examination will be valuable. *Can* you "commune with your own heart upon your bed, and be still"? In that moment between you and your pillow, is there any shadow of a disobedience which robs you of sleep?

Can you face what you see in your own heart, knowing God sees it too? Can you face it and sleep? "Hope springs eternal" from the heart that is one with God. But if there is one single point on which we are not obeying His slightest whisper, we cannot "commune with our own hearts . . . and be *still*."

Most particularly we will not "be still." We cannot.

If something is blocking our oneness with Christ, we are noisy with excuses and alibis and explanations and dodges. And sometimes we are noisy with service! If something is there between you and Christ, you know it. So does He. And "if our heart condemn us, God is greater than our heart, and knoweth all things." We do not need to go on with troubled hearts. With guilty consciences. God is greater than your guilty conscience and actually it is an insult to God to *keep* a guilty conscience. He poured out His own blood on Calvary to free you from sin *and* the *guilt* that follows it. Give it to Him. He is "greater than our heart." Norman Grubb suggests keeping "short accounts with God."

If we do, hope will be a part of our daily peace. If there is "nothing between" we are confident of all things in God.

. . . Commune with your own heart . . . and be still.
. . . If our heart condemn us not, then have we confidence toward God.

133

May 3

Then shalt thou call, and the Lord shall answer; thou shalt cry, and he shall say, Here I am . . . (Isaiah 58:9a).

ALONG with you, I love to sing "Standing on the Promises of God." And we can stand on His promises. But perhaps there is an even deeper truth we should see here.

There is an even more comforting, more faith-building, more hopeful facet to this "blue stone" verse concerning those times of pain and grief and confusion when we call for God in our helplessness. These "blue stone" verses will, if we open ourselves to them, build the very fiber of our faith *for* us.

And so, early in this particular sharing, we must get this perfectly straight: God is greater than His promises!

Please do not misunderstand. I am in no way lessening the value of His promises. But there are times when we are too ill to remember words. Times of grief and shock so intense that words which constitute promises will not arrange themselves into a sentence whose meaning we can grasp. There are times when we are in too much physical pain even to remember that "God is love."

Sleepless nights following one another in a frantic parade can drive an arrangement of words from our memories, but always, under *any* circumstance we can remember a *person*. Perhaps not even the person's *name*. But always the "something" that makes one particular person distinguishable from another comes to mind. The sense of that person's life can be yours even when every promise is forgotten. God's promises *are* completely dependable. But if you forget the promises, He is always there.

Thou shalt call, and the Lord shall answer . . . Here I am. I will never leave thee nor forsake thee.

Then shalt thou call, and the Lord shall answer; thou shalt cry, and he shall say, Here I am. If thou take away from the midst of thee the yoke, the putting forth of the finger, and speaking vanity (Isaiah 58:9).

THOU shalt cry, and he shall say, Here I am. *If* thou take away from the midst of thee the yoke . . ." What does this mean? Isn't God willing to hear our cry, even when we are disobedient? Yes. I couldn't follow a God who only favored me according to my attention to Him. This would make God very much like the conception many people seem to hold of Him, but I believe it to be entirely wrong. In Jesus Christ, and all through the New Testament, I see God as a God who will *never* leave us. Who not only hears our cries, but is right there with us in our troubles. A God who actually falls to the ground *with* a little brown sparrow would not turn His back on me because I failed Him.

No, I merely believe this means we do not *hear* His response to our cry except on the conditions He gives us in this "blue stone" verse. The "yoke" has our attention. And here the yoke seems to constitute criticism and pride or shallowness of heart in us. ". . . the putting forth of the finger" may be arrogance toward the very sacredness of life itself. It may be self-righteousness. Wrong attitudes of heart. And the "speaking vanity" may be our own voices saying, "Well, I'm just like this and that's all there is to it!" Or it may be the self-righteous, calloused heart turned away from the Cross, boasting: "At least I'd never have done a thing like that!"

We will hear Him say "Here I am" when we cry, *if* we are completely open to His voice. One way to remain open is to let other people "off the hook of *your* critical disposition."

Be still, and know that I am God . . .

And if thou draw out thy soul to the hungry, and satisfy the afflicted soul; then shall thy light rise in obscurity, and thy darkness be as the noon day (Isaiah 58:10).

DO you feel ignored by life and is it dark where you are right now? Here is another "blue stone" of hope which can change those depths and that darkness into heights and noonday sun.

But as in yesterday's sharing, there is also a condition which we must meet. There is an *if*. But it is very clear and we need only to meet the condition, then we can forget the darkness and the obscurity.

First of all, let's admit that when we feel cast aside or forsaken or lonely — ". . . in obscurity," it leads inevitably to self-pity, unless we meet God in it. And I am convinced that *nothing* clogs our joy in God like self-pity. It is exactly the opposite of what we see when we look at Jesus hanging on the Cross blessing His enemies who were laughing at His agony. And during the time in which we are indulging in it, we are cancelling in our own lives the power for victory let loose on that Cross for us. We do sink into obscurity. We are in darkness. And God knows these things. Since He created us, He knows how we react to everything and so He carefully reminds us that "*if* thou draw out thy soul to the hungry, and satisfy the afflicted soul; *then* shall thy light rise in obscurity and thy darkness be as the noonday." If you are lonely or feeling cast aside, pour yourself out to someone else today. All around us hearts are crying just to be loved. Satisfy someone's need to be loved, by letter or by a telephone call or by a visit. You won't need to preach a sermon to them. Just say "I love you." And watch the results. Satisfy their hunger and affliction and —

. . . . THEN shall thy light rise in obscurity, and thy darkness as the noon day.

MAY 6

And the Lord shall guide thee continually, and satisfy thy soul in drought, and make fat thy bones: and thou shalt be like a watered garden, and like a spring of water, whose waters fail not (Isaiah 58:11).

THE Lord wants to guide us continually. He wants us to remember He is continually saying "Here I am." And the promises He makes if we meet the conditions for hearing His voice and being willing to take His guidance are the loveliest of promises.

If you and I will "draw out" our souls to someone who is afflicted or hungry, if we will drop our cloaks of self-pity and self-righteousness, He will not only bring light into our obscurity and drive away our darkness, He will satisfy our souls in drought and we will "be like a watered garden."

I'm glad He put it that way.

". . . and thou shalt be like a *watered* garden."

Then I know God Himself will be doing the watering. My needs will be met by His own dear hands. My heart will be mended by the pressure of His Heart against it.

"He shall feed His flock like a shepherd . . ."

But more than this direct, personal attention, He also *becomes* our "spring of water, whose waters fail not." He cannot fail. He is God. We will be fulfilled — in full.

. . . the water that I shall give him shall be in him a well of water springing up into everlasting life . . . Ye are complete in him.

And they that shall be of thee shall build the old waste places: thou shalt raise up the foundations of many generations; and thou shalt be called, The repairer of the breach, The restorer of paths to dwell in (Isaiah 58:12).

THOSE of us who have seen *our* part in the crucifixion of Christ, will forever gasp in wonder and glad amazement at this almost unbelievable "blue stone" verse! How my own faith leaps up when I realize He is also talking to me here.

My "waste places" were so many. Just to know that He has put them forever behind me, just to know He has forgiven me for my destruction is enough. But here is this "Lord of all" pouring down His love in an *overflow* of promises. My "waste places" were many. My years were eaten by many locusts. But here now is the God who forgave me, adding adoration to adoration in my heart, as He declares that even *I* "shall be called, The repairer of the breach, The restorer of paths to dwell in."

I dare to claim this promise for you too, as you read this page. ". . . they that shall be of thee shall build the old waste places . . ." As I claim it for you, who read my book, you may claim it for your friends or your children or for anyone who falls under your influence. Anyone who "shall be of thee."

Dare to look at the person you were when Jesus Christ saved you. Ask the Holy Spirit to cause you to realize your part in Calvary.

Remember the times you shook your fist in God's face and grabbed your rights. Recall the screech of your own raw moments of self-defense. See yourself at the foot of the Cross of Calvary and realize that He not only has forgiven you and made you new, He is now saying:

. . . thou shalt be called, The repairer of the breach, The restorer of paths to dwell in . . . I will cause thee to ride upon the high places of the earth . . . for the mouth of the Lord hath spoken it.

MAY 8

A little one shall become a thousand, and a small one a strong nation: I the Lord will hasten it in his time (Isaiah 60:22).

WE have already said there are no little things with God. He cares about every little thing as though it were not at all small. And if there are no small *things* with God, surely there are no small, insignificant *people* with Him.

Not long ago, I was with an outstandingly capable and successful woman just minutes before she walked like a trusting child into a personal relationship with her new Saviour, Jesus Christ. But before she made the glorious transaction, she looked at me and asked: "How do you expect me to believe God cares about one bit of protoplasm like me?"

Just one or two words about Jesus as He hung on the Cross and her heart melted. She already wanted Him. Her need was great. As was mine. But when one is for the first time aware of God as a Person who loves, one is at the same moment struck with the appalling thought that a God who could create the macrocosm *and* the microcosm could possibly care about one "little one."

Only a look inside the heart that broke on Calvary can convince our hearts. But one look does convince us. And here is a "blue stone" whose every facet holds a promise that He not only cares, but cares enough to make good, creative use of *each* one of us. Especially the "little ones" among us.

God has had a marvelous plan for your life from the moment He conceived you in His mind. A plan especially for you. One no-one else can complete. Only you. Here is a promise to lay hold of with great expectation. ". . . I the Lord will hasten it in his time." Knowing Him, we know He is never late nor early. And He does have a plan for each one of our lives, if those lives are *in* Christ.

For we are his workmanship, created in Christ Jesus unto good works, which God hath before ordained that we should walk in them.

> And it shall come to pass, that before they call, I will
> answer; and while they are yet speaking, I will hear
> (Isaiah 65:24).

TUCKED between the words of this "blue stone" verse, I have always found amazing assurances. I cannot adequately put these assurances into words. They are much more than a promise to me from God that He will hear my prayers.

They are much more than a promise that He already has my answer ready for me, even before I make the request.

These assurances are strangely nameless.

During the time my dear friend, Ellen Riley, was guiding me carefully and kindly to an acceptance of Jesus Christ as my personal Saviour, I read this verse for the first time. I did not read it in the Bible. I had never read the Bible. She knew I was adamant about "text-flingers." She had to talk to me and write to me for a long, long time without using any Scripture verses at all. But once at the close of a very lighthearted letter, way down at the bottom of the page, she wrote simply:

". . . before they call, I will answer; and while they are yet speaking, I will hear."

I felt my heart squeeze a little. Desperately I needed to be answered! Desperately I needed an answer. And a new longing was begun with that verse which I didn't even know was from the Bible.

If your heart longs, *He has answered.*

All along He has known your longing and He has known just when you would call. He has been waiting for you to voice your longing. Go ahead and ask Him with no fear that He will not understand or that He will not hear. Ask Him right now.

> . . . and while they are yet speaking, I will hear. Ask, and
> it shall be given you . . .

**Thou wilt keep him in perfect peace, whose mind is stayed
on thee: because he trusteth in thee (Isaiah 26:3).**

THIS "blue stone" verse is perhaps one of the most familiar verses in the Bible. People hang it on their walls and send it in sympathy telegrams and sign it at the end of letters and use it in psychology books.

Certain groups use it as a kind of mental therapy. Psychologically it is a very strong verse. The new thought books recommend it as a way to "find" peace.

How to think peaceful thoughts: ". . . whose mind is stayed on thee." This much is widely used. It is a mental discipline. Focus your mind on your own concept of God, the new thought books say, then you will find peace.

But, true peace cannot be found. It is a gift of God. "He is our peace," says Paul, and the "He" is Jesus Christ who has "made peace by the blood of his cross." There is psychological value in the very act of keeping one's mind fixed on something outside oneself. Something "higher." But when your heart is smashed you can't focus your mind most of the time. When your body is trembling with pain, you can't practice concentration. This is a power-filled verse under *all* circumstances only because of who Christ is. It is not the fixing of the mind alone that brings peace. It is the character of the One on whom we fix our minds. And God does not promise to keep us in perfect peace because we have done Him the honor of trusting Him. It isn't a reward. It is an inevitable *result*.

Peace comes when we fix our minds on God and enter into oneness with Him and we can *only* do this when we know what He's like! We trust Him because we know Him. We trust Him, not because we are experts in the art of trusting, but because He is trustworthy.

**Jesus Christ the same yesterday, and today,
and forever . . . He is our peace . . .**

He shall feed his flock like a shepherd: he shall gather the lambs with his arm, and carry them in his bosom, and shall gently lead those that are with young (Isaiah 40:11).

IT is a relief to know that the life of faith is *not* dependent upon our ability to trust, but upon His trustworthiness.

The sheep can trust their shepherd if He is a good shepherd. And we are the sheep of His pasture. His sheep may safely graze.

All of His sheep.

The lambs which He gathers with His arm may certainly graze safely and know that even if they stumble and fall, the Shepherd will "lay down his life for the sheep." He will "gather the lambs with his arm . . ."

Those of us who have known Him over a period of time, know that He will care for those new in His love. We can assure them that He gathers the newborn Christian in His bosom with great tenderness and great gentleness. But for those who have been the sheep of His flock for a longer time and who have been given the sometimes painful work of carrying young Christians or non-believers as a sheep carries her young, here is great hope for us in this "blue stone" verse too.

"He shall . . . gently lead those that are with young." The enemy is also very watchful over "those that are with young." Traps are everywhere. Storms blow up suddenly and we try to rush and push past the others to the safety of what we *think* is the fold. On the way, in our foolish haste, we may drop the "young." Only the Shepherd knows how to lead us safely. Only He can recognize the false traps of the enemy. I was led to Christ by one who had never before brought anyone to Him. She led me safely because she listened to the Shepherd. She let Him lead *her*.

He shall . . . gently lead those that are with young.

Thus saith the LORD that made thee, and formed thee from the womb, which will help thee; Fear not . . . For I will pour my spirit upon thy seed, and my blessing upon thine offspring (Isaiah 44:2a, 3).

THOSE of us who are commissioned to be an active part of the great reconciliation of God — and everyone who belongs to Him *is* to be a part of this reconciliation — should look long and deeply at this "blue stone" verse.

First of all, if you feel discouraged in your Christian service, this promise is from "the Lord that made *thee*, and formed thee from the womb . . ." No doubt, He is not at all surprised at this seeming failure. At your present discouragement. And this same Lord "which will help thee" also commands that you "Fear not . . ."

In all things, even this present trial, He is there.

"It is I; be not afraid."

He is in this thing with you. If those whom you are sent to guide and watch over in their spiritual infancy seem to be ill unto death; if they are stumbling and making alibis and showing the deceitfulness of every human heart, "Fear not . . ." the Lord is saying right now, "For I will pour my spirit upon thy seed, and my blessing upon thy offspring."

Those whom God uses to reach others for Himself know the travail of watching silently and praying for these babes "until Christ be formed in them." It is an agony not expressible in words. But the Lord reminds us that we are not to be afraid for them. We are just to go on belonging to Him ourselves. In one sense they are our "children." In the ultimate sense they are His children. And His responsibility. Just as we too, are His responsibility. We can simply rest and belong because "Thus saith the Lord that made thee . . .":

And all thy children shall be taught of the Lord; and great shall be the peace of thy children.

MAY 13

For ye shall not go out with haste, nor go by flight: for the LORD will go before you; and the God of Israel will be your rereward (Isaiah 52:12).

HERE are many things which are easily missed without careful seeing into the very depths of this deep "blue stone" verse. Many things which increase our faith. Which cause us to be willing to enter into the very rhythm of God's life.

And once we have entered into this oneness with Him, we begin to see how simple life becomes. Not easy, but simple. It is only when we stumble back into our own rhythm that we begin to grab wildly for "more faith." Faith is being one with God. Then we know about Him. Then whatever He does is all right.

"For ye shall not go out with haste, nor by flight . . ." How is this possible? What keeps us from running ahead of God? What prevents our "going out by flight"? What causes us *not* to try to escape? The answer to all of these questions is simply that God has already gone before us. "The Lord will go before thee."

He knows what's up ahead. He's been there. And if we are obedient and with Him in fellowship each step of the way, it is more ridiculous to think that we *would* run ahead than to think we would not. He knows. He knows about the causes for our thinking we need to escape. He knows about the enemies of our soul's peace. We have no need to escape. No need to try any way other than the way of just being with Christ. He Himself "will be your rereward." No need to flee to the edge of the world for peace or protection.

. . . Your life is hid with Christ in God.

144

> For the mountains shall depart, and the hills be removed;
> but my kindness shall not depart from thee, neither shall
> the covenant of my peace be removed, saith the Lord that
> hath mercy on thee (Isaiah 54:10).

THIS tells me that *anything* can happen and the Lord will not only remain with us, but He will remain kind. We tend to think of the "mountains" and the "hills" as perhaps trouble from outside ourselves. But to me, at least, my world has never shaken more violently than under the impact of my own willful disobedience to Jesus Christ. After I have disobeyed Him, my grief is intense. My remorse and shame could destroy me, and the devil could have the time of his evil life feeding my black discouragement *if* I weren't absolutely sure that the Lord's kindness would *not* depart from me.

Actually His kindness leads me to repentance.

And even as I cry out for forgiveness, deep at the center is the assurance, not only that peace will return, but that it has never really departed from me. I have merely lost my awareness of it. It is His peace which He left me and it is a part of Himself. He has said He will never leave me nor forsake me and so, of course, His peace will not leave either. It cannot. "He is our peace." The covenant of His peace shall not be removed, because the Lord "hath mercy on thee." He knows that without Him we are bereft. "His mercy endureth forever."

> . . . Without me, ye can do nothing. (But) . . . Lo, I am
> with you alway.

MAY 15

The secret of the LORD is with them that fear him; and he will show them his covenant (Psalm 25:14).

WHAT is the "secret of the Lord"?
As in all of the Christian life, there is a "secret" on both sides. This is true because there are two wonderfully balanced sides to reckon with in all things pertaining to victorious living.

There is God's side.

And there is our side.

As we shared our "red stone" verses, we looked at God's side. We gazed in awe at His love, His unending mercy, His longsuffering which *is* our salvation (II Peter 3:15). And we looked deeper to see that this life which is God's has come to dwell within our lives if we have received Him there by faith.

God's side then is to be Himself *in us.*

Our side is to *let* Him be Himself in us.

Perhaps we could say that the "secret" on God's side is the very fact of His presence within us. Giving us all we ever need for every minute of our lives.

Then could we say, as we look into this "blue stone" verse above, that from our side, "the secret of the LORD" is *obedience?* The word "fear" here implies trust to me. Trust enough in His character to obey when He speaks.

Those who have tried the obedient life, know that it is true that ". . . he will show *them* his covenant." It is a lovely secret between you and God. In another delightful aspect, it is —

   . . . Your life . . . hid with Christ in God.

146

MAY 16

I will instruct thee and teach thee in the way which thou shalt go: I will guide thee with mine eye (Psalm 32:8).

IF deep searching of these "blue stone" verses is to deepen our faith, read this one at least five or six times and read it slowly and confidently. Hear God say it to you. Each time you read it, you will be strengthened in the depths of your being.

This is God speaking to us.

"I will instruct thee and teach thee in the way which thou shalt go: I will guide thee with mine eye."

Each one of us in each one of our sometimes confused "ways"? Yes. Each one of us can claim this amazing promise from the One who cannot lie!

God *will* instruct us. God will teach us. He will guide us with His own eye in the way He knows is the very best way for each one of us to go. This is too high for me. I cannot grasp it, but I can somehow understand it with my heart when I am willing to follow Him. When I am willing not only to know that He will guide me, but when I am willing to *be* guided. When I am willing to "be not as the horse, or as the mule, which have no understanding; whose mouth must be held in with bit and bridle . . ."

As I obey, I understand.

And the more I learn of the very character of Jesus Christ, the more I am willing to obey.

God has not only promised to instruct and teach us in the way we should go, He *became the way* in Jesus Christ. Oneness with Christ will keep me on the way. He *is* the way. When I am one with Him, I am already there.

. . . I am the way, the truth, and the life; no man cometh unto the Father, but by me.

147

MAY 17

There is a river, the streams whereof shall make glad
the city of God, the holy place of the tabernacles of
the most High (Psalm 46:4).

THERE *is* a river.

We need not cry out for supply. The river is already there. ". . . the streams whereof shall make glad the city of God." Not only are we promised always adequate supply, but we are promised gladness too.

There *is* a river.

And it is to "make glad . . . the holy place of the tabernacles of the most high." We are His tabernacles. "Know ye not that your body is the temple of the Holy Ghost?"

It is impossible for us to conceive being glad when our hearts are breaking, but God has said it. We don't need to conceive it. We can conceive very little of what God has in mind for us anyway. "It is too high" for us.

It is a waste of time to try to reach it. We can only receive.

The river is there.

In you. To "make glad . . ." The adequate supply seems to be taken for granted in this "blue stone" verse. God feels it necessary only to remind us that not only will our needs be met, but the river is full enough to make us glad too.

There *is* a river.

No matter what is tearing at you right now, remember, "There is a river . . ."

Be still, and know that I am God . . .

MAY 18

But that ye may know that the Son of man hath power on earth to forgive sins . . . Arise, take up thy bed, and go into thine house (Matthew 9:6).

HERE is a "blue stone" verse to increase even the feeblest faith.

Jesus, Himself saying: ". . . that ye may *know* . . ." He longs for us to be really *sure*. To know. In this account He is speaking to the man brought to Him "sick of the palsy, lying on a bed." It worked for him. It will work for us.

Jesus said to him, ". . . Son, be of good cheer; thy sins be forgiven thee." Then, with strong, gentle reassurance, He said: ". . . that ye may *know* that the Son of man hath power on earth to forgive sins . . . Arise, take up thy bed, and go into thine house."

Jesus says to us: ". . . be of good cheer; thy sins be forgiven thee." And when He sees our shifting faith even after His forgiveness, He gives us a practical suggestion which we ourselves can try. Even though He is the Son of God, He understands us so well, that He gives us something we can do to prove His power to forgive. Something we ourselves can do to prove that we have been given a new life. That we have been healed.

". . . Arise, take up thy bed, and go into thine house."

Whatever that thing is which symbolizes your doubt and fear, grasp it with both hands. Try it. ". . . Take up thy bed and walk."

"And he arose and departed to his house." When the sick man did this, he knew he had been healed. Try Him, however timidly. "If I may but touch his garment, I shall be whole." Touch Him now and know.

. . . and as many as touched (Him) were made perfectly whole.

149

MAY 19

But Mary stood without at the sepulchre weeping: and as she wept, she stooped down, and looked into the sepulchre John 20:11).

THIS Mary is Mary of Magdala, the courtesan whom Jesus touched and turned into a saint. This is Mary, who loved Him much because she had been forgiven much. Mary, who did not have a religious heritage behind her.

She was a woman in great need, who had met the Son of God and had found to her everlasting joy that the Son of God could meet her every need. And here she stands weeping outside the grave where they had just buried Him

Without a "good background," Mary was forced to lean *only* upon the Person of Jesus. Her own moral life was no stay to her. Her immoral life forced her to His feet. She had only Jesus to depend upon. "Nothing in my hands I bring . . . simply to Thy cross I cling." Mary had nothing to bring. She *had* to cling.

And here she stood weeping beside His grave. She didn't understand the theology of what He had just done for her. Somehow her joy was all in His Person and they had crucified Him and her very soul cried out in protest and agony! But, loving Him as she did, she stood by everything she knew of Him. "Mary stood without at the sepulchre . . ." where all she knew of Him had been buried.

If you are a new Christian, stand by all you know of Him. Soon you, like Mary, will be prompted to "stoop down and look into the sepulchre." And when you do, you will find that He, your Lord, is exactly who He claims to be. The *living* Son of God. He is not dead. Stand patiently by all you know of Him now, remembering that He showed Himself *first*, not to an "advanced Christian." Jesus showed Himself first to Mary.

. . . Woman, why weepest thou? Whom seekest thou? . . . I am he that liveth, and was dead; and . . . am alive forevermore.

150

Grace and peace be multiplied unto you through the knowledge of God, and of Jesus our Lord. According as his divine
power hath given unto us all things that pertain unto life
and godliness, through the knowledge of him that hath
called us to glory and virtue (II Peter 1:2, 3).

HERE is a "blue stone" verse which I prize highly. It
has made it simpler for me to lay hold of the faith I
have been given.

Peter has used the word "through" in two instances here,
both of which let enough light shine through to make this a
noticeably brilliant "stone." "Grace and peace be multiplied
unto you *through* the knowledge of God, and of Jesus our
Lord." This lets me know once and for all that grace and
peace will be mine *only* through finding out what God is
really like. When I am sure of His intention toward me, I
am peaceful. When I am sure of His intention toward me,
I am willing to *take* the grace which this knowledge of Jesus
Christ assures me is always flowing toward me.

Using the same word "through," Peter goes on to say that
"according as his divine power hath *given* unto us *all things
that pertain unto life* and godliness *through* the knowledge
of Him," we are to accept this gift and begin at once to
partake of the very life of God which has been put within us.

Whereby are given unto us exceeding great and precious
promises: that by these ye might be partakers of the divine
nature . . .

MAY 21

And beside this, giving all diligence, add to your faith . . . .
(II Peter 1:5a).

W E are to begin to partake of the life of God within us. We can see how to do this only *through* knowledge of God Himself. We can only know God by knowing Jesus Christ.

"And this is life eternal, that they might know thee the only true God, and Jesus Christ whom thou hast sent."

The small "blue stone" at the top of this page reflected a long, bright shaft of new light for my friend, Ellen Riley, only yesterday morning, as I write these pages. In her own devotions, she was reading the first chapter of II Peter. For a long time I had *almost* seen into verses 5 through 7, but the most I had seen so far was that here was an excellent list of moral choices which we have to make before we can know victorious Christian living. However, Ellen was shown the key. I hadn't gone far enough. The key is in verse 9. We shall share that "blue stone" tomorrow. May I urge that you read and reread the first nine verses of the first chapter of II Peter during these four days of sharing among them?

And for today, we look at this one small fragmentary "blue stone" above in order to see once more that faith has been given to us already. Now *we* have a part to perform. We will be able to perform it once we begin to gain a knowledge of what Jesus Christ is really like. This will give us our tools with which to begin to obey this verse. And this is our part: we are to *add to* our faith which has already been given to us by God Himself. And we are to do this diligently.

We must first receive our faith as a gift from God. This we do when we receive Christ Himself. Now we see that there is more.

And beside this, giving all diligence, add to your faith . . .

> And beside this, giving all diligence, add to your faith
> virtue; and to virtue knowledge; and to knowledge temper-
> ance; and to temperance patience; and to patience godliness;
> and to godliness brotherly kindness; and to brotherly kind-
> ness charity (II Peter 1:5-7).

THESE are the things we are to add, "giving all diligence" to the doing. When I look at this list, I still see a list of important moral choices we are to make. But now, I also see a rather vivid description of the very character of Jesus Christ!

If this is true, then aren't these traits all a part of me already? If He has come to live within me, why do I have to *add* them, "giving all diligence"? Isn't this self-effort? Isn't this trying to tie fruits onto my own tree? No. It is simply letting yourself see what amazing characteristics are available to you when you begin to *partake* of this life of God within you. It is not imitation. It is realization. God comes in with all that He is. But we must let this life show forth. We must "work it out" in our daily lives. We must let Him be Himself under all circumstances. Even when it causes us great inconvenience.

"Add" means to "give diligence" in staying out of Christ's way as He lives these characteristics out through our hum-drum daily lives. We must "give diligence" to doing this too. It is not natural. It is supernatural. In short, we must obey. When we really find out what He is like, then we will be watching for an impulse within us to abide by this amazing list of character traits. The impulse within you will be the pressure of the very life of God within you. Daily you will know more about Jesus. Daily, the supernatural life will become more familiar to you. Daily, you'll feel more at home with Christ.

> For if these things be in you, and abound, they make you
> that ye shall neither be barren nor unfruitful in the knowl-
> edge of our Lord Jesus Christ.

> But he that lacketh these things is blind, and cannot see afar off, and hath forgotten that he was purged from his old sins (II Peter 1:9).

THIS is the key verse. Here the bright shaft of new light showed me what God was really driving at through Peter in these amazing verses. I have seen this verse proven and reproven in my own life and in the lives of those with whom I work and live. There are two glowing facets in this "blue stone" verse.

Reread the list of characteristics (in verses 5 through 8) which we are to add with diligence. And now look at the first gleaming "facet" in the verse above. "But he that lacketh these things is blind, and cannot see afar off . . ." If you're in the dark about something, if you're confused and stay confused in trying to find God's will about something, check back over this list. God never tries to mix us up. ". . . he that lacketh these things is blind, and *cannot* see afar off . . ." Something is casting a shadow.

The second "facet" can change your entire life if you will face what it really says: ". . . he that lacketh these things . . . hath *forgotten* that he was purged from his old sins." He is *not* growing. Have you become self-righteous? Self-defensive? Have you a little hidden sin? Are you refusing to control your appetite? Are you allowing God to do His own loving through you even with those who are repulsive, to you? If not, you may be proving this key verse. According to the Word of God you are one of those who "hath *forgotten* that he was purged from his *old* sins." If I am not showing these traits Peter has listed, then I too am one who has forgotten what Jesus did for me on Calvary. God will forgive us quickly in the Name of Jesus and we can go on and never stumble on that weak point again.

> Wherefore the rather, brethren, give diligence . . . for if ye do these things, ye shall never fall.

There is therefore now no condemnation to them which are
in Christ Jesus, who walk not after the flesh, but after
the Spirit (Romans 8:1).

OUR collection of "pleasant stones" (for September and
and October) is composed of "green stone" verses which
ring with the victory cry of God's redeemed ones. This
"blue stone" verse above could rest easily among the green
ones. But I have put it here among our verses pertaining to
faith because it is so sure. In chapter 7 of Romans, Paul has
described the depths of us all. He has laid his finger on
every weakness and he has cried out in despair for every man
and woman and young person who has ever tried to be con-
sistently good under his or her own power:

"O wretched man that I am! who shall deliver me from
the body of this death?"

And then Paul sighs deeply, relieved for all eternity to be
able to say quietly and surely that he thanks God that Jesus
Christ has delivered him from that "on-again, off-again" battle
of ever-failing faith. And now, our shining "blue stone" above
to remind us that "there is therefore *now* no condemnation
(no *need* to fail) to them which are *in* Christ Jesus." I'm
glad, knowing how true is the description of myself in chapter 7 of Romans, that Paul adds here: ". . . to them . . . who
walk not after the flesh, but after the Spirit." *We always
choose.* We can choose to walk after our own desires, or
after the desires of the Spirit within us. If you and I choose
to walk *our* way, we both know sooner or later, we'll stumble
and fall. If we walk His way, we will get there. He is the
way.

Can two walk together, except they be agreed?

MAY 25

For the law of the Spirit of life in Christ Jesus hath made
me free from the law of sin and death (Romans 8:2).

HERE is another "blue stone" verse which could as easily
be a "green stone" victory verse. And yet, I chose to
put it here because my own faith leans against it so
often.

Our "blue stone" verses open the way to steady faith. If
we open ourselves to them, we will begin to see that the law
of faith is as absolute and as dependable as the law of gravity.

That very analogy has helped me greatly here.

"For the *law* of the Spirit of life in Christ Jesus hath made
me free from the law of sin and death."

Sin is a down pull.

Gravity is a down pull toward the center of the earth.

Both are dependable. No-one likes to think of sin as being
"dependable" but it is! "Who shall deliver me from the . . .
law of sin and death?" What can break the law of sin in me?
The down pull?

"There is therefore now no condemnation . . . For the law
of the Spirit of life in Christ Jesus hath" broken the down
pull of sin. Sin is a powerful law. *But* the "law of the Spirit
of life in Christ Jesus" is more powerful. He overcame sin on
the Cross. The power to break the law of sin has been let
loose in the world and it is ours for the taking and for the
using. When you lift your arm, you overcome the law of
gravity by the *higher law* of life in your body. Power to *lift*
your arm. Choose not to use that power and your arm falls,
obedient to the law of gravity once more. Choose to use the
power of Christ in you and you are free from the law of
"sin and death."

. . . God sending His own Son . . . condemned sin . . .
[and] if the Spirit of him that raised up Jesus from the
dead dwell in you, he that raised up Christ from the dead
shall also quicken your mortal bodies by his Spirit that
dwelleth in you . . . if the Son therefore shall make you
free, ye shall be free indeed.

But now in Christ Jesus ye who sometimes were far off are made nigh by the blood of Christ (Ephesians 2:13).

HERE is a "blue stone" verse to bow the hearts of those of us who know both what it is to be "far off" and to be "nigh."

Those of you who have belonged to Him for so long that it is almost impossible to remember what it is like to be "far off," may rest your faith on *our* knowledge of the darkness out there away from Him.

Darkness and quiet, helpless desperation. And longing.

Longing to be "nigh" but perhaps not knowing it.

Those of us who have been "made nigh by the blood of Christ" after having lived "far off" for much of our adult lives, wonder sometimes at indifference to this blood. We wonder more at the indifference to the One who shed His blood that we might be "made nigh."

That He might be close to us.

That we might be close to Him.

That we might be *one* with Him who "hath broken down the middle wall of partition . . ." My faith rests lightly against this lovely, depthless "blue stone." I, who was once "far off," have been "made nigh" to Jesus forever. Brought near to Jesus Christ. Jesus Christ.

In whom we have redemption through his blood, the forgiveness of sins, according to the riches of his grace.

Let no man therefore judge you in meat, or in drink, or in respect of an holyday, or of the new moon, or of the sabbath days: which are a shadow of things to come; but the body is of Christ (Colossians 2:16,17).

I know I have been redeemed by the blood of Jesus Christ. I know that any effort on my part to make myself Christian by observing this and that, is futile. I have the Word of God for that. God tells me that all these things, rituals and holydays and sabbath days and new moons, are *shadows*.

Unreality.

Reality is Christ Himself. The real thing casts the shadow, but we are not to depend upon the shadows. My faith rests upon the One who Himself has already redeemed me and what I drink or what I eat or when I do either is now beside the point.

". . . which things are a shadow of things to come; but the body is of Christ."

Here I understand the word "body" to mean the reality of Christ Himself. The substance which casts the shadows. Men followed the shadows until reality in the Person of Jesus Christ came to earth and died on the Cross, pouring out very real blood to redeem men once and for all from their very real dispositions of sin.

Let the shadows flee away now.

. . . now Christ is risen . . . The Lord is risen indeed.

MAY 28

Peter and his companions had been overcome by sleep, but when they awoke they saw His glory . . . (Luke 9:32, Berkeley).

HERE is another fragment of "blue stone" which settles my faith more firmly. I need this verse.

I am so often "overcome by sleep"!

And not only as I pray, but in the very attitudes of my heart toward Christ. I am so often aware of His need to teach me from the Scriptures as I ride along on a train, and before I know it I am awaking from a nap. I am so often aware of His need for someone I find tiring and almost as I begin to talk about Him, my heart has been "overcome with sleep." I have lost interest.

Before this "blue stone" lighted up for me, I scolded myself for falling asleep in His hour of need, thinking only of the bad example set before me by the sleepy disciples in the Garden of Gethsemane. But here in Luke 9:32 is another time they fell asleep. Just at the moment of Christ's transfiguration, the three beloved ones whom He chose to go with Him that day up to the top of the mountain, dozed off! "And while He was praying, the appearance of His face underwent a change and His garment turned a dazzling white . . . [and] Peter and his companions had been overcome by sleep!"

I am like all the rest. It doesn't seem to matter what the Lord is doing. He may be suffering in the garden or touching glory for my sake, *if I'm sleepy* in my heart, I'll doze off.

This is not admirable. It is simply true. But the wonder of this "blue stone" verse is this: even though, at the very moment of His transfiguration, all three disciples went to sleep, "when they awoke they saw His glory!" He never changes. We may sleep. But when we awake, we can still *see Jesus.*

. . . The Lord thy God is with thee, whithersoever thou goest.

159

> . . . Peter remarked to Jesus, "Master, it is well that we are here. Let us construct three booths, one for you, one for Moses, and one for Elijah," not knowing what he was saying. Even while he said it, a cloud came and overshadowed them and they felt awestruck as they entered into the cloud (Luke 9:33, 34, Berkeley).

DEAR, impetuous Peter saw something that amazed him and filled him with awe, and right away he wanted to begin building buildings! Launching programs. Right away Peter wanted to "promote."

". . . it is well that we are here. Let us construct three booths, one for you, one for Moses, and one for Elijah!" Peter blurted this out "not knowing what he was saying."

Does this sound familiar to you?

Have you sallied forth to do some tremendous work for God, with all your verbal banners flying, only to find that no-one seems to listen to you? No-one seems to take you seriously? Or, if this has not been your experience, have you never known of a sincere, zealous, misguided soul who has experienced it?

Big talk. "Not knowing what he is saying."

Perhaps the motivation for the lofty dreams is very real. Surely Peter had seen Jesus transfigured before his own eyes. And standing right there with Jesus, Peter had also seen Moses and Elijah. It seemed a marvelous idea to begin work at once on something magnificent enough to fit the occasion. But God knew about Peter's rushes of misguided enthusiasm and "Even while he said it, a cloud came and overshadowed them . . ."

The cloud that has come and overshadowed your plans just might be God's way of stopping you. Of getting your attention so He can guide you in His way. ". . . they felt awestruck as they entered into the cloud." This is good. God must re-remind us that He is God. We must sometimes be stopped from charging ahead with our own ideas.

My soul, wait thou only upon God.

> Then a voice came out of the cloud, that said, "This is my Son, My Chosen One, listen to Him!" And with the dying away of the voice Jesus was found alone. At that time they kept still and told no one what they had seen (Luke 9:35, 36, Berkeley).

GOD caused a cloud to overshadow the eager disciples. Peter, particularly, needed to be stopped in his impulsive plans. Gently, but firmly, God stopped him with a cloud.

"Then a voice came out of the cloud . . ."

God never stops our headstrong actions without offering an alternative. When we hear none, or see none, it is because we have been made deaf from the explosion of our egos.

"My soul, wait thou only upon God . . ."

When we do wait upon God, the voice comes out of the cloud around us. That day on the mountain, the voice said: "This is My Son, My Chosen One, listen to Him!" That was all. That was enough. God had spoken the one thing which covers all confusion. He directed their attention back to Jesus.

"And when they had lifted up their eyes, they saw no man, save Jesus only."

This is what God intended. Everything He has to say to us is *in* Jesus, His Son. Apparently, after they looked back at "Jesus only" once more, they must have *known*. The account says "they kept still and told no one." They evidently had something to tell. They had looked at *Jesus only*.

> . . . behold a voice out of the cloud, which said, This is my beloved Son, in whom I am well pleased; hear ye him.

And Jesus came and touched them, and said, Arise, and be
not afraid. And when they had lifted up their eyes, they saw
no man, save Jesus only (Matthew 17:7, 8).

MATTHEW'S account of this mystery on the mountain,
which James and John and Peter beheld that day, throws
one more shaft of light on our "blue stone" verse and
another "facet" appears.

Yesterday we saw that the disciples were balanced again
after they "lifted up their eyes" and "saw no man save Jesus
only."

Here we see that something else had to happen *before*
they could lift up their eyes from their own confusion. We
get so tangled among the ropes of our own "tremendous
plans," our own confusions, our own anxieties, our own fears,
that we forget to lift up our eyes to look at Jesus alone. Or
even if we remember, somehow we seem powerless to do it.
Here again, we must remind ourselves that what gets our
attention gets us!

There were the three disciples "on their face, and sore
afraid," completely overshadowed by a cloud. A cloud that
seemingly did not disappear *until* they lifted up their eyes
and "saw no man save Jesus only."

Here then, is the newly exposed facet of this "blue stone."

Jesus knows you are in that "cloud." He knows about your
fears and confusions. He knows what caused them. Perhaps
you wanted to run ahead like Peter. Perhaps there is another
cause. At any rate, God has had to quiet you. But in the
cloud that overshadows you, God is speaking. And He is
speaking as He always speaks, of His Beloved Son. If you
are powerless to raise your own eyes to look back at Jesus
once more, rest there, because Jesus stands right beside you.
And He knows the depths of your trouble. In a moment, He
will touch you and say, "Arise, and be not afraid."

. . . It pleased the Father that in him should all fullness
dwell . . . Ye are complete in him . . .

June 1

Being confident of this very thing, that he which hath begun a good work in you will perform it until the day of Jesus Christ (Philippians 1:6).

HERE, to begin our sharing for the month of June is a "blue stone" verse which can cause our faith to leap with joy!

Hold it to the light.

Turn it.

Happily, Paul doesn't instruct us to "be confident," he is again simply witnessing. He speaks of himself and Timothy as "*being* confident." Absolutely confident that Jesus Christ will continue His "good work" in the Philippian Christians. Paul seems pleased with their progress. "I thank my God upon every remembrance of you." He longs to be with them. "For God is my record, how greatly I long after you . . ." And yet, the fact that these particular Christians are growing does not in any way lessen the tremendous faith-enriching impact of our "blue stone" verse above.

Neither does it apply only to the Philippians. Nor to those among us who are growing visibly. It applies to *anyone* in whom Christ has begun His "good work." He will continue what He has begun. Not because we deserve it. But because of who He is!

I can trust Christ to continue His "good work" in me, not because my faith is high, but because "I know whom I have believed . . ." The point is not our spiritual temperature at the moment, but the identity of Jesus Christ.

. . . for I know whom I have believed, and am persuaded that he is able to keep that which I have committed unto him against that day.

For the which cause I also suffer these things: nevertheless I am not ashamed: for I know whom I have believed,
and am persuaded that he is able to keep that which I
have committed unto him against that day (II Timothy
1:12).

THROWING still more light upon yesterday's "blue stone"
verse, this one, placed beside it, rests me with the great
quiet I see in its very depths. Knowing Him, we can
rest. Because of His character.

This builds faith of itself.

But a light dances above this verse which shows me *how*
to lay hold of this quiet in the depths of my own sometimes
troubled heart. Paul uses the word "suffer" often. He suffered often. He could use it. But following the use of the
word "suffer," he invariably uses a word which at least implies "nevertheless."

". . . nevertheless, I am not ashamed: for I know whom I
have believed." Paul has "believed" the One who never
stops working in our behalf. But here the new light forces
me to face this: "I must have truly *committed* something
before I can rest. Jesus Christ *is* able to keep it, whatever
it is. But if the torment or the pleasure or the person or the
thing which causes our spiritual unrest is still in our hands,
there is no rest. Jesus Christ remains the same. Still able to
"keep that which we have committed." But if you've taken
it back, if I've taken it back, we are once more thrown into
confusion of heart, even though Jesus Christ remains trustworthy. He does not change. He is every minute and forever *able* to keep whatever we commit to Him. But He will
not grab it from us. We must give it to Him willingly. We
may be weeping when we do it, but until we do it, we know
no rest.

. . . I . . . am persuaded that he is able to keep that
which I have committed unto him . . .

But I would ye should understand, brethren, that the
things which happened unto me have fallen out rather
unto the furtherance of the gospel; So that my bonds in
Christ are manifest in all the palace, and in all other
places; and many of the brethren in the Lord, waxing
confident by my bonds, are much more bold to speak the
word without fear (Philippians 1:12-14).

HERE is a "blue stone" passage which contains so many
facets we cannot see them all at once. But from it
I have come to see that Paul found a creative *use* for
everything that happened to him.

In our collection of "purple stone" verses which light up
God's answer to human suffering, we will speak much more
of this great fact of the continuing redemption of Jesus
Christ. A fact too often overlooked by even the most sincere
Christians.

He *is* a Redeemer.

He will continue to be a Redeemer.

Paul longed for the Philippians to grasp this truth.

". . . I would ye should understand, brethren, that the
things which happened unto me have fallen out rather unto
the *furtherance* of the gospel . . ." Others near Paul saw that
his bonds were "in Christ." He accepted his bonds as from
the hand of the One who meant for him only the very best.
Then others took courage and began to speak for Christ without fear.

Paul never wastes anything. "Nevertheless . . . not I, but
Christ liveth in me . . ." This was Paul's secret. He literally
"wasted" human lives before Christ came to live within him.
Now, he is living because of this same Christ, and therefore
nothing is wasted in his life. Not even his bonds. Not even
death.

For to me to live is Christ, and to die is gain.

Wherefore be ye not unwise, but understanding what the will of the Lord is (Ephesians 5:17).

I F we could understand the will of the Lord in the trouble-some areas of our lives, we would indeed not only be wise, but peaceful. Do you doubt this? Or do you believe it?

Over and over I have heard persons say, "I'm afraid to give in to God's will on this. I'm afraid I'll be unhappy."

That would seem to indicate that we really don't believe God's will is always sweet.

It may not *seem* sweet at the time we are obeying. Surely the nails which bored into Jesus' hands on the Cross were not "sweet." But He had agreed with the Father in the garden. He was *in* the will of God as He hung on the Cross, and that was enough. We have already seen that when He had gone through the Cross and come out of the tomb, the first thing He said to His beloved disciples when He met them again near the empty tomb was, "O joy!" The will of God had turned out to be sweet. Jesus' own heart leaped with joy at what He had been able to do for His loved ones.

Obedience to God is the beginning of wisdom.

Wherefore be ye not unwise, but understanding what the will of the Lord is.

JUNE 5

Wherefore be ye . . . understanding what the will of the
Lord is (Ephesians 5:17). And be not conformed to this
world: but be ye transformed by the renewing of your
mind, that ye may prove what is that good, and acceptable,
and perfect, will of God (Romans 12:2).

THE will of God is always sweet in the end.
If we truly believed this, wouldn't we just follow Him
anywhere from this minute on, if we knew this to be true?
We can know it to be true.

The will of God is "good and acceptable and perfect . . ."
One look inside the great heart of love that broke on Calvary
and we can know this. But perhaps right now you're fighting
this Heart. Perhaps there's something you want to do so
much that you're trying to forget all about Calvary. Forget
it, at least for a few days or weeks until after you've overcome this forbidden thing.

All right. You are free to take it, whatever it is. But from
my own experience, I know you will not be able to *forget*
Jesus Christ. Not for long. You see, *He won't leave you.*
You just can't forget Someone who is still right there! And
He, of all people, completely *understands* your fighting God's
will in this thing. He struggled in the garden in an agony
of aloneness and rebellion, but He stopped struggling at last
and said the glorious thing that set *us* free! "Not my will,
but thine . . ."

You and I may do that too. We have the same power
available to us. But we must be willing *not* to be "conformed
to this world" in this particular thing. We must be willing
to have the mind of God in it. It may seem too hard. It probably is for *you*. But you are not alone. And if you obey, you
won't need to take someone else's word for the fact that God's
will is sweet. You can prove it for yourself.

> . . . be ye transformed by the renewing of your mind, that
> ye may prove what is that good, and acceptable, and perfect,
> will of God.

167

Speaking to yourselves in psalms and hymns and spiritual songs, singing and making melody in your heart to the Lord (Ephesians 5:19).

H ERE is a great faith-building secret. Sing and make melody to the Lord. And not just with your vocal chords, but with your heart too.

I will never be through thanking God for one particular album of old-fashioned Gospel songs recorded by Blanche Thebom some years ago. Miss Thebom sang "Softly and Tenderly," and through that song I was called back into fellowship with Christ. When I'm overly tired or confused, to this day nothing lifts me quite like playing Mahalia Jackson's Gospel songs. Mahalia "speaks to me in . . . spiritual songs" and so thoroughly turns my attention back to the joy of belonging to Jesus that the things which seemed so troublesome a few minutes before fall out of sight (or at least into place!), and I find myself "singing and making melody in my heart to the Lord."

My faith leaps up because it has *looked* up to Him again.

The next time you want to cry or lash out at someone or sink into the luxury of a black mood, force yourself to sing something like "More Love to Thee, O Christ." This very day, as I write this, I had to visit someone in deep trouble. I needed the time to write. I didn't want to go at all. But the Lord needed me there. And as I dressed, I sang "Where He leads me I will follow . . ." Soon I was rejoicing that He had given me this unexpected way of showing my love for Him. I dressed, singing with my *vocal chords* only. I returned to the typewriter a few hours later listening to my own *heart* "making melody to the Lord." There is no melody like the melody of an obedient heart. Even when it has been so recently a stubborn heart!

Giving thanks always for all things unto God and the Father in the name of our Lord Jesus Christ.

Giving thanks always for all things . . . in the name of our
Lord Jesus Christ (Ephesians 5:20).

IN the past I have found myself giving "lip service" to
God's Word here. I "gave thanks," but not from my heart.
From my mouth.

And, of course, the joy that always follows obedience to
God's Word did not reach my heart. My heart was not involved in the transaction at all.

I have called this a "blue stone" verse because at last I
believe I am learning what "God is up to" here. And what
I have seen in these brief glimpses has caused my faith to
grow. There is no exercise at all in doing easy things. If
God had said, "Giving thanks always for all the easy things,"
no-one would be challenged enough even to try to find out
what He really means. But He said, "Giving thanks always
for *all things*. . ."

Humanly speaking, this is an impossibility.

And Jesus warned us that without Him we could do nothing. We will share much more along this line in our collection of "purple stones" where I will attempt to show *how to*
give thanks. For now, let me promise you that a deeper
faith always follows obedience to this divine instruction.

A deeper faith and a better look at the face of Jesus Christ.

We are forced to look at Him in it! Otherwise we are
snowed under by the "things" themselves. Our part is to be
willing to look at Jesus. And the more we look at Him, the
more we are drawn to Him, and the more quickly we are
enabled to be willing to begin even that first feeble, "Thank
you."

. . . we all, with open face beholding as in a glass the
glory of the Lord, are changed into the same image from
glory to glory even as by the Spirit of the Lord . . . and
Jesus lifted up his eyes and said, Father, I thank thee . . .

JUNE 8

Submitting yourselves one to another in the fear of God
(Ephesians 5:21).

NO doubt someone is wondering how this verse became a faith-building "blue stone" verse to me. Someone may be thinking, "I've tried submitting myself to someone, and *I'd* put this one in the collection of 'purple stones' on the subject of human suffering!"

I quite agree that genuine suffering can be involved in "submitting yourselves one to another."

I've tried it too.

And yet, here is the Word of God telling us to do it. And to do it "in the fear of God." Could we be misreading that word "fear"? Could that have something to do with our human desire to skip this "blue stone"? Perhaps. But I believe "fear" here means *respect* or *reverence* for the fact that what God says really works. And He says over and over and over again that we are to "turn the other cheek," "submit yourselves one to another," "go the second mile."

Once more we must remind ourselves that Jesus warned us carefully, that without Him we can do *nothing* He asks us to do! We need His power, available to us through the Holy Spirit, even to receive Him as Saviour in the first place. So of course, we cannot "submit ourselves" to someone who makes us see red, *unless* He empowers us to do it. But He does. And I can also promise you from my own experience, that if you will this day "put yourself at the feet" of that person who is so difficult for you even to think about, you will find, as you actually feel your faith grow, that here is a true "blue stone" verse. Bow your stiff neck to her or to him and then thank God in your *heart* for the closer look you've just been given into *His* heart.

> . . . Even the Son of man came not to be ministered unto, but to minister, and to give his life . . .

170

I am the vine, ye are the branches: He that abideth in
me, and I in him, the same bringeth forth much fruit: for
without me ye can do nothing (John 15:5).

W ITHOUT me ye can do nothing."
How does this build faith? Simply because it causes
us to step aside and let Him *be* what He wants to
be to us. It forces us to open our eyes in wonder and say,
"So *that's* what He means!"

Victorious Christian living is based entirely upon our remembering that Jesus was kind enough to remind us that
without Him we are spiritually helpless. This is a source of
great joy to me now. Because He has brought me at last
to see that I want "victorious living" far less than I want
Him!

Faith seems automatic when I am in fellowship with Christ.
I have His word for it that if I abide in Him and He in me,
I will bring forth fruit as a simple, inevitable *result*, of our
being together.

I believe Him.

Now and then He allows us stunning glimpses into the
meaning of what faith really is. This morning, as I climbed
the stairs to the room where I write, I almost stopped climb-
ing halfway up. Suddenly I felt the tremendous *benefit* of
my own need. Without Him I can do nothing. And how
glorious this is! It keeps me with Him minute by minute. It
forces me to His heart. I must stay there. Where else would
I go now? If only we would walk into each day rejoicing
in our desperate need of Christ.

Abide in me . . . continue ye in my love . . . without me
ye can do nothing.

As ye have therefore received Christ Jesus the Lord, so
walk ye in him (Colossians 2:6).

H ERE is a "blue stone" verse that relieves me of the al-
together futile attempt to whip up my own faith.
"*As* ye have therefore received Christ Jesus the Lord..."
How did I receive Him?

In a wonderfully helpless condition! I couldn't have explained
it theologically, but suddenly I saw to my great horror that I
was in desperate *need*. I was *lost* in every sense of the word!
I was thirty-three years old and ashamed to begin running this
way and that, crying at the sky, "Do something. Somebody do
something to find me!"

But I felt that way. And in that moment of utter need, I
threw myself upon Christ! I received Him as my Saviour, knowing in my heart that I could do absolutely *nothing* to save
myself.

But knowing that I needed desperately to be saved.

I received Him in complete need. In helplessness. And the
inevitable, quiet relief followed only minutes later. At last
I could stop running. At last I could rest. I could stop being
embarrassed at my need.

Since then I have seen that I can rest as I walk with Him
too. In the midst of anything. I have come to Him and as
He promised, He has given me rest. I realize and benefit
from this rest *as long* as I walk as I received. In complete
and entire dependence upon Christ. Rejoicing in my need.

If ye abide in me, and my words abide in you, ye shall
ask what ye will, and it shall be done unto you.

JUNE 11

I know both how to be abased, and I know how to abound: every where and in all things I am instructed both to be full and to be hungry, both to abound and to suffer need (Philippians 4:12).

FAITH is an inevitable *result* of a witness like this one. Anything less brings an inevitable *consequence*. Nothing shatters faith quite so much as a complaining nature. Just a few days ago I watched one of my dearest friends begin to fight God. She is a comparatively new Christian, and we had one night not long before, been amazed at her poise and sweet temper when a tire blew out on her car on Chicago's Outer Drive in the midst of a blizzard. She changed it herself and proved the indwelling Christ to us in a still deeper way. She was in close fellowship with Him that bitter, winter night. She was willing to let Him hold her close to His heart even when the jack kept slipping on the icy street. She was a benediction.

At this writing she is fighting Him over a new temptation in her life. In this mood she drove me to another speaking date and another tire went bad. This time she banged the doors and kicked the jack and complained bitterly, even though there was a mechanic available to change this tire for her and it wasn't even raining!

How typical this is of us all! *He* is always the same. But only those who are really obedient to Him are *willing* to let Him take over *in all things*. Are willing to be instructed by the Holy Spirit to "be full" or to "be hungry." Either way, Jesus Christ remains the same. Only when we are grasped by this truth, are we willing to stop fighting.

Human nature usually fights a long, long time. This is not necessary. Anyone can choose to become obedient at any time. Victory in all things is always God's will for us. And He is always within us to take over when we choose to let Him.

I can do all things through Christ which strengtheneth me.

173

JUNE 12

... for I have learned, in whatsoever state I am, therewith
to be content (Philippians 4:11b).

CAN we look to the very depths of this little "blue stone"
verse and say this of ourselves?

Have I learned to be content in Christ in the midst of
anything?

Have you learned to be content in Christ no matter what's
going on around you?

Have you?

Have I?

We can learn. Paul did not have a "corner on the market"
of the obedient heart. Anyone can obey God. Even the
weakest among us. Particularly the weakest among us, according to Paul. Because the very same man who wrote our
"blue stone" verse at the top of this page, also wrote: ". . .
when I am weak, then am I strong." God had proven to Paul
that His "strength *was* made perfect in weakness." *Our*
strength only gets in God's way.

Bring it down to a very everyday matter. One which can
be really tragic as well as laughable. If you're overweight
(as I have always been), have *you* "learned *in whatsoever
state I am,* therewith to be content?" Or do you look at that
thin person eating piles of whipped cream and grind your
teeth in discontent? Does your heart as well as your stomach
growl, "This shouldn't happen to a dog, much less to me"?

God has a word for *all problems.* Especially for yours. And
especially for mine. And with each word He supplies the
power to obey. You and I *can* learn to be content under
any circumstances *with Him.*

... my God shall supply all your need according to his
riches in glory by Christ Jesus.

174

Not that I have already gotten ho
perfection, but I am pressing onwა
because I have been laid hold on b
3:12, Berkeley).

HERE is my favorite translatiᴄ
Upon it my faith rests easi
standing opens. I need my
cause I have often confused my๋

How is this possible? Simply
writer concerning the things of ꞓ
about Christ and when we reread
want to hide our faces in shame
what God has shown us.

My understanding of this seem
opened and my faith lifted in
Verkuyl of Paul's humble statem
such heights, it often seems to leᴀ
times he is always writing about
Paul *had* to write the verse aboʋ
his humility, but to free himself ꞇ
more than go on with the One
on" him.

Paul is "pressing onward in hoⱷ
he has been "laid hold on by ꞓ
caught up with. Right there on ꞇ
Christ "laid hold upon" the Christ
we are "laid hold upon" by the Sᴇ
fact that hate is merely twisted
turn to loves, because our hatred
been "laid hold upon" by the One
to forget the past and go on wi
is here.

Brothers, I do not infer that I
one thing I do: Forgetting what
for what lies before, I push on
of God's heavenly call in Christ

175

peace of God, which passeth all understanding, shall
ur hearts and minds through Christ Jesus (Philippians

ten we try to keep our own hearts and minds in
ceful condition. Quite naturally, we usually fail.
ey is in the phrase "quite naturally." We are
it by "natural" means.

earts and minds, always sensitive to pain and hu-
d scorn, *cannot* keep themselves peaceful.
st *be kept.*

must be kept *supernaturally* by God Himself. This
" verse assures us that "the peace of God" will
arts and minds. God's peace is God Himself. He
be unpeaceful than He can be other than Himself.
afflictions, he is afflicted." He feels our pain and
our heartache, but He knows what He is about!
ith us does not cause God to lose peace. "For
ace . . ." (Ephesians 2:14) He knows His ultimate
we are told in this "blue stone" verse that our
minds are to be kept "*in* Christ Jesus." This is
er. Not only because one day "at the name of
y knee shall bow" but because He Himself *is*
ing and the end."

is our peace . . . (and) he has said, I will never
hee, nor forsake thee.

... whatsoever things are true, whatsoever things are honest, whatsoever things are just, whatsoever things are pure, whatsoever things are lovely, whatsoever things are of good report; if there be any virtue, and if there be any praise, think on these things (Philippians 4:8).

HERE is a large, exceedingly brilliant "blue stone" verse, which, if it were observed by us all, would result in a calibre of faith that would change the world!

Contrary to the often heard interpretation, by which followers of the "moonlight and roses" cults go about *trying* to declare that *all things are* true, honest, just, pure, lovely and of good report, Paul is being almost brutally realistic here.

Christianity deals entirely with reality. The Cross was real and the blood Jesus shed on it was real and tragedy is real and so are the pain and tears that follow it. No use dodging the issue; sin and suffering *are here*. God does not intend for us so to distort the brilliance of this verse by attempting the entirely unrealistic and impossible method of *declaring* ugliness into beauty. You may be in a situation now where there is no beauty whatever. Only ugliness and pain and suffering and sin. How ridiculous to try to bend your mind out of shape by telling yourself it's all lovely! That's just what you will do if you try — bend your mind out of shape. God is not saying that. He is realistic. He says, "*if* there be any virtue, *if* there be any praise, [then] think on these things." Perhaps in your situation there is some. Then think on those aspects of it. Psychologically, the advice in this verse is perfect. We should exercise our minds to think on a higher level. *But,* God faces facts and admits that in some instances, there is only ugliness and at times terror. What then? Christ is still there and we can think on Him. He is true, honest, just, pure and altogether lovely. Everything about Christ is "of good report." Think on Him. Think on *Him*.

Thou wilt keep him in perfect peace, whose mind is stayed on thee ...

In whom we have redemption through his blood, even the forgiveness of sins: Who is the image of the invisible God . . . (Colossians 1:14, 15a).

WE only have a few more "blue stones" left to share. But perhaps these will do much to show us how to step aside and stop hindering the flow of faith in us toward God. Faith is God's idea, just as we are God's idea.

We did not "think ourselves up."

God did.

And then He did the most glorious thing of all. He came to earth to be one of us in the person of Jesus Christ.

"In whom we have redemption through his blood, even the forgiveness of sins . . ."

In all our "pleasant stones" we find facets which point us to the wonder of what God did when He revealed Himself in Jesus. It is before and behind all Christian faith. Unless we know this, we have no creative faith.

We can only lay hold of God through Jesus Christ. And here, once more, my own faith rises within me as I look deeply into the "blue stone" verse at the top of this page. Here I see, not only the story of a Redeemer who bought me back from myself by His own blood; I see also that this Redeemer *is* the "image of the invisible God"! I can know nothing of God for sure, except what I see in Jesus. My heart sings because of this. The more I look at Jesus, the more I see I never need to know any more about God than what I see in the face of Jesus Christ.

For God who commanded the light to shine out of darkness hath shined in our hearts, to give the light of the knowledge of the glory of God in the face of Jesus Christ.

For by him were all things created, that are in heaven, and
that are in earth, visible and invisible, whether they be
thrones, or dominions, or principalities, or powers: all things
were created by him, and for him (Colossians 1:16).

A LL things."
"Without him was not anything made that was made."
Faith is created for us even as we read these lines, if
we are open to the working of the Holy Spirit. Faith upon
faith until it springs alive and becomes a living awareness
of this One literally dwelling within us.

This One who created all things, including us. The music
of heaven and the dandelions that grow beside our rocky paths.
This One lives within us.

This One who created invisible thought and the visible
human brain *and* the vast unknown which links them together!

This One who Himself created all things and *for whom*
all things were ever conceived in the mind of God in the
beginning.

This One who breaks out of all word patterns.

This One who is God.

This Jesus Christ . . .

... who is the express image of his person.

And he is before all things, and by him all things consist (Colossians 1:17).

OVER and over again I have placed my fingers on the keys of my typewriter to write of this "blue stone" verse. Nothing came until I stopped long enough to ask God to turn off some of His glory.

Words are such feeble, stubborn things at best. And God is God and indescribable. He will not "remove his kindness" from us, however, and so here is something of what comes to me as I look at this little, power-packed verse.

I see into the words of Jesus Himself: "Before Abraham was, I am."

Only God could have made such use of such small words. I see also into more words of Jesus Himself: "I am the beginning and the end."

I see that I can trust Him most especially when "all things" around me are in ghastly, nerve-tearing turmoil. I can trust Him and I will trust Him in quiet, confident faith *if* I remember this "blue stone" verse.

"He is before *all things* . . ."

I can give thanks in "all things" and fear *nothing* because before "all things" were, Jesus *was!*

And I rest my faith still deeper in the assurance that "by him all things consist." By him all things hold together. Are held together. By Him.

And He is the head of the body. . . . who is the beginning, the first-born from the dead: that in all things he might have the preeminence.

For it pleased the Father that in him should all fulness dwell (Colossians 1:19).

I have been writing and speaking on this verse for many months. I sit hour after hour on trains and think about it. And yet I know so little of what it really means.

". . . it pleased the Father that in him should all fulness dwell."

All fulness.

In Jesus Christ. *In His person.* How can it be that to those of us who know Him, He *is enough?* How can one life fill the emptiness in every human life? How is this possible? We cannot know. We can only experience this fulness by emptying ourselves of ourselves and by receiving Him fully.

No-one can tell anyone else how to do this. Only each individual person knows what it is that prevents the complete capture by Christ. He is in pursuit. Every minute. He is near now, pressing in upon us from within and from without. He would be "fulness" to each person in the world. Fulness includes everything. And it pleased the Father that all fulness should be *in* the person of Jesus Christ, His Son. In Him is everything we ever need. Our part is to "learn of" Him.

In whom are hid all the treasures of wisdom and knowledge.

And, having made peace through the blood of his cross, by
him to reconcile all things unto himself; by him, I say,
whether they be things in earth, or things in heaven
(Colossians 1:20).

EVEN if there is something or someone in heaven in need
of reconciliation, it has been provided for by Jesus Christ.
". . . by him, I say, whether they be things in earth or
things in heaven."

I don't pretend to know what that means in its entirety.
But my faith draws rich nourishment from it. I see that this
Jesus Christ, whom I worship, "is beyond conceive of books
or mind."

He is understandable only to the heart.

Only the heart can truly conceive reconciliation. My heart
can tell you what He did for me on the Cross. So can yours,
if you have allowed Him to become real to you.

Jesus Christ not only *is* peace, He has "made peace through
the blood of his cross" and we need to ask the Holy Spirit
to lift this out of the doctrinal labyrinth and give our *hearts*
access to it! We may be frolicking absently about the foot of
the Cross right now, never once looking up toward the One
whose blood has made peace *for* us with God. He has reconciled you to Himself by the blood of His Cross. He has
reconciled me to Himself by the blood of His Cross. To be
reconciled means to be *harmonized*. We must check ourselves. Perhaps the jarring unevenness of our lives springs
from the fact that the music to which we stubbornly frolic
around the foot of the Cross is *our* own tune! Therefore *out*
of tune with the melody of heaven. But we can get into
God's rhythm again. We have already been *harmonized* "by
the blood of His Cross."

And you, that were sometime alienated and enemies in your
mind by wicked works, yet now hath he reconciled.

And above all these things put on charity (love), which is
the bond of perfectness. And let the peace of God rule in
your hearts (Colossians 3:14, 15a).

ABOVE all these things."
If you will read Colossians 3:12 and 13, you will find
Paul's list of Christian behavior patterns which we are to
adopt. And then, having been changed from a Christ-hater
to a love-slave of the Lord Jesus, Paul says:

"Above all these things put on love . . ."

Love covereth.

And after we have "put on love," we are to "let the peace
of God rule in our hearts." Just putting on love *once* does not
complete the operation. After that, minute by minute, we
are to "let the peace of God rule in our hearts."

Just as Jesus said, "*Let* not your heart be troubled . . ." so
we are to "*let* the peace of God" take over in our *hearts* first,
and then it will inevitably be in command of our *actions* and
our *words*.

We have already seen that our heart, as the Bible speaks
of it, is far more than the seat of our emotions. It is the seat
of our wills and thoughts as well. It is the "description" of
our very characters. We are exactly what our hearts show us
to be. And if we are to be obedient, we will —

. . . let the peace of God rule in our hearts . . . and
be ye thankful.

And whatsoever ye do in word or deed, do all in the name
of the Lord Jesus, giving thanks to God and the Father by
him (Colossians 3:17).

I have been guilty of excusing my lack of faith on the
grounds that I was "confused" as to what God really
meant. Was it wrong to do a certain thing? Was it wrong
or merely "acquired conscience?"

A friend once said at our table, "I just think maybe I'm
meant to be overweight, I crave food so!" Pleading confusion
as to what God is really driving at with us.

But here is a "blue stone" verse which allows no such
hedging where faith is concerned. God never tries to mix
us up, and if we would only obey this verse verbatim, we
would find He has even made a neat little outline for us to
follow in finding out "what's right and what's wrong."

Here is the outline:

1. Do *everything* you do and say *everything* you say "in
   the name of the Lord Jesus . . ."

2. Do *everything* you do and say *everything* you say in an
   attitude of thanksgiving to God.

Now, can you eat that extra piece of pie in the name of
the Lord Jesus? Realizing that "in His name" means "in
His nature"? Can you write that letter "in the name of the
Lord Jesus"? Can you scream at your children and nag your
husband all the while your heart is giving thanks to God?
Can you deceive your wife or turn that shady business deal
in an attitude of thankfulness to the One who poured Himself out on a Cross for your eternal life? God has made
finding out His will very, very simple.

Whatsoever ye do, do it heartily, as to the Lord, and not
unto men . . . for ye serve the Lord Christ.

And the Word was made flesh, and dwelt among us, (and we beheld his glory, the glory as of the only begotten of the Father,) full of grace and truth (John 1:14).

IN this "blue stone" verse we can find the very heart of the the Gospel. God revealing His heart in Jesus Christ. But for our purposes in sharing verses which settle our faith, one word lights up: *grace.*

"And the Word was made flesh, and dwelt among us . . . full of *grace* and truth."

"Grace" is an almost undefinable word. It has been well called God's unmerited favor toward us. G. Campbell Morgan calls it God's activity toward us and in us. But when I begin to try to explain it, I seem only able to do so by quoting Paul: "Where sin abounded, *grace* did much more abound."

Grace is a look into God's heart.

Grace is a carrying out of God's intention toward us as we see that divine intention in Jesus Christ. He is "full of grace," therefore as in every other riddle in the Christian life the riddle of *grace* is only answered in a closer walk with Jesus Christ Himself. Certainly explaining grace poses a riddle. But just as certainly receiving it does *not!* Anyone can receive God's grace. It is a gift. As His Son is a gift. Grace comes when Jesus comes. "He is full of grace and truth." When Jesus Christ is on the scene, grace is abounding! It flows out of Him. Ever toward us. There is the Saviour for every sinner and grace for every sin.

. . . Where sin abounded, grace did much more abound.

And he said unto me, My grace is sufficient for thee . . .
(II Corinthians 12:9a).

WHO said this?
Jesus Christ said it to Paul. And He called it
His grace.

"*My* grace is sufficient for thee."

Not only in quantity, but in quality. It is the grace of Jesus Christ Himself. And He is "full of grace and truth." All grace has already been given in Him. We do not need to ask for special grace for this or that. In fact, we belittle God's great gift when we plead for grace to endure a hardship. All grace has already been given and it is always available to us according to our exact need for it. Grace always flows toward us. We never have to reach for it. It has been given, but God releases it according to *His* estimate of our need. If He did not, we would always take a little more than we need at the moment and then try to store it up for some future time.

This is impossible.

And it is a good thing that it is, because then we would begin to depend upon our storehouses of grace, rather than upon the One who Himself is "full of grace." He wants us totally dependent upon Him. This is the glory of belonging. This is the freedom of belonging. Utter and entire dependence upon Jesus Himself. We cannot store grace. We are given "grace for grace" as we need it. According to *His* perfect knowledge of our need. And we have His own word for it that there will always be enough.

. . . My grace is sufficient for thee . . .

And with great power gave the apostles witness of the resurrection of the Lord Jesus: and great grace was upon them all (Acts 4:33).

MOST of us have been looking with longing into the depths of these "blue stone" verses, hoping fervently that we'll find *something* to increase our faith. To give us power in our Christian lives.

In this one is a simple answer to that need.

"And with great power gave the apostles witness of the resurrection of the Lord Jesus: and great grace was upon them all." We are to begin to witness and *then* the power will come. "Great grace" is already upon us!

Most of us have no power in our Christian lives because we have a subnormal concept of grace. Jesus Christ declares that His grace is sufficient for us. And this means it is sufficient to *forgive every sin*. This means it is sufficient to *cover every failure*. This means it is sufficient to *cleanse every conscience*. We can know the joy of a *forgiven heart*. We can know the creative joy in having learned how to *fail* in the Lord's strength. Everyone cannot win. Some must lose. But in His name, because of grace, we can learn how to fail. And we need never carry around the useless burden of a *guilty conscience*. Grace covers! Our part is to open ourselves and obey as much as we see right now. This always opens the way for more grace to pour in and as it operates within us, our vision opens and new obedience becomes our privilege. We have God's own word for it; there is always bound to be more grace than sin! Jesus Christ has broken the power of sin. He has come to live within us, if we have received Him there. And with Him has come an all sufficient supply of an all sufficient grace.

[He is] full of grace and truth.

My soul, wait thou only upon God; for my expectation is from him (Psalm 62:5).

IF impatience is blinding your vision, hold this little "blue stone" before you — and wait upon God. Impatience is lack of love in us. And only by *waiting upon God*, can we know love. Love is shed abroad in our hearts by the Holy Spirit of God, as we are willing to open our hearts to God's touch.

Last autumn I made a note beside Psalm 62:5, and I want to share that note as we share this "blue stone" verse which has so directly to do with your faith and mine.

I made the note while riding on a train, from Chicago up through Wisconsin to Minnesota and across North Dakota and Montana to the west coast. It was the middle of September, and as I looked at the lovely rolling hills in the Wisconsin farmland, I had a distinct feeling that the trees were *waiting*. Their green was dark and lifeless, but it was still green. And yet, I knew that perhaps two weeks later, when I would ride by them again, their waiting time would have passed and all the storm of color would be there. As I understand it, the other colors are always there, only not in as much intensity as the green manufactured by the chlorophyll in the leaves. But when the sap begins to go down in the autumn, the green-making process stops and the *waiting* period of summer and early autumn comes to an end.

The waiting colors appear and our eyes are dazzled each year as though we were seeing them for the first time. As my train entered the wild beauty of Montana and edged up, up across the Continental Divide, I saw another waiting period at an end. The beauty was almost too great to see alone. Just the day before, I saw Wisconsin trees still green. But in Montana, the waiting period was over. The time of color had come! And I marked my Bible here . . .

My soul, wait thou only upon God.

188

And the Lord direct your hearts into the love of God, and into the patient waiting for Christ (II Thessalonians 3:5).

ONCE more Paul lifts my faith in another "blue stone" verse which directs my heart "into the love of God." If we will only remain aware of His love, we will find it much easier to "lift up the hands which hang down."

We can lift hands of praise to a God whose heart *is* love. Whose intentions toward us *are* love.

We find it easier to enter "into the patient waiting for Christ," if we know God's heart is all love. I believe we can use this "blue stone" verse in two ways to strengthen our weak hands of faith and our "feeble knees." First of all, of course, Paul urges the Thessalonian Christians to "direct their hearts into the love of God" so that they could wait more patiently for Christ's return. Surely, this is a wise word to us now as well. He is coming back. And especially those of us who have glimpsed His *real intention* toward His creations await that time eagerly. But if we know of this LOVE, we will be able to wait *patiently* for Jesus to come back and reveal His ultimate purpose to everyone.

There is a second word of nourishment for our faith in this little "blue stone" verse too. If our hearts are directed "*into the love of God*," we will be more willing to wait patiently for Christ to work out His perfect will in our lives here on this earth. We will be willing to wait for Christ to act, so that "the word of the Lord may have free course, and be glorified."

Rest in the Lord, and wait patiently for him . . . [for] the Lord is faithful, who shall stablish you, and keep you from evil.

JUNE 28

Now the Lord of peace himself give you peace always by all means (II Thessalonians 3:16a).

THIS little "blue stone" verse is another of Paul's letter closings which we so easily overlook. But look again. Here is light for your faith. And light for mine.

"Now the Lord of peace himself give you peace always *by all means.*"

I read this at a most unpeaceful period of my life not long ago. I had read it before many times during calm periods and saw nothing but a prayer for peace in it.

When I needed peace, I saw more!

Surely the prayer for peace to the One who Himself *is* peace, is the main theme of this verse, but the last three words open the heart of it to me.

". . . by all means."

Perhaps we have a part here which we have overlooked. God and God alone can give us peace. "He is our peace." But are we refusing His gift of peace because He sees it is necessary to use a "means" which does not please us? Paul prays for peace for his spiritual children "by all means." Could he be telling them that they must be willing to grow through some hardship God permits to come, in order to make more room for the peace He is sending? Could it be *we* are to make room for peace? He has "made peace by the blood of his cross." It is ours for the taking. But if a wrong attitude has crowded our hearts, where is the room for God's peace? He has made peace possible for us. We must make room for the peace which He chooses to send however He chooses to send it.

Now the Lord of peace himself give you peace always by all means . . . by all means.

190

Pray without ceasing (I Thessalonians 5:17).

HERE is a tiny "blue stone" verse with great depth of meaning. Such depth, in fact, that many pass it by as impossible. Or mystical. Or out of reach.

As not for today.

For antiquity, perhaps, when people had time.

But not for today.

Yes, it is for today. In fact, this little verse and its equivalent verses which assured me I could live minute by minute in direct contact with Christ, drew me to become a Christian in the first place! I was a rank materialist. But the psalmist tells us the "Lord hath fashioned our hearts alike." My heart, like every other human heart, was fashioned to be *near* the heart of God. It is restless and empty and cold as long as it is alone and wandering. *We need constant contact with God.*

I have found in my own experience that I can "pray without ceasing" and still get my work done. I can "pray without ceasing" and still catch trains and write books and wash dishes and make beds and press clothes and sleep and eat and pack and unpack and laugh and weep and answer letters and live out my days as a member of the human race. Thomas Kelley, in his lovely "Testament of Devotion," calls it living on two levels at once. Praying is being aware of God. Praying without ceasing is being *constantly* aware of Him.

He has a part in our relationship with Him, and so do we. Our part is to "pray without ceasing." To be inwardly aware of Him, even though we are in the midst of a board meeting! This requires practice for us, but it is gloriously possible. His part is kept faithfully second by second. His promises are trustworthy because He is God. And He has said, that for His part, He —

. . . will never leave thee, nor forsake thee . . .
Lo, I am with you alway.

Faithful is he that calleth you, who also will do it
(I Thessalonians 5:24).

THIS is our last "blue stone" verse, and in it is all anyone ever needs for an established faith in Christ. A
workable faith. A constant faith.

·Our "blue stone" verses have all pointed toward the way
of faith. These "pleasant stones" are laid by God Himself
all along this adventurous way and they are there for our *use*.

The "pleasant stones" laid along the way of faith may seem
another color to you. To me they are "blue." Therefore, I
have placed them in this collection of "blue stones." But, as
with the physical make-up of sapphires, they are of ordinary
stuff until formed, (as we have seen them) by the Holy
Spirit. Sapphires are made of specially crystallized *common
clay!*

And here in this last "blue stone" we see the power which
formed our "blue stone" verses in this special way.

The power is God Himself.

"Faithful is he that calleth you, who also will do it."

Our faith grows strong and is useful *only* as we recognize
and rely upon His faithfulness! God is faithful. "Great is
thy faithfulness," O Christ. And we lean our wavering faith
against Thy faithfulness and draw upon it. Everything is
here. Everything needed. "Faithful is he that calleth you,
who also will do it." We can rest and live.

God is faithful, by whom ye were called into the fellowship
of his Son Jesus Christ our Lord.

PURPLE STONES

Amethysts, or "purple stones," like most other gems, reflect a long and legendary past. In fact, the amethyst is so surrounded by legend that I find it impossible to relate it to our spiritual quest, except by its color. It was the ninth stone in the breatsplate of the Hebraic high priest, symbolizing the tribe of Dan. In Greek mythology, both Bacchus, the god of the grape, and Diana, the moon goddess, are players in the legendary drama of the lovely "purple stone."

I have found several accounts of the amethyst having been believed to prevent intoxication. For this reason, the ancient Greeks often drank from cups made of huge amethyst crystals. In the days when men believed utterly in witchcraft, many also believed utterly in the amethyst's magic power to safeguard them from the evil machinations of witches. If worn as a pendant from a string made from the feathers of a swallow, it supposedly formed perfect protection from hailstorms and lightning.

The color purple, however, is to me at least, related to SORROW *and* SUFFERING. *Not darkly, but* VICTORIOUSLY *in Christ! We forget the ancient legends now and begin to search these "pleasant stones" for God's answer* TO US *in our very real and inevitable times of human suffering. Perhaps these "stones" may be wet with our tears. But God is in them, calling us to Himself. For your time of sorrow now, or for the time still to come . . . share my "pleasant purple stones."*

In all their affliction he was afflicted, and the angel of his presence saved them: in his love and in his pity he redeemed them; and he bare them, and carried them all the days of old (Isaiah 63:9).

IN all their afflictions he was afflicted . . ."

"And he went up *unto* them *into* the ship; and the wind ceased." When Jesus got into the ship *with* his frightened disciples, the storm stopped!

The value of this first "purple stone" verse to us is, however, the unalterable fact that Jesus is *in* our troubles with us. "In all their afflictions he was afflicted." A marginal reading tells us: "He does not afflict." He is *sharing*, not *causing* our suffering.

At the beginning of these "purple stone" meditations on God's answer to our human suffering, I believe it is of the utmost importance that we realize that God does not send suffering. Surely He *permits* it, and as we shall see as we go on sharing these verses, He very definitely *uses* our suffering, *if* we give it to Him to use. But not only does He not afflict, He is actually involved *in* our suffering Himself. I do not mean that the suffering of the Cross continues, but the same heart still beats in the breast of God, and in a very definite sense, Christ suffers *with* us. Someone expressed surprise when I said I believed this. Their surprise "surprised" me. How could we believe Christ could be so contradictory as to yearn over lost sinners and suffering Christians and still be shut away from us in paradise where He feels no pain? His identification with us is complete. It in no way diminishes the glory or the power of the ascended Christ to know that in all our afflictions He is also afflicted. It gives me great courage. I rejoice that I have God's own word for it —

In all our affliction he was afflicted . . . and he went up unto them into the ship.

Are not two sparrows sold for a farthing? and one of
them shall not fall on the ground without your Father?
(Matthew 10:29).

WE have looked at this stone in another collection,
but let's look at it again here among our "purple
stones."

Not only is God actually *in* our sufferings, Jesus tells us
that not even a little sparrow can fall to the ground without
the Father.

And *two* sparrows are not even worth a farthing now.

How much then, do we underestimate God's heart-deep
caring about our sufferings! I cannot conceive how much He
cares. But I can open myself, as you can open yourself now,
to the Holy Spirit and allow Him to reveal more of God's
intention toward us.

More and more I see that He is always in motion *toward* us.

He never stops.

Minute by minute, Christ is *in motion* in our behalf. And
sometimes only in tragedy and times of great weeping, do
we pay enough attention to Him to realize this. It is my prayer
that as we share these "purple stones" together, we will come to
recognize His everlasting, minute-by-minute activity toward us.
If this is true, then we *can* rejoice in our need.

If your heart is breaking now, Jesus Christ not only knows
exactly why, but He cares with all the love there is in
existence.

God is love . . . God is love.

For he knoweth our frame; he remembereth that we are
dust (Psalm 103:14).

PERHAPS your sorrow has already come. Perhaps a second
sorrow has come upon the first. Perhaps there seems no
end to sorrow and you feel as though your very heart
will crumble if help does not come.

Perhaps your sorrow is still up ahead.

One thing we must accept. And that is that none of us is
immune to sorrow. None of us is immune to suffering. None
of us is immune to tragedy and grief.

"Jesus wept."

We are not immune. We do not weep, however, simply
because Jesus wept. If you, in your weeping, find little or no
consolation in the fact that He wept too, look at it this way:
Jesus wept because He became perfectly human. He does
not force us to weep because He wept. He wept because
there is weeping in all *human* life. He was identifying Himself *completely* with us. He was partaking of *our* life so that
we could partake of *His*. He knew we were dust, because
He created us. He did not need, for His own understanding,
to become man, but He needed to become man so that we
could understand *His* heart. He knew that we would know
His heart, if He "got in this thing" with us! God became a
man in Jesus of Nazareth. He knows. And be very, very
sure that —

. . . he remembereth that we are dust.

JULY 4

For I know that my redeemer liveth . . . (Job 19:25a).

NOTHING that could happen to us could be worse than what happened to Job. And in the midst of his ghastly pain and sorrow and perplexity, he still cried: ". . . I know that my redeemer liveth . . ."

This little "purple stone" holds the key to God's answer to all of human suffering. I have only begun to see into this answer, but I am convinced that one word in this verse opens our vision. As I see it, there is no other way to begin to understand where God is in our suffering.

The word is not "know" as some might believe. We need to *know*, to exercise our faith. But we cannot do this when our hearts are smashed *except* we have first come to see that God *is still a redeemer!* The word is *redeemer*.

Mysteriously, but certainly, He redeemed our sin as He hung on the Cross, pouring out His own blood for our sake. A redemptive power was let loose in the world when Jesus cried: "It is finished." And more and more I see that the redemptive power is operative in our *circumstances* as well as our sin! Before these "purple stone" verses reveal their deepest meanings to us, we must be convinced that Jesus Christ is a redeemer of our every *circumstance* as well as our sin.

Whatever He touches He changes and makes new. Whatever He touches He redeems and makes *useful*.

Nothing is ever wasted in the presence of Jesus Christ. Not even your great weeping. Not even your physical pain. If you give it to Him, He will redeem it and make truly creative *use* of it.

> For brass I will bring gold, and for iron I will bring silver, and for wood brass, and for stones iron . . . A little one shall become a thousand, and a small one a strong nation: I the Lord will hasten it in his time.

A bruised reed shall he not break, and the smoking flax
shall he not quench . . . (Isaiah 42:3a).

SOMETIMES when our suffering is so intense, words from
well-meaning friends are like rude bits jerked into our
mouths. Our friends want so much to help, they force
words of "comfort" upon us. They quote Scripture verses
which tell of God's ability to comfort in time of need and
although we try to follow them, we are soon using up more
of our waning energy trying to control our rising desire to
cry out, "Go away and leave me alone!"

I once heard a woman shout, "Just let me cry in peace,
please!"

People, too often, "break the bruised reed" by trying to
straighten it out. They want to help, but they end up, jerking cheerfully at the already bruised heart, only to bruise it
more deeply.

Job's well-meaning "religious" friends almost added insanity
to his pile of troubles, by their feverish attempts to *explain*
his suffering.

God never does this.

God never wastes time with explanations and He always
knows when to speak and when to be silent. Perhaps right
now, you need *only* to be held in His arms. Remember they
are "everlasting arms" and they are always underneath to
hold *you*. He knows you so well, He will never do the wrong
thing.

A bruised reed shall he not break and the smoking flax
shall he not quench . . .

JULY 6

Whereas thou hast been forsaken and hated, so that no man went through thee, I will make thee an eternal excellency, a joy of many generations (Isaiah 60:15).

WE have all felt forsaken at one time or another in our lives.

Perhaps you feel forsaken now.

Feeling forsaken may be a new tragedy in your life.

Feeling forsaken may be old to you and too familiar.

You may feel forsaken because you have had to break certain friendships for Christ's sake. Or because death has taken the one who was always there when you needed someone to be there. Yours may be a solitude that is as old as your life. You may *never* have felt wanted.

Whatever the history of your aloneness, turn this lovely "purple stone" in the light of the love of God and look deeply into its heart.

"Whereas thou hast been forsaken and hated . . . I will make thee an eternal excellency . . ." This is God speaking to *you!* God, recognizing *your* feeling of having been forsaken and promising at the same moment to "make thee an eternal excellency." This may mean a different thing with each one of us. But it is a thing which is well known to God. Whatever He has in mind as an "eternal excellency" for *you* will be the very most desirable thing of all. And if your feeling of desolation has been the cause of your aching heart, He also promises you that *if* you will leave it to Him, He will not only give you joy, He will "make thee . . . a joy."

No-one can tell you how God will do this. This is one of those lovely secrets between you and God. One He longs to reveal to you, as He longs to possess you completely. Give Him yourself, including your bitterness at being forsaken, and let Him make you an "eternal excellency . . . and a joy."

Thy sun shall no more go down; neither shall thy moon withdraw itself; for the Lord shall be thine everlasting light, and the days of thy mourning shall be ended.

Violence shall no more be heard in thy land, wasting nor
destruction within thy borders; but thou shalt call thy walls
Salvation, and thy gates Praise (Isaiah 60:18).

WHATEVER your life has been like in the past, however filled with violence and destruction, all that is at an end! Here is a "purple stone" verse particularly for those of us who came to Christ as adults. Or for those who knew Him once and turned away and then came back.

There is always violence and destruction without Him.

Sin destroys and tears down. Christ creates, and recreates. Yours may have been an inner-violence which showed itself only in the quiet desperation on your face. Or it may have been a quiet, bitter destruction at work on your own heart because you refused to forgive. It may have been raw self-fired violence.

No matter what it was and no matter what it is, "violence shall no more be heard in thy land" if Christ is possessor of that land. There will be no more "wasting nor destruction within thy borders" because where Jesus Christ is, *nothing* is wasted and nothing is destroyed, except the power of sin!

It has been said that "there is no cement in sin."

But "by Him (Jesus Christ) all things consist." By Him, all things *hold together*. The time of destruction and waste is over. Your life has become of one piece, if it is all in the hands of the one Son of God.

And they that shall be of thee shall build the old
waste places: . . . thou shalt be called, The repairer
of the breach . . .

The Spirit of the Lord God is upon me; because the LORD
hath anointed me to preach good tidings unto the meek; he
hath sent me to bind up the broken-hearted, to proclaim
liberty to the captives, and the opening of the prison to
them that are bound (Isaiah 61:1).

JESUS rose one day in the synagogue and read these lines
from the prophet Isaiah. What He read is our "purple
stone" verse for a few days of sharing.

"(And he came to Nazareth, where he had been brought
up: and, as his custom was, he went into the synagogue on
the sabbath day, and stood up for to read . . . he found the
place where it was written,) The Spirit of the Lord is upon
me, because he hath anointed me to preach the gospel to the
poor; he hath sent me to heal the brokenhearted, to preach
deliverance to the captives, and recovering of sight to the
blind, to set at liberty them that are bruised."

This is the passage Jesus chose to read. And as He read
those ancient lines, He gave them life. He added to them, not
only the phrase, "the recovering of sight to the blind," but He
added a *quality* which He backed up with His own life less
than three years later!

Not knowing the original, I have no explanation for the
New Testament addition of Jesus' line, "recovering of sight to
the blind." Perhaps this was written in the scroll from which
He read that day in the synagogue. This much I do know,
however, and would share with you, as we look at the different
facets of this ancient "purple stone" verse from Isaiah: Jesus
Christ did "come a light into the world"! Having been one
of the "people who walked in darkness," I have now seen "a
great light." I know He has come and I know He is light.
In His presence, all darkness has lost its power. I rejoice that
it is Jesus Christ —

Who hath delivered us from the power of darkness . . . in
whom there is no darkness at all. [Who came] to preach
. . . recovering of sight to the blind.

. . . the Lord hath anointed me to preach good tidings
unto the meek . . . (Isaiah 61:1).

WHEN Jesus read from the ancient scroll in the synagogue in Nazareth, He used the word "poor" instead of "meek."

". . . because he hath anointed me to preach the gospel to the *poor*." This merely gives more light on the word "meek." When Jesus finished His great invitation to "Come unto me . . . and rest," He added that we were to learn of Him. And He gave only one reason for this learning.

". . . learn of me; for I am meek and lowly in heart."

"Poor" in heart. Not arrogant.

He did not say that we were to learn of Him because of His creativity or His power, but because He is "meek and lowly in heart." True meekness does not have to be *proven* right. True meekness is always willing to be *made* right.

"Though he were a Son, yet learned he obedience by the things which he suffered . . ." (Hebrews 5:8a). The Spirit of the Lord God was upon Jesus Christ. He had been anointed to preach the good tidings. I believe He was anointed to preach them to *everyone*. "Come unto me, all ye. . . ." (Matthew 11:28a). But knowing what He knew about human nature, Jesus realized that only the meek, only the teachable, only those who were open God-ward, would *learn!* Only those could grasp the *humility* of God.

If, according to the Word of God, Jesus Christ Himself "learned . . . obedience by the things which he suffered," might it not be that our sufferings are the gate to the obedient life in Christ?

Beloved, think it not strange concerning the fiery trial which is to try you, as though some strange thing happened unto you: But rejoice, inasmuch as ye are partakers of Christ's sufferings; . . . [who] Though he were a son, yet learned he obedience by the things which he suffered.

The Spirit of the Lord God is upon me; because the LORD
hath . . . sent me to bind up the brokenhearted . . .
(Isaiah 61:1).

IF your heart is broken, look long and deeply at this facet
of our ancient "purple stone" verse. Look long and re-
ceptively at the reason Jesus came.

He came to bind up your broken heart.

". . . he hath sent me to heal the brokenhearted . . ."

The Spirit of the Lord was upon Jesus and He was anointed
specially to heal *your* broken heart.

Does this seem farfetched to you as you sit there perhaps
more aware of the ache in your heart than of the presence
of Christ? Does your heartbreak seem so big that you have
lost your sense of perspective?

I am not attempting to diminish or belittle the pain in your
heart. I know about broken hearts too. But I also know that
it is so easy for us to look so long at our heartache that we
lose our perspective on Christ Himself. He is somehow
dwarfed by the hugeness of our trouble.

If not that, we are at least likely to think that He can't
quite know how much it all hurts.

He does know, though. And He did what He did on
Calvary to make a way to heal your heart. You and I can
lay our wounded hearts up against His. He knows. He went
to the Cross, healing as He went. The same Lord who created
the universe and who holds it in place at this moment, is
giving equal attention to *your* broken heart.

> He healeth the broken in heart, and bindeth up their
> wounds, He telleth the number of the stars; he calleth
> them all by their names.

JULY 11

The Spirit of the Lord God is upon me; because . . . he hath sent me . . . to proclaim liberty to the captives, and the opening of the prison to them that are bound (Isaiah 61:1).

HERE is another facet of this "purple stone" verse which throws still more light on Christ's connection with human suffering.

"He hath sent me . . . to proclaim liberty to the captives," we read in Isaiah. "To preach deliverance to the captives . . . to set at liberty them that are bruised," Jesus read that day in the synagogue in Nazareth.

When Jesus came, He came *proclaiming* liberty!

He did not come to show the way *to* it, He came bringing it *with* Him. And He saw that those who are in prison are of necessity "bruised." And so He declared that He had come to "set at liberty them that are bruised."

Paul spoke of himself as a "bondslave of Jesus Christ." Those outside of Christ wonder at us when we say we have been set free by Christ. I understand their wondering. Before I became a Christian, I believed myself to be free. I was free. Free to get into trouble! I now know that the only real freedom is in being totally mastered by Jesus Christ. Only then are we masters of our circumstances. "If the Son therefore shall make you free, ye shall be free indeed." Jesus said this of Himself. It is true. The alcoholic may think he is free to drink. He is. But he is not free. He is owned by his bottle. I once thought myself free to take what I wanted when I wanted it. I was. But I was not free. I was owned by my own slightest whim and desire.

Christ has already come to set at liberty those who are bruising themselves against the walls of their various "prison houses." Only in Him can anyone be truly free. Only in Him can we *own all things*.

For all things are yours . . . and ye are Christ's and Christ is God's.

JULY 12

**Bring my soul out of prison, that I may praise thy name
. . . (Psalm 142:7a).**

IN this little "purple stone" fragment we find the heart-cry
of a captive humanity. Humanity captured by its own
hostile heart. Humanity held captive by its own rebellion
at being set free!

We can be free.

Each one of us. *If* we want to be.

If you are locked in a prison right now as we share these
"purple stones," you can come out. Perhaps we won't mention your particular prison. But you know it. You've lived
in it. If it isn't mentioned by name, the way *out* of it will
be made clear anyway. The type of prison is not the point.

Coming out is the point.

The "purple stone" verse above does not mean that we are
to bargain with God. We are not asking God to let us out
of prison just so we can praise His name. We are merely
facing the fact that until we have been willing to come out,
we *cannot* praise Him. Perhaps you are objecting to that
word "willing." Perhaps you believe yourself to be willing
now. I understand this. You feel you are a victim. As we
share together these next few days, we'll see, if we are open
to see, that it is not God's will that anyone should stay in
prison. We have Jesus Christ's own word for that:

**. . . he hath sent me . . . to preach deliverance to the
captives . . . to set at liberty them that are bruised.**

JULY 13

Bring my soul out of prison . . . (Psalm 142:7a).

THIS is a very small "purple stone." But it *is* the heart-cry of every imprisoned human heart, and so we will turn it for these next few days, and share what we see. "Bring my soul out of prison . . ."

What is a prison? The souls of men who are actually behind iron prison bars, may be in need of deliverance. Perhaps most of them are. But just as many men and women behind bars have been delivered by Christ, so many outside actual stone and steel walls are nevertheless "in prison."

We will look at a few "prisons" in which so-called free citizens may live. What about the prison of *selfishness?*

Has anyone ever escaped serving time in this most crowded of all "soul prisons"? Have you? Are you in it now? Am I in it now? We will never get out, until we are absolutely honest. Surely, the alcoholic is a striking example of a human soul in the prison of selfishness. Anyone will agree with this. Particularly anyone who is not an alcoholic. But there is another human type as frequently locked in the stuffy shadows of the prison of selfishness and that is the selfish mother whose mother love has turned to smother-love! She is usually excused by society. But not by God. *He loves her as much as He loves the alcoholic and He wants them both free.* In His heart, it isn't so much a matter of "excusing" either one as of breaking both their captivity. Captivity is captivity and we are of no use to God when we are locked up in our own selfishness. And days passed in this airless prison lead invariably to bitter *rebellion,* but there is great hope. Great hope. A promise, in fact:

> Thou hast ascended on high, thou hast led captivity captive; thou hast received gifts for men; yea, for the rebellious also, that the Lord God might dwell among them.

JULY 14

Bring my soul out of prison . . . (Psalm 142:7a).

JESUS Christ has already led captive, the "captivity" of your selfishness and mine.

We don't need to go on being selfish. We can come out of the prison of selfishness. But before we share the practical steps to coming out in His strength, perhaps we should consider a few more prisons by name.

Here is another very crowded prison. *Anyone* — good or bad — may get into it. But anyone can come out of it too.

It is the prison of *sorrow* and *grief*.

And days and months and years spent in this dark prison lead to a kind of cold, relentless *rebellion* against all of life. Tears can, after a while, freeze inside us and our very souls are made brittle. Natural grief turned hard in the frigid air of self-pity. One young woman looked at her husband's coffin standing at the same altar where they had stood to be married three years before. She looked and fled, weeping, into the "prison" of *grief*, and stayed there, until by her own admission, her friends could no longer bear to visit her. She was a Christian, but she had retreated completely into the prison of grief and sorrow. Her consequent rebellion vanished and she came out into the clean air of the free life, *only* when she came to see that He had led *her* "captivity captive" too! She saw that Christ *meant her well*. She began to let Him *use* her tragedy redemptively. And through her He drew other grieving widows to Himself. When all captivity has been led captive, that includes the captivity of grief and sorrow too.

. . . yea, for the rebellious also, that the Lord God might dwell among them.

Bring my soul out of prison . . . (Psalm 142:7a).

W E often forget God when we aren't aware of a need. "Bring my soul out of prison . . . ," our hearts cry, and we turn to Him again. He knows that some of us won't truly turn to Him until we are desperate, and so He *uses* the tragedies that come to every imperfect human being in an imperfect world, to draw us to Himself.

He *is* a Redeemer.

Nothing is wasted with Him. Not even unbelief. Here is a prison about which I know a great deal. It is the prison of *unbelief*. The prison of "seeking and refusing to find." It is cold and bare and there is no place even to sit down to rest for a moment. Its walls seem to me to be lined with stainless steel! I find stainless steel an ugly metal. Cold and relentless. Like the walls of this prison of unbelief. So hard are the walls of this prison that you can't even stain them! Here walk round and round those whose intellects won't *receive* truth as a little child. Here walk those who refuse to "find" because they refuse to be found by the shepherd heart of Jesus Christ. Here walk round and round, weary and puzzled and chilled, men and women whose souls are starving to death on their logical diet of lifeless principles. They are *rebelling* quite violently inside, but grimly they refuse to show it. Christ doesn't need to be shown, of course. He already knows. He created them too. And He fashioned their hearts also to be loved. He waits for them to come out through the same door of love.

He fashioneth their hearts alike . . . yea . . . the rebellious also.

Bring my soul out of prison . . . (Psalm 142:7a).

IN looking deeply into this "purple stone" verse we not only see that there are as many prisons as there are human rebellions; we see that much of the human suffering in the world is a result of captivity.

We *can* all come outside our prisons and be free. The way has been cleared. But before we look at the way, I believe we should look at two more prisons. This one is also crowded. Ironically, it is crowded with Christians as well an non-Christians. This is ironic when we see that this is the prison of "*having* to be right"! How many Christians do you know who just can't bear to admit to being wrong? Perhaps you're one of them. We can all slip easily and with such good intentions into this stuffy prison. If you and I see the truth about Christ and then explain it to someone in our *own* dogmatic spirit, we are *in* this prison! Oswald Chambers says there soon appears "a smell of gunpowder" around this type of two-fisted saint. Said saint may be running around "evangelizing" but most likely the "fruit does not remain" because the hard-hitting saint's own soul is in the prison of "having to be right." The love of God *melts*. He never uses a hammer. If your temper flares, if you are easily insulted or shocked, look around you carefully. You may be in prison and not know it. True humility, true meekness is not easily shocked or insulted. It does not flare. There is no aroma of "gunpowder" around true humility. Only the aroma of Christ.

. . . learn of me; for I am meek and lowly in heart; and ye shall find rest unto your souls.

Bring my soul out of prison . . . (Psalm 142:7a).

MUCH of the suffering in the world springs from, or results from, someone's imprisonment in the prison of the *dread* or *fear* of *death.* This is such a crowded prison, we will spend two days sharing it.

There are three kinds of prisoners in this place.

Those who fear death because they fear what lies "out there" beyond it; those who dread it because they believe nothing is out there but extinction; and those who fear it because of loved ones they leave behind.

My friend and companion, Ellen Riley, who led me to Christ, was seriously ill a few years ago. She asked to talk with our dear friend, Anna Mow, to whom this book is lovingly dedicated. Ellen told Anna she was afraid she was going to die. Anna looked at her and smiled as only one who knows God so well can smile, and replied, "Well, if you die, that's all right." If you know Anna Mow, you know *how* she said this. You know that her certainty of God is so great, that when she said it, all my friend Ellen *could* do was smile! But she went on to tell Anna that while it would be "all right" with her to die, she was worried about what would happen to *me.* Anna smiled again and said, "Well, Genie will be all right. The same Lord who gave her that new life, will still be the same Lord." Anna's voice was so quiet, and her heart so calm and sure, Ellen went right to sleep. And then she got well. No need to stay in the prison of "worrying about your loved ones" if you die.

> . . . for I know whom I have believed, and am persuaded
> that he is able to keep that which I have committed unto
> him against that day.

July 18

Bring my soul out of prison . . . (Psalm 142:7a).

T HEN there is the prison of the fear of what's "out there"
beyond death.

I will have to share with you on this one, out of the experiences of other people. Before I became a Christian I believed there was nothing "out there." And so I feared nothing. My dread of death was a different kind and I will share that with you tomorrow.

But perhaps this prison of the "dread of what's out there" after death, is the most crowded prison of all. I have heard of certain saints who have trembled in fear at the brink of the "valley of the shadow," even though they have believed the "correct doctrine" all their earthly lives. This is understandable. Those who *smile* at death, don't mention their doctrine very often. They just mention Jesus!

And even though they don't have a blueprint of exactly what happens when they stop breathing, they know He will be there and that is all that matters. Whatever He has worked out will be lovely. Most likely we won't notice it all much anyway, because He will be there and we shall "see him as he is"! Christ is the Lord of the road to eternity. He has already been there. He died as we will die. He was buried as we will be buried, and then He came back to show us His hands and to assure us that it's all right all the way there and back.

The way out of this prison is the same way as the way out of all the others. We will be specific later on. But those who smile at the thought of physical death, do it because they're so eager to see Jesus as He is. The sting has turned into a smile because they know what He's really like.

For to me to live is Christ, and to die is gain.

Bring my soul out of prison . . . (Psalm 142:7a).

PERHAPS some of the deepest suffering is the lot of those who live, as I lived for so many years, in the prison of the "dread of *extinction*" by death!

When you believe in absolutely nothing beyond this earthly life, you are, as Paul says, "of all men most miserable." God has built right into us a desire to live!

Even an injured bug will fight and fight for its little bug-life. Human beings fight to live when their physical bodies are eaten up with disease. Something deep inside us, if we are in our right minds, throbs with an almost desperate desire to *keep going!*

"*Continue* ye, in my love," Jesus said.

He knew about this longing to live forever because He is also the Creator God. He put it in us in the first place. For all the eighteen years of my adult life in which I believed in *nothing* after this life, I *resented* deeply the idea of dying. I looked at my grandmother's body lying in her coffin and wished that I could believe in some kind of God so I could hate Him for creating her and then letting her die. She loved living and then she was dead. Or so I believed. My grandmother was a Christian, and of course, she had merely stepped fully into life, with no limitations. But I didn't believe that. I believed that this earthly life was the end of life. I "lived up" every minute of it. Never condemn anyone who "lives it up" in this life because that person most probably believes in nothing beyond this life. He or she is trying to get what's available here and now! But Jesus Christ breaks the power of rebellion (sin) in our lives by giving us eternal life. The kind of life we were created to enjoy. The prison of the "dread of extinction" is a shadowy, desperate place. But the way out has been provided. Jesus *cries:*

> . . . I am the resurrection and the life: he that believeth in me, though he were dead, yet shall he live; and whoso-ever liveth and believeth in me shall never die . . .

Thou hast ascended on high, thou hast led captivity captive:
thou hast received gifts for men; yea, for the rebellious
also, that the LORD God might dwell among them (Psalm
68:18).

HERE is a "purple stone" verse which sweeps away all
captivity!

We have been speaking of prisons. Perhaps we have
not named your particular prison as such. But you know it.
You live in it. And you are a victim of the particular kind
of rebellion which is characteristic of your prison.

God has done something for you. He has opened the door
to that prison two thousand years ago! If you've been sitting
there all this time, nursing your injury and complaining because of your confinement, I share your feeling of dismay.

I've done it too.

But now I see once and for all that the *door has been open
all the time!* I have the word of the risen, glorified, ascended
Son of God for this:

". . . Behold, I have set before thee an *open* door, and no
man can shut it . . ."

"I am the door," says Jesus, "by me, if *any* man enter in,
he shall be saved, and shall go in and out, and find pasture."
Jesus Himself is the door. And it was torn open forever,
when they tore His body on the Cross of Calvary. If we
continue to sit huddled in our prisons, feeling ourselves to
be victims, we are saying that the Cross of Christ was for
nothing!

We are saying that ours is a special case. Too hard for the
Son of God. We are claiming to be victims of circumstance.
No-one who follows a risen Lord is a victim of anything.
He has already become a victim for us on the Cross. The
door is open. We can come out. If we do not, we are either
too comfortable in prison, too lazy to walk out, or, like the old
Prisoner of Chillon, we are afraid of freedom!

. . . Behold, I have set before thee an open door, and no
man can shut it . . .

And he said to them all, If any man will come after me, let him deny himself, and take up his cross daily, and follow me (Luke 9:23).

IN the gleaming facets of this "purple stone" we find the practical way *out* of prison.

We have established the fact that anyone can come outside to freedom, not because of achievement, but because Jesus has opened the door. Because Jesus, Himself, *is* the door. We can either come out or He is wrong.

We can either be free from every prison-house, or Jesus Christ died in vain. *But we have a part too.* And the deepest principle involved in our part of coming out of prison is *in* this "purple stone" verse at the top of this page. Read it again and see for yourself, that Jesus offers Himself to anyone — *if* that person will give up the right to himself and follow! *Ours is the choice.* And since the door is open to your prison and mine, *we* can decide whether or not we will come out. Here are three things I have found *I* must do, after I have believed what Christ has done:

(1) *I must call my prison by name.* If it is jealousy, I must call it "jealousy." If it is self-pity or sorrow or stubbornness, I must put an honest sign over the door.

(2) *I must be willing,* once I have been honest with God, *to leave my prison.* Many of us think we are willing, but when we actually start to walk out, realizing that the door *is* open, we find ourselves pulling back. It is dark, but it's familiar in there. We've been there so long.

(3) *I must be willing to stay out,* once I come out. Even though the air is sweet and Christ is outside with me, my old thought patterns are deeply made. I have felt "at home" in the dark, foul nest of my prison. At the most unexpected times I long to run back. But I must not. *This I decide.* God is always ready to *keep* me free, *if* I choose to stay free.

[For] God is faithful . . . God is faithful.

As for me, I will behold thy face in righteousness: I shall be
satisfied, when I awake, with thy likeness (Psalm 17:15).

T HIS is a "purple stone" verse to me, because its meaning
became real to me out of much suffering. While we
are still "in prison," we are alone.

Even if our prison is crowded, even if most of the others
in the world are in it, we are still alone. We can suffer there
creatively and eventually come out into the sunshine of freedom in Christ, or we can suffer there in self-pity and stay
inside in the airless shadows.

No-one is immune to suffering. Jesus Himself is the supreme sufferer. It has been said that the "red thread of suffering is woven into the very fabric of the universe."

But there are *two* ways to suffer.

Creatively and *defensively.*

If we suffer *defensively,* we complain and pity ourselves.
If we suffer *creatively,* we have come a long way into the
wonder of the redeemed life. Creative suffering is *expectant*
suffering. You will suffer. I will suffer. But when our weeping is too great for words, our hearts can still *expect* Jesus
Christ *to be Himself in it.*

We can choose about all this. If we choose to complain,
He permits our complaints. If we choose to suffer expectantly,
He gives us the grace to do it. When a certain suffering in
my own life turned *expectant,* I began to understand our
"purple stone" verse at the top of this page. I began to
understand *creative suffering.* As I stopped complaining, even
though the suffering continued, I found my own heart able
to whisper this and mean it:

. . . I shall be satisfied, when I awake, with thy likeness.

JULY 23

O my soul, thou hast trodden down strength (Judges 5:21b).

FROM the dynamic experience of his own changed life, Paul writes: "When I am weak, then am I strong."

And yet we go on complaining in weakness, and wonder at those who seem able to "lay hold of the strength" Paul writes about.

The "purple stone" verse from Judges which we are sharing today *explains* much of our seeming weakness. At least, I have come to see that I have "trodden down strength" in my own life by refusing to *act* as though I really believe Jesus Christ.

Perhaps it is God's infinite wisdom in operation in my life in these days as I write through our "purple stones," perhaps not. But He is certainly making *creative use* of the somewhat ironic seeming events in my own life as I write. In His infinite wisdom, *He is redeeming fresh suffering* which I am experiencing as these pages are set down. I must finish this book at a certain date and there is no time for the "luxury" of a period of dramatic conflict. No time for rebellion. But at any other period of my Christian life, I probably would have fallen rather willingly into the pit of discouragement. Sharing these pages with you has shown me that I don't *need* to "tread down strength" like that ever again. With the vicious, thumping little hoofs of discouragement, over and over again "my soul . . . hast trodden down strength."

There is so much more for us to see about redemption. And we must be *willing to see for ourselves* and not wait any longer to be shown.

> And he said unto me, My grace is sufficient for thee: for my strength is made perfect in weakness . . .

Hast thou not known? hast thou not heard, that the everlasting God, the LORD, the Creator of the ends of the earth, fainteth not, neither is weary? there is no searching of his understanding (Isaiah 40:28).

PERHAPS this depthless "purple stone" verse can be grasped only through suffering. Days may pass, and then suddenly, out of the shadows springs a light so clear and a meaning so simple and vast we wonder at our having waited so long to see it.

Suddenly we ask ourselves, "Hast thou not known? hast thou not heard, that the everlasting God . . . fainteth not, neither is weary?"

In our weariness we have forgotten as though we never knew, that God never sleeps! Never grows weary. His care is never diminished by constant watching. Minute by minute, He has been aware and is still aware of our suffering. Of our weariness, of our faintheartedness. Even when we sleep, we can rest our troubled depths in His hands. We can trust our shadow-darkened subconscious minds to His re-creative care. Our subconscious minds never sleep and neither does He. If we truly come unto Him, He will *give* us rest. He *is* the "everlasting God, the LORD, the Creator of the ends of the earth," *and of us*. And wonder of wonders to our aching hearts is the fact of His endless *understanding*. When our hearts cry, it is understanding we want above all else. Human understanding is sweet. But there are times of shadowy confusion in all our lives when we can't express ourselves even to our dearest friends on earth, because we don't understand why our own hearts are aching. We only know about the longing to be understood. If the pain is intense, we need understanding more than we need to understand. And in this, over the pain, we can say with great relief, to God—

Thou knowest my downsitting and mine uprising, thou understandest my thought afar off . . . thou . . . art acquainted with all my ways.

217

Thus saith the LORD, which maketh a way in the sea, and a path in the mighty waters (Isaiah 43:16).

IN the moments when we need to be understood even more than we need to understand, this "purple stone" verse is a suddenly opening gate.

"Thus saith the Lord."

And we are empowered by the Holy Spirit to know that whatever He says is *fact*. The Holy Spirit is always willing to make this known to us. But it is only through suffering that He is sometimes able to get our attention.

Once we know that the Lord's word for it is enough, we somehow don't need to know the nature of the path we are to follow from this point on. It is enough to know "Thus saith the LORD, which maketh a way in the sea, and a path in the mighty waters."

If the Lord says He will do it, He will do it.

How He does it no longer matters. We know about the "sea and the mighty waters." They have beaten against us for so long. About the way through them, we do not know. But He knows. And that is enough. He will make the "way in the sea, and a path in the mighty waters."

And thine ears shall hear a word behind thee, saying, This is the way, walk ye in it, when ye turn to the right hand, and when ye turn to the left.

Behold, it is written before me: I will not keep silence, but will recompense, even recompense into their bosom. Your iniquities, and the iniquities of your fathers together, saith the LORD, which have burned incense upon the mountains, and blasphemed me upon the hills: therefore will I measure their former work into their bosom (Isaiah 65:6, 7).

THIS is a strange and puzzling "purple stone" verse until we see that God is a consistent God. If your present suffering is because of your own selfishness, if my present suffering is a consequence of my own willful action against God, then it is no great mystery that we suffer!

God is absolutely consistent.

When your heart aches, it is the *natural* thing to feel sorry for yourself. To pity your poor aching heart. It is just as natural to feel sorry for ourselves when it is *our own doing.* Self-pity is natural. And it is deadly.

Face the facts in the light of the Cross. God cannot dismiss His own constancy. He cannot suddenly become quixotic and keep you from suffering the consequences of disobedience. You and I will reap the consequences of our actions and God will not hold back those consequences. God does not "measure their former work into their bosom" from spite. He simply permits the consequences to fall according to the moral laws which He has built right into life. God is in all our afflictions *with* us. He "became sin" on the Cross for us. He has gone the entire distance. When we refuse to obey Him, He can do nothing but let things remain as He created them. We break ourselves *over* His laws. *He does not break us.* He wants to *mend* us when we come to Him with contrite hearts. But He is consistent:

There is no peace, saith my God, to the wicked.

JULY 27

And I will bring the blind by a way that they know not;
I will lead them in paths that they have not known: I will
make darkness light before them, and crooked things
straight. These things will I do unto them, and not forsake
them (Isaiah 42:16).

IN yesterday's "purple stone" verse we saw the basic need
to discover whether or not our suffering springs from our
own disobedience. If we admit that it does, we can know
we have taken a step in the right direction. We have been
honest before God and with ourselves. We can then ask and
receive forgiveness. By His grace, we can put the disobedience behind us and go on.

However, perhaps your suffering is *not* from conscious disobedience on your part. But still you feel as though you are
in utter darkness and in all honesty do not know which way
to turn. This terrifying darkness can be a consequence of any
kind of suffering: self-inflicted suffering or unmerited suffering.
The density of the darkness remains the same. The terror is
the same. Your very heart seems to *be* condensed darkness.

Even if you have received forgiveness, you still stand
bereft, not knowing where the light is for *you*. You know
intellectually that God is light, that Jesus said, "I am the light
of the world," and yet in your abject suffering you truly don't
know where the light is *for you*. Even if someone explained
it you might not understand. You might try, but your despair
is so wide and your darkness so deep you seem blocked.

Whatever the cause of your suffering, it is *here*, at the
point of blank despair that we *can* feel the pressure of God's
love upon our hearts. It may be the first time we have ever
been sure of it. Stop and *expect* His touch. There are no
words. God does not need words to communicate with us.
He created us. Stop trying to *hear* Him. Just be with Him
and *know*.

I will make darkness light . . . and crooked things straight.
. . . Fear not: for I have redeemed thee, I have called thee
by thy name; thou art mine.

JULY 28

The voice said, Cry . . . (Isaiah 40:6a).

D O you feel no need to cry to God as we share this strange little "purple stone" verse? If you feel none, I pity you.

All we ever need to come to Him is need.

And here, in His kindness, He reminds us to *cry!*

"The voice said, Cry . . ."

Why is this? Why does God urge us to cry? How nonsensical that sounds in this era of "chin-up, keep-smiling"! How backward in this era of "gloss-it-over"!

Why does God say, "Cry"?

I believe the answer is very simple. God knows, even if we have never known, how needy we are. He came so that we could have life and have it more abundantly. Therefore, He wants to supply our needs. Since He cannot supply needs we don't recognize, He speaks this strange little "purple stone" verse to us: "Cry . . ."

Perhaps your present suffering is due to your ignorance of your need on some point. If you spend hour after hour dwelling on the great wrong someone has done you, *what is your real need?* To have God change that person so much he will never wrong you again? To have God change that person so much he will make the past wrongs up to you? No. This is not your need. Your need is to let go of *your resentment* against that person. Begin to pray for him. Give God the resentment as a love-offering and let Him change *you* where this person is concerned. This we cannot do in our own power. Face this need in yourself in the light of the teachings of Jesus Christ and then "Cry"!

And it shall come to pass, that before they call, I will answer; and while they are yet speaking, I will hear.

Comfort ye, comfort ye my people, saith your God. Speak ye comfortably to Jerusalem, and cry unto her, that her warfare is accomplished . . . (Isaiah 40:1, 2a).

SUFFERING is stacked upon suffering in our lives because we do not recognize that the "warfare is accomplished."

The war is over!

The "middle wall of partition" has been broken down.

No need for your life and mine to be "divided against itself" because of these ugly walls of resentment and bitterness and fear and anxiety and self-pity.

We run away to be alone. We run away to find "peace."

No-one can live "a life within itself that breathes without mankind."

"Whither shall I go . . . whither shall I flee . . .?"

There is no place we can go to *find* peace as such. There is only one place we can go to *receive* it. And that is to the foot of the Cross of Jesus Christ. The peaceful Christian *stays* there. That is why he is peaceful.

Jesus "made peace by the blood of his cross" and in this great act the walls fell down. The warfare came to an end. Peace became available. The tragedy now is not the Cross of Christ. That has become victory. The tragedy now is that those of us who receive this peace He made there, walk away from the Cross and forget it. We forget we have no *right* to resent. No *right* to be bitter. No *right* to be afraid. We have *no rights* if we follow Christ. This is the freedom. This is the comfort. This is the peace.

Comfort ye, comfort ye my people . . . [the] warfare is accomplished . . . For he is our peace, who hath broken down the middle wall of partition between us.

And even to your old age I am he; and even to hoar hairs will I carry you: I have made, and I will bear; even I will carry, and will deliver you (Isaiah 46:4).

I have spoken at homes for the aged and have found suffering there of a specialized nature. Along with the pain and weakness of an aging body, there hovers around some beds and wheel chairs a deep rebellion. This is almost a child's rebellion. It *is* childlike in the sense that it justifiably cries "Something is twisted! I'm old now. I know my body is wearing out, but I should be peaceful. Where is my peace? Someone has done something with my peace! I should have my peace of mind and heart now that I'm old!"

Children justifiably expect to be cared for. This is normal. It is also normal for the aged to cry out in rebellion if they're not peaceful. I will be a very old woman one day, if God leaves me here. And my heart, even now, longs to store up peace for my old age. I cannot. But I can remind you, if you're old, that no-one took your peace away. It is still there. You've misplaced it in your mind. Perhaps you're giving your attention to some worry, when you should be giving it to Jesus. *He is your peace.* "Remember the former things of old." Has God ever let you down? Even once? Then, will He now? It's very, very easy for anyone to misplace peace. Peace is not departed from us. He said He would never leave us nor forsake us. We have only forgotten Him.

And He reminds us at any age, that —

. . . even to hoar hairs will I carry you: I have made, and I will bear; even I will carry, and will deliver you . . . Remember the former things of old: for I am God, and there is none else; I am God, and there is none like me.

Art thou not it which hath dried the sea, the waters of the great deep; that hath made the depths of the sea a way for the ransomed to pass over? (Isaiah 51:10).

I remember one particular visit to a home for the aged where Miss Mary McFarland, one of my dearest prayer partners, lives a life by cheerful miracle. Only a few people have the marks of my dear Mary McFarland's "cheerful miracle" on their faces.

I shall never forget the fear I have seen raging in some dim old eyes. Fear and worry and anxiety storm often within the quiet breasts of the very old with a raging to rival the "waters of the great deep."

Mary McFarland's "cheerful miracle" is merely a life any Christian can experience. It is the "miracle" of a life lived deep in God. She prays without ceasing. And her face glows and her life is the "path in the mighty waters" for many with whom she lives. Through her, during a single brief visit, I can walk straight out of my own busy confusion back into the peace of His presence. It seems to me that especially older people, who may *seem* laid aside, can be very straight ways "in the sea," if they accept their age and allow the One who has ". . . made and will bear," to make *creative use* of their advancing years. Mary McFarland prays for me every day. It is one of God's clear paths "in the mighty waters" for me. If you who are aging will permit Him to do it, He will make your last years a "cheerful miracle" too. He will use your life to make "the depths of the sea a way for the ransomed to pass over."

. . . I am the Lord thy God, that divided the sea . . .

Then I said, I have labored in vain, I have spent my strength for nought, and in vain: yet surely my judgment is with the Lord, and my work with my God (Isaiah 49:4).

HERE is a "purple stone" verse dear to my own heart and by God's grace, I mean never again to be deceived by my own failures. *Anyone* can fail. Anyone can weep in despair at an apparently wasted effort.

But God longs to wipe away these tears too and to teach us one of His loveliest lessons as He does so. ". . . my judgment is with the Lord, and *my work with my God.*"

Nothing is ever wasted in the presence of Jesus Christ. Not even work which has failed. We cannot repeat too often that He is a redeemer and His every intention toward us is redemptive. We have often been reminded that Jesus was a "failure" too as far as the world knew. Our own self-preoccupation causes us to forget this, however, and when our work seems in vain, we suffer foolish but very real pain over it. His identification with us is absolutely complete. He has *already* identified Himself with your even seeming *failure.* But here the *paradox* of the Gospel is its glory. Our failures *can* become our victories.

This truth broke upon my consciousness one night as I stood alone leaning my head wearily against the wall of an inquiry room after I had spoken in a beautiful new church on the west coast. I *knew* my message had fallen flat. And wilting there against the wall, I cried in my heart: "Lord, forgive me for failing You!"

Then I smiled suddenly and said: "All right, forgive me for asking You to forgive me. Just take over and make something lovely out of it." He did. I have "failed" since, however, when nothing at all seemed to happen. We are not to look for signs. We are to look at Jesus. Not at ourselves.

. . . in the shadow of his hand hath he hid me, and made me a polished shaft; in his quiver hath he hid me.

Behold, I have graven thee upon the palms of my hands: thy walls are continually before me (Isaiah 49:16).

A more accurate translation of the word "walls" is "ruins." "Thy ruins are continually before me."

At first glance, this could depress us desperately. But it becomes a "purple stone" to lift the suffering of depression when we realize that, although God does see our "ruins," He relaxes our *hearts* in this "purple stone" verse by *first* assuring us that He has literally carved us on the palms of His hands.

The old song reminds us that we shall know Him "by the print of the nails in His hands." We shall. And in those prints *we ourselves* are graven. He took the very violence in the heart of man and used it to carve man's initials forever on the palms of His hands!

". . . thy walls (ruins) are continually before me."

They are before Him, but no longer are they half-crumbled "walls" standing uselessly by to remind us of our failure. Our very "ruins" have become monuments to the triumph of Calvary, *if* we have walked away from them in the power of Christ.

If we have allowed Him to touch them and turn them to triumph-gates.

If we have allowed Him to "build the waste places."

Jesus Christ *is* the Redeemer.

I know that my Redeemer liveth.

When my father and my mother forsake me, then the Lord will take me up (Psalm 27:10).

THERE is no feeling of forsakenness to compare with having been forsaken by one's father and mother. I do not know this from my own experience, but over and over again I have seen the wounds and scars of this singular loneliness on the hearts of those who have never known or have lost the security of mother and father love.

A child has every right to cry out for this love.

Every right to rebel when the safety of that love has been taken away or has never been there at all.

My heart still twists at the memory of one little girl, who clung to me sobbing her five-year-old rebellion at her Mommie and Daddy's impending divorce.

"Why can't we go back where we used to live and be together again the way we used to be? Why can't we? *Why can't we?*"

I had no answer. I could only hold her in my arms and let my heart break against hers.

A child loves *both* its mother and father. When they separate, the child is forsaken. And only the touch of the heart of Christ on that wretched little heart, can restore it to wholeness. Our hearts remain wretched to "hoar hairs" without the touch of the love of Christ upon them. If your heart rebels at having been forsaken by your mother and father, you don't really need God's warning that "the rebellious dwell in a dry land." You know it. You're *in* that dry land. But you can come out. "God setteth the solitary in families."

He has a word just for *you*. Hear it now.

> Behold, I have graven thee upon the palms of my hands; . . . I have redeemed thee, I have called thee by thy name; thou art mine.

The Lord is my light and my salvation; whom shall I fear? the Lord is the strength of my life; of whom shall I be afraid? (Psalm 27:1).

THERE is no greater suffering than the suffering from *fear*. Your fear may differ from mine, but the same tightness squeezes your heart and the rhythm of your life jerks along at the same uneven tempo. You feel you will be able to soar again when the light returns. "When it's daylight," you say, "I'll be all right." But the sun comes up and you are still afraid. You may go on to work, acting as though your fear has gone. But your heart knows better, and so does God.

If we are Christians, how do we reconcile this continued suffering from fear, with the fact that God Himself is our light and our strength? Doesn't the Bible say this? Yes, it does.

"Fear not, for I have redeemed thee . . ."

Then why don't we act like it? I am more and more convinced that fearful Christians are simply partially *unbelieving* Christians. We can be Christians and still not believe *all* God has to say. And the Lord Himself said, "Fear not," *before* He reminded us that He had redeemed us. "*Fear not, for* I have redeemed thee . . ." We are to "fear not" *because* He has redeemed us!

It is up to Him to see through both the dark nights *and* the nervous days. The psalmist is merely *witnessing* from his own experience when he declares: "I sought the Lord, and he heard me, and delivered me from *all* my fears."

I rejoice that David included that word "all." I am also relieved that David admitted his own fears. Fear is common to everyone. The devil likes to discourage us with it. Don't fall in that trap. "What time I am afraid," sang David, "*I will trust thee*." We do not *need* to endure the suffering of *fear*.

. . . whoso hearkeneth unto me shall dwell safely, and shall be quiet from fear of evil . . . when thou liest down, thou shalt not be afraid: yea, thou shalt lie down, and thy sleep shall be sweet.

Let not your heart be troubled . . . (John 14:1a).

J ESUS said this.

To those who have never received Him as their very *life* this is an impossible and almost ridiculous statement!

When every fibre of our being cries out under the load of suffering that comes when the troubles press, we *cannot* be peaceful. It isn't that we do not want to be peaceful.

We simply cannot.

And yet, here is the Son of God saying "*Let not* your heart be troubled."

Our rebellion at this command of the dear Lord Jesus, on the night before they killed Him, comes from a careless misunderstanding of what He is really saying, I believe. He faced the world's greatest tragedy as He spoke these words to His disciples that night. His Cross was very real. He did not for one minute imply that it was not real. That it would never happen. "He set His face *toward* Jerusalem." His entire earthly life had been filled with trouble and He still faced the darkest hours up ahead.

And yet, wanting so to warn His beloved ones about life as it *is*, but also to instruct them of the victory soon to be made possible by His death and resurrection, He said this apparently contradictory thing: "Let not your heart be troubled . . ."

Jesus did *not* say we would have no troubles in life.

He said that when trials and suffering come, we are not to allow them to *trouble our hearts*.

We are to believe in Him and we are to *act* as though we believe in Him. And believing in Him means believing in His love because He *is* love. Face these great simplicities right now in your time of suffering from trouble and care. Face them in the light of what Jesus has already done on Calvary. "Let not your heart be troubled . . ."

. . . he careth for you.

The Lord looketh from heaven; he beholdeth all the sons of men. From the place of his habitation he looketh upon all the inhabitants of the earth. He fashioned their hearts alike; he considereth all their works (Psalm 33:13-15).

THOSE who know the suffering which can come along with feeling *different* from other people will find great help in this "purple stone" verse.

Some *try* to be different. This also causes us to be misfits, but we are not so quickly aware of our oddities when something in our own egocentric personalities drives us to be unlike other people.

It is for those among you who feel "different" and don't want to feel that way, that I share this "purple stone." Perhaps you are crippled or physically disfigured in some way. Perhaps you *are* not quite like other people. I could never for one moment believe God caused your affliction. There is nothing in the Heart that broke on Calvary that indicates He sent it willfully. Where it came from, no-one can clearly explain. But, as with the man born blind from birth (whose blindness Jesus said was not caused by the sin of his parents or himself), you too can begin to see beyond your handicap (John 9). He didn't know *how* it was that Jesus healed him but he did know that while once he had been blind (different from other people) suddenly, after the touch of Christ, he could see! "The Lord looketh down from heaven; he beholdeth *all* the sons of men." You too. *Just as you are.*

And if you will drop your resentment and questioning long enough to experience the touch of Jesus upon your life, you too will begin to see as you've never seen before that "He fashioneth their *hearts* alike." *In* your affliction, He is also afflicted. Recognize that Christ is *in it* with you. Look at Him *in* your suffering, and you will begin to trust Him.

. . . none of them that trust in him shall be desolate.

AUGUST 7

They looked unto him, and were lightened; and their faces were not ashamed (Psalm 34:5).

ANYTHING about us which we have not acquired of our own free wills, and which causes others to turn to look at us, causes suffering of an indescribable nature.

We "stick out" from among our fellow human beings like "society's sore thumb" and we suffer bitterly. This is understandable. The more people look at us, the more we are twisted in upon ourselves. We become ingrown and moody and resentful.

God knows this.

He knows what happens in your heart every time you "catch" someone trying *not* to look at you. The same thing happens in His Heart *for* you. He is ever with you in all of it.

With you, urging and wooing you to Himself.

Urging and wooing *you* to *look at Him*. To look away from yourself to the One who loves you so intensely that His own Heart aches *with* yours in your humiliation.

I cannot tell you how He frees us from this humiliation.

His ways cannot be explained. But I *can* plead with you to look long into the depths of the "purple stone" at the top of this page. And I can beg you to allow your long-looking into that verse, to cause you to look at Jesus. *Look at Him.*

Look at *Him*.

They looked unto him, and were lightened; and their faces were not ashamed . . . looking unto Jesus . . .

. . . Thine arrows stick fast in me, and thy hand presseth me sore. There is no soundness in my flesh because of thine anger; neither is there any rest in my bones because of my sin. For mine iniquities are gone over my head; as an heavy burden they are too heavy for me. My wounds stink and are corrupt because of my foolishness. I am troubled; I am bowed down greatly; I go mourning all the day long . . . I am feeble and sore broken: I have roared by reason of the disquietness of my heart (Psalm 38:2-6, 8).

WHO but David has ever so described the suffering that dogs the self-indulgence of the disobedient child of God?

Those of us who have ceased living by the rhythm of the *giving* heart and have *taken* for a period, know what David means. Those of us who have taken that which our flesh has desired, know the singular pain from the "arrows" of God which "stick fast" in our hearts.

We cry out against what we think is the anger of God, and yet those disobedient hearts of ours remind us monotonously that it is our "iniquities that have gone over our heads" *seeming* to cut us off from the love of God.

". . . as an heavy burden" these hearts *are* too heavy for us. They condemn us. We cry "Lord, all my desire is before thee; and my groaning is not hid from thee." After we have *taken* what our flesh desired, we complain to God over our heavy hearts.

"Come unto *me*, all ye that labor, and are heavy laden . . ."

Our hearts turn back at the sound of that familiar voice! We cry "I am ready to halt, and [yet] my sorrow is continually before me." Then we grow honest and specific with God: "I will declare my iniquity; I will be sorry for my sin."

The arrows fall from our battered hearts and the blood from His Heart covers the wounds our iniquities made. We hear the dear familiar voice once more . . .

Come unto me . . . my burden is light.

The sacrifices of God are a broken spirit; a broken and a
contrite heart, O God, thou wilt not despise (Psalm 51:17).

THIS "purple stone" verse lies close to the center of the
answer to all human suffering. Our tendency is to *complain* about our broken hearts. We despise them!
But God does not.

". . . thou delightest not in burnt-offering . . . a broken
and a contrite heart, O God, thou wilt not despise."

Broken hearts can be light-filled entrance ways into the
victorious Christian life. The fashion today is for arrogant
hearts. "Head held high" is the boast of most of us.

"Bloody but unbowed" is the *closed door* to God.

Our blood can avail nothing. His blood has already been
shed. "Unbowed" hearts are not contrite hearts. And "a
broken and a contrite heart" give us *entrance* into the life
deep in God.

This is not because God is trying to smash us. It is because we cannot be made new *until* we see our *need* for
being new. Until our broken hearts force us to Christ for
healing, we too often forget Him and His Heart that broke
on the Cross for love of us.

Until we know contrite hearts, we do not know our need
of a Saviour.

If your heart is broken and contrite, give thanks. You are
among the blessed who are in a position to be healed. Don't
complain.

Be still, and know that I am God . . . I will heal thee.

AUGUST 10

... **Be not highminded, but fear** (Romans 11:20b).

THIS is the "purple stone" which shows the *other side* of the suffering caused by our disobedience. We complain and chafe at the mere idea of "a broken and contrite heart."

We are "highminded" because we *want* to be.

It is our very nature to be "highminded." To possess hearts "puffed up" with pride of our own virtues and doings. This is natural.

Once more, may I remind you we are dealing with the *supernatural.*

"Without me ye can do nothing," said Jesus. Therefore when God's Word admonishes us to "be not highminded, but fear," we are being asked to do what we can *not* do naturally.

Invaded as we are, however, with the very life of God, with whom. *all* things are possible, this becomes possible also.

Invaded as we are, by the very life of the One who demonstrated the humility of love on the Cross so clearly that even we can grasp it, we *can* learn to welcome the contrite heart. We can learn to go quickly with our broken hearts to the Heart that has already poured itself out at the moment it broke for our sakes at the place called Golgotha.

"Be not highminded, but fear."

"Watch and pray, lest ye enter into temptation." And entering *into* temptation, means we have refused to flee it. Embracing it, we fall into sin and our highmindedness is seen to be what it is: "a stench in the nostrils of God," because it leads His dear ones back into the miry pit. "Highmindedness" leads *down* to the pit. The affliction of the "broken and contrite heart" leads *up* to glory.

For thou wilt save the afflicted people; but wilt bring down high looks.

Flee fornication . . . (I Corinthians 6:18).
. . . Flee from idolatry (I Corinthians 10:14).
Flee also youthful lusts . . . (II Timothy 2:22).
. . . having escaped the corruption that is in the world
through lust (II Peter 1:4).

TWO verbs stop us here in these terse "purple stone"
warnings from God: *flee* and *escape*. Temptation can
come like a sudden wind-driven fire. We are not looking for it. In spite of the warnings of Jesus. We are preoccu-
pied with Christian service or our families or our work.

"Watch and pray." But we do not. We've been busy.

And the temptation-bolt strikes and we are set aflame with
a quick new desire to *take* or to *become* or to *possess!*

We have not "escaped the corruption that is in the world
through lust." We have walked right into it and we are
more surprised than anyone else. We hadn't even been
thinking about it.

That's the whole trouble. Had we been watchful, we
would have carefully obeyed the other verb so prominent in
our "purple stone" fragments above. We would have fled
this thing.

"Flee from . . . flee from . . . *flee.*"

But we were busy or lonely or tired. We were unwatchful
and "our adversary, the devil" knew it and struck when *his*
time was right. We mistook him for someone else and followed him.

This thing just couldn't have happened to us, but it has!
And our hearts are broken at what we've done to Christ.
This is a peculiar kind of suffering known *only* to those who
know Christ personally. The kind of suffering we can avoid
only by *fleeing* temptation in the strength of God. You may
want to stay and nurture it just a moment or two, but turn to
Christ deliberately and say:

I will GO in the strength of the Lord God.

**Looking unto Jesus, the author and finisher of our faith
. . . (Hebrews 12:2a).**

THIS "purple stone" is related in a piercing way to the suffering that always follows taking the "reins of our lives" back into our own hands.

In order to take them back, even for a moment, it is necessary that we jerk them from the hands of the Son of God. And to do this causes us to look *away* from Him quickly.

When we yield to the temptation of desire for something to which we have no right as followers of the Crucified One, we seem immediately to *forget* Him. For the time of indulging our selfish desire, *He becomes quite unreal to us.*

He has not gone away.

"Lo, I am with you alway."

But we forget His Presence in the flush of our *taking.*

We have fallen on the way because of the wrong *look.*

And only when we begin to try to pick ourselves up from the ground, do we realize we have almost *forgotten* about the Lord. Only when we try to look back, do we realize how *far* we have looked *away.* He has not turned from us. We have turned from Him, and our shame and sorrow and remorse team up to cause a kind of suffering only His loved ones know. We haven't *hated* Him during our time of self-indulgence. We have *forgotten* Him. And this burns into our hearts and we cry "All my powers forsake me"! "Against thee, and thee only, have I sinned, and done this evil in thy sight." How can I get back as I was before:

> Return unto the Lord . . . Come unto me . . . look unto
> me and be ye saved. Let him return unto the Lord, and
> he will have mercy upon him; . . . he will abundantly
> pardon.

O wretched man that I am! who shall deliver me from the body of this death? (Romans 7:24).

UNTIL *this* cry of agony rises from the loved one who has fallen back into the pit, God cannot fully answer the cry of our heart.

It isn't that God doesn't want to answer *before* we reach desperation. He does. But He loves too much to do it that way. We would soon become heavenly spoiled brats.

He is about the dreadful and painful task of remaking us in His image so that although we live on earth we will feel at home in heaven when we get there.

As long as we are crying "O, pathetic creature that I am! who shall deliver me from my unmerited mistreatment?" God cannot do one thing for us but *wait*.

And He will do that.

We can be sure He will wait.

"His mercy endureth forever." He will stop at nothing, not even waiting, to finish the work He has begun in His loved ones.

"I am weary of my crying: my throat is dried: mine eyes fail while I wait for my God." Most of us know that feeling. But have we been crying in the right way? Have we cried from a "broken and contrite heart"? Have we cried the honest, openhearted, desperate cry of the "wretched man" who really *wants* deliverance from the "body of this death"? Just crying until your "throat is dried" is not enough. God is *not* waiting for our cry for sympathy and pity in our dilemma there in the bottom of the pit!

He waits only for the genuine cry for deliverance from those who really long to get out of that pit and who are willing to "live in the house of the Lord forever."

. . . who shall deliver me? . . . I thank God through Jesus Christ our Lord . . .

237

I would hasten my escape from the windy storm and tempest (Psalm 55:8).

GOD will wait for us until we are honest. Until we truly cry for deliverance. Until we are ready to receive it. And use it.

"I am the beginning and the end."

God is not in a hurry. He lives in eternity. But He also understands about our *time*. A day and a thousand years are the same in His reckoning, but He never forgets for one minute that you and I are bound and held by one minute following another in a certain way we have devised.

He knew when we began to live in "time." He is God. He lived in it once Himself for thirty-three years.

He "remembereth that we are dust" also and so He is not surprised at the heart-cry in the "purple stone" verse above.

"I would *hasten* my escape from the windy storm and tempest."

God knows when we are suffering and longing for escape from the suffering. "God was in Christ" on the Cross – *suffering*.

In time and in eternity too.

"The lamb was slain before the foundation of the world."

And then one day in "time," John the Baptist "seeth Jesus coming unto him, and saith, Behold the Lamb of God, which taketh away the sin of the world. *This is he . . .*"

God completely understands about the hang-rope of time and about our suffering when we cannot escape it. God hears your cry to escape. He hears and He replies:

In the beginning was the Word, and the Word was with God, and the Word was God. The same was in the beginning with God . . . and the Word was made flesh, and dwelt among us . . . Before Abraham was, I am . . . I am Alpha and Omega . . . I am with you alway . . . I have called thee by thy name; thou art mine . . . wait thou only upon God.

AUGUST 15

But when he saw the multitudes, he was moved with compassion on them, because they fainted, and were scattered abroad, as sheep having no shepherd (Matthew 9:36).

ARE you perhaps suffering the loneliness of what you quite honestly feel is a consequence of *your* having been misunderstood?

Has a wall been raised between you and someone you love due to a "stand" you feel you just had to take? This is often true. As Christians we cannot compromise what we know to be the Christian position. The estrangement brings acute suffering. Christ knew it. His own family said He was "beside Himself."

He was shut away by the wall of their misunderstanding what He was about.

As Christians we must learn from Him, to be misunderstood and remain true to His Spirit in us. "If we have not the Spirit of Christ, we are none of His." We long to resemble Him. But if we are not willing to be misunderstood graciously as He was, we do not have a family resemblance to Him.

But, with this "purple stone" verse above, let's take it farther than merely being willing to be misunderstood. Here we see Christ "was moved with *compassion*" for the multitude, although they were acting like scattered, unruly sheep without a shepherd. Are we perhaps suffering this current loneliness because our motives were not clear? Did we perhaps become moved with *condemnation* instead of *compassion?* Perhaps someone *did* act unkindly toward us. Does this give us a right to condemn and defend ourselves? No. As followers of the Crucified One, it gives only the right to be "moved with compassion" realizing that our part is to point *to* the Shepherd and not *at* the sheep who are acting up.

. . . When he saw . . . he was moved with compassion . . . For God sent not his Son into the world to condemn the world; but that the world through him might be saved.

239

When Jesus heard of it, he departed thence by ship into a desert place apart: and when the people had heard thereof, they followed him on foot out of the cities. And Jesus went forth, and saw a great multitude and was moved with compassion toward them, and he healed their sick (Matthew 14:13, 14).

HERE is a "purple stone" verse for you to hold if your present suffering is because someone you loved deeply has died.

Jesus was in deep grief here. "When Jesus heard of *it*" refers to the murder of his beloved friend and cousin, John the Baptist. "When Jesus heard of it," He did just what you wanted to do. He did just what you may be doing right now.

". . . he departed . . . into a place apart . . ." His heart ached with sorrow. He wanted to be alone. Of all times, humanly speaking, He did not want crowds of people pulling at Him, demanding His ministry.

He wanted to be alone *away* from the demands of His work.

And He went. But "when the people had heard thereof, they followed him on foot out of the cities." How would we react to this? With a heart freshly burdened with grief at the death of a loved one, what would we do if we were followed into our secret place of mourning, by a mob of people demanding our attention?

We can only look at what Jesus did. And then be willing to let Him do the same thing through us when He wants to!

This same Christ lives within us and His heart of compassion has not changed because of our present sorrow any more than it changed that day because of His own.

After they followed Him, with His own heart still heavy with grief, he was again "moved with compassion toward them, and he healed their sick."

Hereby perceive we the love of God, because he laid down his life for us: . . . we ought to lay down our lives for the brethren.

Then cometh he to Simon Peter: and Peter saith unto him,
Lord, dost thou wash my feet? . . . Thou shalt never
wash my feet . . . (John 13:6, 8).

IF Peter had not made a quick change of attitude after
this seemingly humble statement, he would have suffered
as many of the rest of us have suffered the inner agony of
pride.

A proud heart causes a particularly acute type of suffering
because it invariably leaves its owner *alone*.

Peter sounded humble enough when he gasped, "**Thou shalt**
never wash my feet."

But the Lord Jesus saw through Peter just as He sees
through us, and I'm sure He is greatly displeased when we
call ourselves worms and appear to cringe in abject nothing-
ness when someone is giving us a perfectly normal compliment.

Have you not heard this again and again? "Oh, I did nothing! The Lord did it all!" As with Peter's remark in the
upper room, it *sounds* humble enough, but it points directly
to our own *fancied* piety of soul.

If I'm humble, I don't need to tell you. You know it. If
you're humble, you don't need to tell me. I know it.

Pride is devastatingly subtle. Check your motives when
you cringe in the background. Could it be because you
unconsciously long to call attention to yourself? If we run
ourselves down as Christians, we are not only running down
the redeemed of Jesus Christ, we are still pointing to *ourselves!* Christians who are really off their own hands, can
quite quietly receive a compliment and simply say "thank
you" and go on. They are *off* their own hands. Nothing
needs be done about them one way or another. They are
about their Father's business, not their own.

Looking unto Jesus, the author and finisher . . .

And they that stood by said, Revilest thou God's high priest? Then said Paul, I wist not, brethren, that he was the high priest: for it is written, Thou shalt not speak evil of the ruler of thy people (Acts 23:4, 5).

I doubt if there is any monotonous form of suffering more destructive than the suffering that accompanies pride of heart. This "purple stone" verse proves that Paul escaped this form of discomfort. Filled to overflowing with pride in his old life, as Saul of Tarsus, here we see the glorious, almost hilarious freedom from pride available only to the love-slave of Jesus Christ.

Standing trial before the Sanhedrin, Paul took his critics' abuse in a lovely spirit. He found a way to agree with them and in effect, corrected his own bad form.

"Then said Paul, I wist not, brethren, that he was the high priest: for it is written, Thou shalt not speak evil of the ruler of thy people."

Paul *could* apologize.

Many people cannot. Pride is the reason. They are simply too *aware* of themselves to be able to *observe* themselves as proven wrong in anything.

Paul's attitude of heart as he apologized, is the attitude of his Lord's heart. He called those who were tormenting him "brethren." "I wist not, *brethren* . . ." He was not above them in his own opinion. He knew himself to be "the chiefest of sinners." He knew nothing among them "save Christ and him crucified."

Therefore, Paul could not be otherwise than humble. He had been made that way by the One who "humbled himself, and became obedient unto death, even the death of the cross." Paul *could* apologize because he had *laid hold* of the freedom of this death for his own earthly life:

I am crucified with Christ . . by whom the world is crucified unto me, and I unto the world.

And the night following the Lord stood by him, and said,
Be of good cheer, Paul: for as thou hast testified of me
in Jerusalem, so must thou bear witness also at Rome
(Acts 23:11).

WHEN we have been through the suffering of any
"trial" before the "sanhedrins" of our daily lives,
we are *ready* to rest. We cry out to God in our
weariness that surely this is enough for now.

But after "there arose a great cry" and after "there arose
a great dissension" and after Paul had been "taken by force,"
he was not *allowed* to rest. "*The night following* the Lord
stood by him, and said, Be of good cheer, Paul: for as thou
hast testified of me in Jerusalem, so must thou bear witness
also at Rome."

There was no let-up. His next call came ". . . the night
following . . ."

But, when it came, ". . . the Lord stood by him . . ."
We have all known the suffering of fatigue and nervous exhaustion. Many go down under it. Many of us bring it on
ourselves by trying to do God's work. But at the time,
when we are asked by God to "bear witness also at Rome"
on ". . . the night following," Jesus is always *right beside us.*
Standing by us. When *He* calls, He supplies the means to
answer His call. If we are looking too intently at our *work*
for Him, we can easily miss His Presence beside us. And this
brings *great suffering.* It is all much too hard without Jesus.
But He's there. Our part is always to expect Him and to
look for Him. Knowing that before He gives the next order,
He always says "Be of good cheer." When we hear this, the
suffering is all right. We welcome it. Because Jesus is standing by everything He asks us to do.

. . . he dwelleth with you, and shall be in you.

And when Paul's sister's son heard of their lying in wait, he went and entered into the castle and told Paul (Acts 23:16).

ONE of the hardest things for us to do sometimes is to work behind the scenes. To be unnoticed. This is often hard for us because of our pride in our work.

But it is also hard because we genuinely feel at times that what we are doing is so small, it just couldn't possibly count in anything as big as God's plan.

Paul's enemies were "lying in wait" to kill him. The entire New Testament would have been altered and the Gospel would not have been spread as it was, if a little fellow whose name is not even mentioned, hadn't done his mighty bit!

His Uncle Paul was in danger. Perhaps this is all the lad realized. ". . . when Paul's sister's son heard of their lying in wait, he went and entered into the castle and told Paul."

Paul's life was saved.

The boy had fulfilled his destiny.

One of God's saints whose name I remember only as Carrie, made such an impression on me early in my own Christian life, that I have thanked Him again and again for *her* life. She sat quietly in a prayer room one night *loving* a raucous alcoholic woman as I *talked* with her. What I said was unimportant. Carrie had loved this woman in tangible ways through the years, when others had pulled aside their skirts. I may never know Carrie's last name, but like Paul's nephew, she fulfilled her destiny with God.

Whatever comes our way, we are to "do it as to the Lord."

. . . he . . . entered into the castle and told Paul . . .
[Andrew] findeth his own brother Simon, and saith unto him, We have found the Messias . . .

As sorrowful, yet alway rejoicing . . . (II Corinthians 6:10a).
Giving thanks always for all things . . . in the name of our
Lord Jesus Christ (Ephesians 5:20).

THESE two seemingly paradoxical verses fuse to form our "purple stone" verse which can lead you into a new life of freedom from your complaining heart.

Paul wrote so often of rejoicing "in the midst of" that I was finally driven to find out *how* to do this! Sorrow and trouble come to us all. Paul was familiar with them both, and yet he dealt almost recklessly with the holy paradox of "giving thanks *always for all things* . . ."

From contact with those who had learned to give thanks in the face of tragedy and trouble, from my own experience, from time spent on my knees crying to God for a down-to-earth method for learning to do this, I was given some *concrete answers.* First of all, I came to see that the thankful-hearted Christians I knew are those who have *accepted* their lot without complaint. They had nothing in their attitudes or manner which said: "I'm too precious for life to have treated me this way!" Betty Elliot, whose beloved Jim was murdered in a jungle for the cause of Christ, wrote that "He continues to give His joy"! Not that God was enabling her to *endure* it, but He was "giving His joy"!

About that time I read an old book of Oswald Chambers in which he said: "Joy is God in your blood." I saw that God was in the blood of Christ already poured down from the Cross. Then a fresh time of suffering came to me. But this time I "accepted it" with this joy made available to me through the blood of Christ. Allow the Holy Spirit to open *your* heart to this:

Jesus . . . who for the joy that was set before him endured the cross . . . Jesus [who said], My joy I leave with you. Count it all joy. Count it all joy.

Count it all joy . . . count it all joy . . . (James 1:2a).

COUNT it all joy when your very breath seems choked off by the load of grief in your heart? Count it all joy when the house is so empty, you think of beating your head against the wall just to make a sound of some kind? Count it all joy when you can't imagine what it would be like to stop weeping? Count it joy when one ghastly scene *won't* be wiped out of your memory? Count it joy in this pain? In this anxiety? In this uncertainty?

Joy in *this black and endless hour?*

Yes. "Rejoice . . . giving thanks always *for all things."*

Joy as we know it in Christ, has little or nothing to do with laughter or happiness. With tears or sadness. It is, as Oswald Chambers declared, "God in your blood." And *this* joy remains as long as God remains! When I cried from my own heart for a *method* of giving thanks even when my heart was breaking, God gave me *proof* in the lives of some of His rare saints, a *definition* of His joy from the book of His beloved Oswald Chambers, *and* the instruction that I am to "accept" it all *with this kind of joy.* Accept it all with God in my blood. Still my own heart drew back under *certain* circumstances. And God said that I was not to look at the circumstances, but at Him. He reminded me in countless little ways that *He is love.* That He *is* a redeemer. That He redeems every circumstance He is permitted to touch. To my own humiliation, He then pointed me to one of my *own* books, EARLY WILL I SEEK THEE, and I read the last two chapters on pouring out everything to God as a love-offering. Suddenly I saw that when I do this, I can accept *anything.* It is no longer in my hands, *but in His.*

[And] I know that my Redeemer liveth . . .

. . . it was revealed . . . unto us . . . which things the angels desire to look into (I Peter 1:12a, c).

THE two simple steps shared in the last two meditations lead directly to a thankful heart "in all things." And they were "revealed unto *us* . . . which things the angels desire to look into."

(1) *Give the heartache and the cause for it back to the Lord.* "Pour it out" at His blessed feet as a love-offering. This is easier than a *surrender*. It *is* really the same thing, but the word "surrender" implies we are giving up to an enemy. I can pour *anything* out as a love-offering to One who *is* love Himself.

(2) *Accept it with the joy Christ left us.* The joy that is "God in your blood." *God will always be in your blood.* When you are laughing at a good joke or weeping beside a new grave. He will be there as *joy.* "I will never leave you nor forsake you." Accept this thing you can't do, this criticism, that difficult person, the fiery trial, the temptation-flames across your heart, the loss, the weeping, the loneliness, the confusion, the new grave — accept it in His strength and in His joy.

You cannot? I must disagree. "With God all things are possible." And we *can* accept what has happened to us *if we* have really given it back as a love-offering. Not because of our action, but *because of who Christ is!* We can trust *everything* we know about the heart that broke on Calvary. When it is in His hands, we no longer have to cope with it. We *can* "accept it" and we will find that thanks come because of the character of the One before whom we have poured out our love-offering! *He means us well.*

God is love . . . God is love.

David . . . poured it out unto the Lord (II Samuel 23:16).

DAVID wrote many of our "purple stone" verses. He knew suffering and he also knew the One who "continues to give His joy" in the midst of that suffering.

"Thou, O God, didst send a plentiful rain, whereby thou didst confirm thine inheritance, when it was weary."

God never deserted David, and when the pitcher of water from the well at the gate of Bethlehem, was brought to him at the risk of the spilled blood of his friends, David "poured it out unto the Lord" who had never forsaken him.

The most precious thing, he gave to the Lord. *But also the most grievous.* ". . . as for me, my prayer is unto thee, O Lord . . . Deliver me out of the mire, and let me not sink . . . Hear me, O Lord; for thy lovingkindness is good . . ."

David "poured it out unto the Lord," *no matter what it was.* Good or bad. Sinful or holy. He knew even then that the Lord *is* a redeemer! That He is *continually redeeming* everything we give Him willingly. Resentments, grudges, bitterness, heartbreak, pain. The hands with the nail-marks in them will take it, whatever it is, and *redeem* it. Change it into something useful and creative. He is the Creator-redeemer. David knew this, and so he "poured it out unto the Lord." A woman who had just "poured out" her resentment against her young son, reminded me that if we pour something out on the ground, *it soaks in!* We can't get it back. I rejoice in this.

Take hold of that thirst, that agony of soul, that hatred, that temptation, that grief, and pour it out *right now.* If He took our sin *into* Himself on the Cross, can't He take our every circumstance now? Pour it out now onto the ground at the foot of the Cross of Jesus Christ. It will soak in!

[Then] let the people praise thee, O God, let the people praise thee, [and] . . . the earth shall yield her increase.

Bear ye one another's burdens, and so fulfill the law of Christ (Galatians 6:2).

WHEN your own heart is heavy with trouble, this word from God can only seem to *increase* your load.

God knows this. That's why Jesus said: "Without me ye can do nothing." The average life is so full of trouble that it would be the rare thing for a *burdenless disciple* to appear in order to "fulfill the law of Christ."

Christ told us that we were to love our enemies as much as we love ourselves, even if they are our neighbors.

He said this *knowing* how heavy hearts feel. His had been heavy again and again in His earthly life. He said this *knowing* from His own weariness that to take on someone else's load without a moment to rest, is *humanly* impossible. And yet we are told to "bear one another's burdens, and so fulfill the law of Christ."

This is the same Christ who understood trouble and heavy hearts and weariness out of His own earthly experience.

We have already seen that during His own personal grief over the murder of His cousin, John, Jesus wanted to be alone, as anyone wants to be alone at times like that. But we saw also, that He asks nothing of us which it is not in *His* own heart to do. The people came thronging after Him in His secret sorrowing place and "he was moved with compassion" and "he healed their sick." *This same Christ lives in us now.* We *can* bear each other's burdens *if* we let Him do it *through* us.

. . . Without me, ye can do nothing . . . Abide in me, and I in you . . .

For every man shall bear his own burden (Galatians 6:5).

IS this not asking too much of us? When our own load is
heavy with new sorrow or trouble, can God expect us
to "bear . . . one another's burdens" and also bear our
own too? Wouldn't it be only fair for us to expect someone
else to bear ours as we are expected to bear theirs?

This would be "fair" as *we* think of fair-play. But fair-play
has nothing whatever to do with the Gospel of Jesus Christ.
If it had been based on fairness, He would never have gone
to the Cross at all! "For he hath made him to be sin for
us, *who knew no sin* . . ."

There is nothing "fair" about the only sinless Person who
ever walked the face of the earth, *becoming* sin for every
other utterly sinful person in the world.

The Gospel always speaks paradoxes to our hearts from
the human point of view. God paid the price for sin Himself instead of punishing the guilty sinner. Don't hate your
enemies and try to get even with them; love them and bless
them that despitefully use you. Don't strike back; turn the
other cheek and let it be slapped too.

"Bear ye one another's burdens . . ." but don't expect anyone to bear yours! "For every man shall bear his own burden."

This is madness until we have seen *into* the heart that
broke beneath the load of the sin it received willingly *and
with love.* Once we have seen His heart, we know something
of what He means when He tells us in effect to expect nothing for ourselves and to give everything away. We don't
understand it all, but we *know* about it, because He did
it for us. There is an entirely new dimension here. One that
can only be experienced and demonstrated, never explained.
When we *give* we find out it *is* a far more blessed thing than
to receive. When we bear someone else's burden even as we
weep from our own, we know about the joy of His yoke.

Bear ye one another's burdens . . . my burden is light.

Then took Mary a pound of ointment of spikenard, very costly, and anointed the feet of Jesus, and wiped his feet with her hair . . . (John 12:3).

HERE is a "purple stone" verse with many hidden facets, some more easily understood by those of us who waited a long time to begin to worship Jesus.

Mary of Bethany, whom we know and love as Martha's devoted sister, could be the same "woman in the city, who was a sinner" spoken of by Luke. I am not contending that Mary of Bethany had "gone astray" in the big city, I am saying she *could* have. Anyone could. If you think you could not, think again.

But the important thing is that the woman who "chose the better part," *could* once have been an unchaste woman who had met Jesus and had been made perfectly whole at His touch!

This has been happening for almost two thousand years. It would not be at all unusual. A woman's hair was her mark of honor in those days. Mary wiped His feet with hers! Whether or not she had been the "woman in the city," her heart knew that her only *real* honor was His love for her.

The disciple who complained about the "waste" of the "very costly" ointment, missed the point completely. Mary *had* made the highest choice. And she showed Him in the only way she knew how to show Him. He was about to go to a Cross to show His love for Mary and for us. Someday I want to thank Mary for what she did. She did what she knew to do. Mary poured out the ointment "very costly" to show her love for Jesus. To show her *heart's* understanding of His love. She anointed His body to be buried, because He had anointed her to live forever. She poured out her ointment to show her love for Him. He poured out His blood to show His love for her. And for us.

. . . While we were yet sinners, Christ died for us.

And . . . there came a woman having an alabaster box of ointment of spikenard very precious; and she brake the box, and poured it on his head (Mark 14:3).

THIS is Mark's account of this "purple stone" verse, and in it is something special for you if you have recently been forced for any reason to the breaking point.

"There came a woman having an alabaster box of ointment of spikenard very precious . . ." We all have "alabaster boxes" full of things "very precious" to us.

In one sense we ourselves *are* the alabaster boxes.

And because life is not kind, but cruel and twisted by sin, we are broken again and again as it passes us *by* or as we pass *through* it.

You may be broken now because something in life has passed you by. If so, let your "ointment of spikenard very precious" be spilled on Jesus as a love-offering.

The "woman in the city, who was a sinner" wiped His feet with her own tears and her own hair. If your tears have spilled out when your "alabaster box" was broken, let them fall on the feet of Jesus in love for Him.

Perhaps your "alabaster box" broke when you said good-by to someone not long ago. Jesus knows about it and with Him even your heart breaking can be a redemptive act. Mary poured her "ointment . . . very precious" onto her Beloved. She "brake the box" and did what she could for Him. He allowed His body to be broken and His blood "very precious" to be poured out for her.

She did what she could for Him because she loved Him. He did what only He could do for her, because He loved her. He has also done it for you.

> **. . . she brake the box, and poured it on his head . . . For God so loved the world that he gave his only . . . Son.**

August 29

And, behold, a woman in the city, which was a sinner, . . .
brought an alabaster box of ointment, and stood at his
feet behind him weeping, and began to wash his feet with
tears, and did wipe them with the hairs of her head, and
kissed his feet, and anointed them with the ointment (Luke
7:37).

IF you have gone to Jesus in a time of suffering, you understand the lovely progression of action in this "purple stone" verse from Luke's account of the anointing of Jesus.

Perhaps you have come *bereft,* not really knowing just what you would do, but you came because you were bereft and because you had heard that Jesus was there.

If you came "a sinner," as this woman came, at first you just stood behind Him weeping. If you came bereft because of some fresh suffering in your life, you also might have stood for a while "behind him . . . weeping."

Whatever your reason for coming, something about Him changed you a little. Both sin and suffering can eventually force us to *walk around and face Jesus.* ". . . [she] began to wash his feet with her tears, and did wipe them with the hairs of her head, and kissed his feet . . ." She was no longer "standing *behind* him . . . weeping." Still weeping, but now that she had seen *His* face, she found a *use* for her tears! She could wash His feet with them. She could wipe His feet with the hairs of her head. And this much nearness bowed her head still further and over and over again she kissed His feet, preparing them with *her* love, for the nails that could never have held Him to the Cross if it hadn't been for *His* love! To be rid of sin or to be rid of suffering *can* drive us to Jesus. Then He draws us, first around in front of Him, then to our knees to continue our weeping and at last to adoration! *Need is a golden thing.* Seek it always. Let it lead you to where Jesus is.

Come unto me . . . and I will give you rest . . .

253

. . . and the house was filled with the odour of the ointment (John 12:3c).

THIS is almost the last of our "purple stones" which speak to us of God's intentions toward us in our human suffering. My own heart has become more willing as I have shared them with you. Willing to let Him be toward me *only* as He wants to be.

So often I have locked my heart, *unwilling* to see God's movements of love toward me. Unwilling to act as though I really believe He *is* love. Unwilling to open my wounded heart to Him for healing. Unwilling, or unable quite to believe that He is *always in motion toward me* with ministering graces and healing in His hands.

At those times of rebellion in my heart toward God, there was no aroma of Christ in my life. He was there. But His aroma was shut away behind the wall of my refusal to accept His actions of love toward me.

My "house was [not] filled with the odour of the ointment" of my Beloved Lord. I was not treating Him as though He were my Beloved. But He kept on treating me as though I were His.

And then — I broke.

There was great weeping with it.

At first I wasted the tears, but then I remembered the woman with the alabaster box, and I began to wash His feet with them. Once that near, I could not help but kiss the dear feet. And then I *had* to break the box! *I* had to break at His feet. Because only then could I anoint Him with my "ointment . . . very precious." Only then was my "house filled with the odour of the ointment." Only then was the suffering sweet.

. . . Christ also suffered for us, leaving us an example . . . nevertheless . . . not I, but Christ liveth in me.

But we all, with open face beholding as in a glass the glory of the Lord, are changed into the same image from glory to glory, even as by the Spirit of the Lord (II Corinthians 3:18).

I have kept this "purple stone" verse until the last because it has lighted up *my* part in redeeming the sufferings of my life. My part is to *look at Christ in them.*

As I suffer or as I enjoy myself, I am to do both "with open face beholding . . . the glory of the Lord." Only then can I be changed "from glory to glory" back into His image. Only then can I find *willingness* to lay my broken heart up against His broken heart to be healed.

Look what happened to Stephen and be *made* willing to do as Stephen did in the midst of his torment and suffering!

". . . he, being full of the Holy Ghost, *looked up* steadfastly into heaven, and saw the glory of God, and Jesus standing on the right hand of God. . . . And they stoned Stephen calling upon God . . . [Stephen, who] kneeled down, and cried with a loud voice, Lord, lay not this sin to their charge."

Stephen *kept looking* at Jesus in His hour of trial. Gloriously, he *proved* that we can be "changed into the same image from glory to glory," because even as they stoned him to death, Stephen *took on the image* of the One who had also cried: "Father, forgive them, for they know not what they do."

A disciple named Stephen, outstanding for no other reason, kept *looking at Jesus,* and as he was murdered, he didn't *fall* to the ground screaming in self-pity and anguish, ". . . he *kneeled* down, and cried in a loud voice [as his Master had cried], Lord, lay not this sin to their charge." When we keep our eyes on Jesus, we are *given* peace and rest in the midst of our suffering.

When [Stephen] had said this, he fell asleep. He giveth his beloved sleep . . . I will give you rest.

255

GREEN STONES

There are green garnets, green tourmalines and green sapphires. But our "green stone" verses are EMERALD *verses because of all stones, the emerald is the most precious. To bring a high price, the other stones must be flawless. But the true emerald's value depends upon its size and particularly upon its color.*

All of our "green stone" verses are as big as God is. And so, we have chosen them, as one chooses emeralds for their size and their "color." Emerald green has always been to me a "singing color." Once I sat in the office of the art professor at the first college I attended and saw printed in large, ornate letters on the wall: "Green Sings!"

It does.

So do our "green stones."

As with sapphires, emeralds are also the same mineral as the ruby. So, our "blue" and "red" and "green stone" verses are all of the same basic composition: The love and the redemption and the long-suffering of God through Christ.

Machinery cannot be used to mine emeralds, neither do we come by the "singingness" of the victory at Calvary through a pat, mechanized process. Emeralds are picked tediously by hand, from the sharp washed broken rocks which form their "pockets." Victory in Christ is "by hand" too. His nail-pierced hands and our willing hands. When first taken from their greenish quartz "pockets" where they are formed, emeralds are very fragile and must be "toughened" by exposure to the air for some time. So must our "green stone" victory verses be exposed to the air of our daily lives before we can know there's a SONG *in them. Gem-cutters in ancient times kept an emerald near-by to rest their eyes. Green is a* SINGING *color. It is also a* RESTFUL *color. Experience these truths about victory and rest now as you "share my pleasant green stones."*

He that loveth not knoweth not God; for God is love. In this was manifested the love of God toward us, because that God sent his only begotten Son into the world, that we might live through him (I John 4:8, 9).

WHAT better "green stone" for our first day of sharing among the verses that cause our hearts to sing than this one in which we see joyfully that it is impossible to know divine love without knowing God and impossible to know God without knowing divine love!

No-one can truly experience love at its highest who has not truly experienced God. Deceptive imitations of it, perhaps even human love at its very best. But only by knowing God can anyone know divine love because God is love.

God is love.

Not a heavenly sentimentalist, but LOVE.

And this love was made *perfectly plain* to us when God "sent his only begotten Son into the world, that we might live through him."

All we need ever know of the love of God is in Jesus Christ.

All we *can* know of that love is in Christ.

"I and the Father are one."

Jesus Christ and God are one. And God is love.

My heart sings and sings and sings because I am at last convinced of this relentless love of God toward us. My heart keeps right on singing, even when the tears are running down my cheeks, as I am *laid hold of* by the divine love I see looking down at me from the Cross. Divine love that melts my heart and fuses it to His heart forever. Divine love that will *never* let me go.

And we have known and believed the love that God hath to us. GOD IS LOVE; and he that dwelleth in love dwelleth in God, and God in him.

The eternal God is thy refuge, and underneath are the everlasting arms: and he shall thrust out the enemy from before thee . . . (Deuteronomy 33:27).

THE eternal God who *is* love, is our refuge. And every minute of every hour of every day of our lives the arms of this eternal God are *underneath* us.

This is not true because He would not be free to take His arms away. He could take them away any time He chose to do it. This is God and He is omnipotent and that means that all power to do *anything* belongs to Him.

He could take them away right now.

But much joy to all the world, we know He won't!

He could, but He won't. Because this "eternal God" with these "everlasting arms" *is* Jesus Christ. These same arms were stretched out willingly on the Cross because He loved us so much. Why, by the wildest flight of anyone's imagination, would we possibly think that the heart that threw wide those gentle arms at Calvary, would withdraw them now?

"I and the Father are one." The Father will never do anything Jesus wouldn't do. They are one. We are not expected to understand this, but we can make *use* of it. If you feel you have "been dropped" by God, try to imagine Jesus suddenly tiring of the whole process of bringing the little dead girl to life (Luke 8:49-56). Try to imagine that just as He had taken her by the hand to call her back, He suddenly dropped that little hand and turned away to attend to something else!

The same hand that took hold of that little girl has taken hold of you. The same "everlasting arms" are under you. They will *remain* because nothing changes Jesus Christ. They will continue to hold you (even if you *feel* dead) because they are the same arms that stretched themselves across the black space between you and the Father, at Calvary.

And he came and took her by the hand and lifted her up . . . he took them in his arms, put his hands upon them, and blessed them . . . underneath ARE the everlasting arms.

. . . And he shall thrust out the enemy from before thee (Deuteronomy 33:27b).

HERE is another facet from yesterday's "green stone," bright with cause for rejoicing and rest.

"The eternal God is thy refuge, and underneath are the everlasting arms: *and he shall thrust out the enemy from before thee.*"

In looking into this lovely singing stone yesterday, we saw that God's arms are always underneath us because of what His heart is like. No-one could conceive of the arms that were nailed to Calvary ever being withdrawn no matter what we do to deserve it. If no man can pluck us out of the Father's hand, why would this same God withdraw His arms?

". . . underneath *are* the everlasting arms . . ."

To stay.

But this merely gives strength to the fragment above:

". . . and he shall thrust out the enemy from *before* thee."

God Himself is up ahead.

The same arms are pushing aside what must be pushed aside *if* we are laying hold of this promise. It is well to remember that no word of God to us is a fact *for* us until we have taken it for our own use by faith. *If* we have placed our faith in the very *character* of God, then we can be quite sure that He *will* ". . . thrust out the enemy from before" us. And He will know our enemies too. Sometimes we can't recognize them. At other times we *refuse* to recognize them.

God may leave an "enemy" there for our growth and refinement for a while, but *if* we are depending solely upon His character and are resting in His intentions toward us, we can be certain that at the time *He* knows to be right, those same "everlasting arms" will ". . . thrust out the enemy from before" us.

. . . he shall thrust out the enemy from before thee . . . Follow me. Follow me.

> . . . The beloved of the Lord shall dwell in safety by him; and the Lord shall cover him all the day long, and he [the beloved of the Lord] shall dwell between his shoulders (Deuteronomy 33:12).

JUST a few days ago we finished sharing my "pleasant purple stones" in which we saw some of the great wonder of God's minute by minute tenderness toward us in times of our great weeping.

Here is a "green stone" verse whose meaning points toward the reason God *can* give us peace even during the hours of great weeping and pain and heartbreak. He can do this because He is *always with us.* God's peace and comfort and strength in time of trouble are not gifts *from* God, given out as we give gifts. *They are God Himself.* We are peaceful because He is with us and *He is peace.*

"The beloved of the Lord shall dwell in safety by him . . ." because He is there *by us.* ". . . the Lord shall cover him all the day long" because the Lord is *there available* to cover him.

". . . and he, [the beloved of the Lord — you and I] shall dwell between his shoulders." What a cause for singing! This verse could be no other place but among our "green stones" because green *does* sing and surely this is the secret behind *how* God has been able to "put a new song" in our hearts. The cause for the "song" is the glory-filled realization that God has worked out a *way* in Christ so that we, who were once so "far off," *can* "dwell between his shoulders."

> And even to your old age I am he; and even to hoar hairs will I carry you: I have made, and I will bear; even I will carry, and will deliver you.

. . . thou shalt be called by a new name, which the mouth of the Lord shall name (Isaiah 62:2b).

SAUL is to become Paul.

Simon will be Peter.

You and I will be "called by a new name" and there will be rejoicing in heaven over our new name. Because the Lord will name it, it will mean that we have been given new natures too. Just as Paul and Peter were changed from a Christ-persecutor and a thoughtless blasphemer, to a love-slave of Christ and the first disciple with enough spiritual perception to see that Jesus *was* the Son of God!

"Thou art the Christ, the son of the living God." The rough, impetuous, weak-willed fisherman named Simon, did not see the great central truth of Christianity *because* he had been given a new name. He was given a new name *because* he was new enough to *see!*

". . . praying . . . for us, that God would open to us a door of utterance, to speak the mystery of Christ, for which I am also in bonds." The once self-seeking, Christ-hater Saul, did not ask for prayer for an open door to preach Christ for whom he was in bonds, *because* he had been given the new name of Paul. He was given a new name *because* of his new nature which caused him to write ". . . to me to live *is* Christ."

Only "the mouth of the Lord" can name our new names. Only He knows about our new natures because only He can give them to us.

Something to sing about is the *fact* of our new names. The names He intended us to have in the first place. Not old names made new. But *new names.*

> . . . If any man be in Christ, he is a new creature: old things are passed away; behold, all things are become new. And all things are of God, who hath reconciled us to himself by Jesus Christ.

And they shall call them, The holy people, The redeemed
of the Lord: and t..ou shalt be called, Sought out, A city
not forsaken (Isaiah 62:12).

NEW names over which to rejoice in this "green stone"
verse. New names given to us if we have placed our
faith in God's Son, Jesus Christ.

"And they shall call them, The holy people . . ." Having
come to Christ as an adult, I still gasp at the thought that *I*
could be called one of "The holy people." And yet, I answer to
that name without self-consciousness, because at last I have
come to see that *no-one* could ever be called one of God's
"holy people" if Jesus Christ had not redeemed him.

The facets in this "green stone" are formed in a very
orderly way. First we see that "they shall call them, The
holy people." And then, we see that "They shall call them,
The holy people" *only* because they are "The redeemed of
the Lord."

The Holy Spirit heaps joy upon joy here in this "green
stone" when He goes on to tell us through Isaiah that we
shall also be called "Sought out." Who hasn't at least for
some period in his life, felt *unwanted?* Perhaps you feel unwanted right now. But you're *not* unwanted. *God wants you.*
He has redeemed you and now He has given you the comforting, spirit-raising name of "Sought out." Sought out personally
by God Himself. Not only are we called "sought out," but heap-
ing on almost too much gladness, we are told by the Holy Spirit
that we are also called "A city not forsaken." What a lovely
name. "A city not forsaken." A holy people, redeemed by
God Himself. Then "sought out" and forever "not forsaken"
by the God who knew *He* would *have* to "put a new song"
in our hearts so that we would be able to express joy like
this!

Let the people praise thee, O God; let all
the people praise thee.

I the Lord have called thee in righteousness, and will hold thine hand, and will keep thee . . . (Isaiah 42:6a).

THE cause for singing in this "green stone" verse is the use of the past tense in one facet, and the future in another.

"I the Lord have called thee . . ."

"Thus saith God the Lord, he that createth the heavens, and stretched them out; he that spread forth the earth, and that which cometh out of it; he that giveth breath unto the people upon it. . . ."

This Lord called *you!*

"I the Lord . . . who created the heavens and stretched them out . . . have called *thee*."

"I the Lord . . . [who] spread forth the earth . . . have called *thee*."

"I the Lord . . . that giveth breath unto the people . . . have called *thee*."

This same Lord adds another melody to your song by reminding us that He has already *called*. He is not still making up His mind. He has called all who will come — ". . . him who cometh unto me, I will in no wise cast out."

One melody line in the *past* tense in the joyful fact that God has already called and another in the *future* certainty that He will not only keep us, He will do it in a most intimate and personal and reassuring way:

I the Lord have called thee . . . and will hold thine hand, and will keep thee. God is faithful, by whom ye were called unto the fellowship of his Son Jesus Christ our Lord.

Look unto me, and be ye saved, all the ends of the earth: for I am God, and there is none else (Isaiah 45:22).

REASON for rejoicing and rest here. God has already *called* and on Calvary He *acted* and now there remains nothing for us to do but *look!*

Someone has said "we are saved by the right *look*."

We are.

The God who is the Author of simplicity and clarity and *not* confusion, tells us that we are to look at Him and He will save us.

And He declares clearly and simply also that this includes anyone who *will* look.

"Look unto me and be ye saved, *all the ends of the earth*."

"Knock and it shall be opened unto you."

"Seek and ye shall find."

"If *any man* thirst, let him come unto me and drink."

"*Whosoever will*, let him take of the water of life freely."

The love of Christ is universal. It spreads its arms as wide as the Cross. Wide enough to embrace and hold anyone who is thirsty and hungry and helpless enough to come and be loved by the One who Himself is love.

We are to come and we are to look and we will be saved. This is because of *who God is*. God gives a reason for the utter simplicity of *looking*: "Look unto me and be ye saved . . . *for I am God*, and there is none else."

Ho, everyone that thirsteth . . . Come unto me.

In righteousness shalt thou be established; thou shalt be far from oppression; for thou shalt not fear: and from terror; for it shall not come near thee (Isaiah 54:14).

BLESSED are they which do hunger and thirst after righteousness; for they shall be filled."

If you are hungry, the only thing to do is eat. If you're thirsty the only thing to do is drink.

Blessed are those who know this and who believe the supply is always more than the need.

But blessed also, said Jesus, are those who just keep on hungering and thirsting after righteousness, because unless we are hungry and unless we are thirsty, all the food and drink in the world will do us no good.

Dr. Fritz Kunkel calls this beatitude the "hunger riot" of the soul. If you are driven to a reckless search for more righteousness, rejoice! If you cry out, "O God, feed me, I'm starving to death!" — rejoice. He will fill "the hungry with good things." But only the hungry.

And if you are so hungry the pain is intense at times, sing out with your joy at what we see in this "green stone" verse at the top of this page, because here God promises that "In righteousness shalt thou be established." And the more we are filled with God's righteousness, the more immune we are to oppression, fear and terror of any kind.

Christ literally became sin for us on the Cross, and when we believe that He does everything perfectly and completely, this very knowledge gives us great rest. We shall be "far off" from oppression, fear and terror — wrapped in His righteousness.

For he hath made him to be sin for us, who knew no sin; that we might be made the righteousness of God in him . . . In righteousness shalt thou be established.

For my thoughts are not your thoughts, neither are your
ways my ways, saith the Lord. For as the heavens are
higher than the earth, so are my ways higher than your
ways, and my thoughts than your thoughts (Isaiah 55:8, 9).

THIS is a real cause for rejoicing and praise. It may not
seem so at first glance, but look again. If you have
never seen God "turn out to be right" when your highest
plans were all wrong, you most probably have just not been
very observant of results.

It is a great relief to me that my thoughts are not His
thoughts. Not only because my thoughts are so inferior to
His, but because I was created to worship someone outside
and higher than myself. And if my thoughts were equal
to God's, there would be no-one for me to worship.

But more than this, I rejoice in this "green stone" verse because I know the terror inherent in *living one's own life*. I
know this because I lived my own life as I wanted to live
it for eighteen of my so-called adult years. I had nothing
higher than the top of my own head on which I could depend and as a consequence I *died* a little every day I lived.

I was destroying myself by the very fact that my thoughts
and my ways were *not* God's thoughts and God's ways.

He is life.

Anything outside of Him is death.

I love Him and give praise for the magnitude of this utterly simple-sounding statement. ". . . my thoughts are not
your thoughts, saith the Lord, neither are your ways my ways."

Anyone who has ever lived his own life, knows that he
does not really mean himself well. We destroy ourselves by
grabbing, because we cannot *give*. The love of God is a totally
giving love. There is nothing in our nature that is totally
"giving." By nature we "take." Only God *can* truly mean
us well. All the way.

For I know the thoughts that I think toward you, saith the
Lord, thoughts of peace, and not of evil, to give you an expected end.

But we are all as an unclean thing, and all our righteousnesses are as filthy rags; and we all do fade as a leaf;
and our iniquities, like the wind, have taken us away
(Isaiah 64:6).

SOME who read this book will be shocked that I have placed this verse among our "green stones."

If you are shocked or even surprised, the Lord has a lovely surprise of His own in store for you. Do you hate mention of your "iniquities"? Do you loathe thinking of yourself as "an unclean thing"? Do you feel your righteousnesses are not all quite as undesirable as "filthy rags"?

Have you recoiled from this painfully blunt verse? If you are attempting to follow one or another of the so-called "new thought" schools, where you are told over and over again that all good is in you and your part is to affirm it, et cetera, et cetera, then I can easily understand why this is a repugnant verse to you. You've been nurturing your pride so carefully, its muscles have become quite strong and able to resist any "insult" to your *good* name."

But, *our* "good name" is not what matters! Only the name of God. Our righteousnesses are beside the point, as well as being "filthy rags." Our iniquities "have taken us away" from God and nothing but the blood of Jesus Christ can bring us back again. Be open to the *words of God*, not the words of a school of pacifying thought. God says, "All have sinned," and until we see this and embrace it and allow our hearts to be cleansed by the blood that flowed from Jesus' heart on the Cross, we have nothing about which to rejoice. If you are trying to kid yourself about your "innate goodness," weep! But weep in His presence, and He will take your sin and give you His righteousness.

Blessed are they that mourn, for they shall be comforted.

Draw me, we will run after thee . . . (Song of Solomon 1:4a).

HERE is the glorious simplicity of Christianity. In this little "green stone" fragment is the key to the dynamic of the changed life. This does not present a philosophical persuasion or a logical premise. This verse explains why the twelve and all the others since, "left their nets" and *followed*.

We can abide *by* a principle. But we can only abide *in* a person. People will always be more important to people than principles will ever be. God created us that way, and so it is no wonder at all that He invaded our world Himself as a human being, who also cared much more about people than ethical concepts.

God always does things the simplest and clearest way. And since He "fashioned our *hearts* alike," He knew He would never capture and hold us through our *minds*. He knew we would have to be "drawn with cords of love" and that we would have to be drawn by a Person.

God knew He didn't dare depend only upon "verifiable data" or intellectual attraction, when He began to reach toward His loved ones who were so "far off." He depended upon Himself.

God came down here!

God in Jesus Christ is the Beloved who would draw *you* to Himself. He asks more than your mind in agreement with His. More than your heart turned nostalgically toward His. He asks for *you*.

And in return He gives you Himself. The sin-sick, confused man can't concentrate upon a system of theology, but he *can* look at a Person. And when he looks at Jesus Christ, he is drawn *out* of himself *into* the One who has been seeking him. Once he *sees*, he follows. However haltingly.

. . . we will run after thee . . . my soul thirsteth for thee, my flesh longeth for thee . . . Thou art my God.

269

The voice of my beloved! behold, he cometh leaping upon the mountains, skipping upon the hills (Song of Solomon 2:8).

WHAT a lovely place for such a lovely "green stone" verse, some may say. Yes, it is a lovely place here among the "green stones" and it is a lovely verse.

But it is more valuable because of its *depth* than because of its surface beauty.

It may be that this quick verse has only dazzled and intrigued you and you have gone on, not troubling to look beneath the sun-sheen on its surface.

Take it in your hand and turn it now and you will see that this "voice" is the voice of *your* Beloved too. Perhaps you're saying *you* never hear music like that. You're never aware of your Beloved "leaping upon the mountains" nor "skipping upon the hills." Wait. Look upon the "mountains" in your own *life*. Remember the complaining, nagging sound of that neighbor's voice? Or maybe it's your boss's voice.

Remember the drunk relative who called you long distance two weeks ago wanting to make jokes at three A.M. and also to borrow fifty dollars until payday? Recall the baby's voice stabbing you awake for the twelfth time on the third night in a row? The whiskey voice of that beggar on the street, the one you passed by without a look? What does that have to do with this verse? Simply this. If we always look for our Beloved to come skipping and leaping over a sunlit, craggy mountain side, and calling to us joyfully in what we imagine to be the music of heaven, we will seldom see or hear Him at all! But He is always leaping and skipping toward us and He is always calling. We will *see* Him if we look for Him on the monotonous mountains of our own daily lives. We will *hear* His voice if we listen to the heart-cry in *every* human voice. If we recognize *Him*, we rejoice.

Inasmuch as ye have done it unto one of the least of these my brethren, ye have done it unto me.

My beloved spake, and said unto me, Rise up, my love, my fair one, and come away (Song of Solomon 2:10).

T HE voice of my beloved!"
If we have not learned to recognize His *voice* in the cries for help from the unlovely, we have not learned all He wants us to know about His *heart*. If we have not learned to recognize His voice calling us to dull, daily routine, with the same enthusiasm with which He calls us to the top of the mountain — we have not realized that He *wants* to light up drudgery and monotony for His loved ones.

Over and over we stumble here, because we are trying to *endure* the ugly and the routine; we "hurry through" the mundane to get to that "spiritual time" alone with our Beloved, and all the while, He has been calling to us in the doorbell and the telephone and the children.

"The voice of [your] beloved" calling in that friend who has nothing to do but sit by her telephone and tell you about her troubles. "The voice of [your] beloved" in the shrill of your child's scream which tells you the older one "has done it again." "The voice of [your] beloved" in a call to serve on a dull committee with not even the possibility of half-hearted applause because this committee is never recognized at the annual meeting.

"The voice of [our] beloved" calling us to "rise up . . . and come away." Come away from what? Come away to a bright peak of heavenly bliss where the phone won't ring and the children won't cry and there isn't even one hammer or typewriter or dishpan? No. "My beloved spake, and said . . . , Rise up, my love, my fair one, and come away" from self-pity and our own mental moiling! He did not promise to change our daily lives or our lots in them. He promised to change *us. If* we will "come away" *with Him* in the midst of our daily dullness.

Come unto me, all ye that labour and are heavy laden, and I will give you rest. Rise up, my love, my fair one, and come away.

For lo, the winter is past, the rain is over and gone; The flowers appear on the earth; the time of the singing of birds is come, and the voice of the turtle is heard in our land; the fig tree putteth forth her green figs, and the vines with the tender grape give a good smell. Arise, my love, my fair one, and come away (Song of Solomon 2:11-13).

THE voice of our Beloved does not call us to "come away" *because* "The winter is past, the rain is over and gone."

He does not call us *because* "the flowers appear on the earth" and "the time of the singing of the birds is come."

The "voice of the turtle" has nothing to do with the year-long call of the Lord's voice to His loved ones.

He calls knowing as He does, that only *when* we answer Him and "come away" from our self-life, we will be able to look about us and see that "the fig tree putteth forth her green figs, and the vines with the tender grape give a good smell."

Until we "come away," until we follow Him in every area of our lives, we just don't *know* it's spring all over!

It *is* spring.

But we're too deep in the dishwater of monotony to have noticed it. Our Beloved *never* recommends shirking our daily work. One of the ways He has come to me most strikingly is not at the actual "time of the singing of birds," but at the "time of the washing of the dishes"! He has come as I have *remembered* that the presence of Christ puts a glow on *anything.* I have been most aware that "the vines with the tender grape give a good smell" when emptying the wastebaskets in a filthy ice-rutted Chicago alley!

But I wasn't aware of it *until* I allowed the very fact of the bulging wastebaskets to remind me that *in Him,* there were no dirty ice-choked Chicago alleys.

In him . . . the winter is past, the rain is over and gone; the flowers appear on the earth.

As the apple tree among the trees of the wood, so is my beloved among the sons. I sat down under his shadow with great delight, and his fruit was sweet to my taste (Song of Solomon 2:3).

THIS is a lovely "apple-tree" simile. An apple tree in "the woods" is rare. One expects to see almost any other kind of tree but an apple tree growing in a wild stretch of natural woods.

"As the apple tree among the trees of the wood, so is my beloved among the sons."

"He is altogether lovely."

She points to Him with pride. "As the apple tree among the trees of the wood, so is my beloved among the sons."

It is a quiet, deep joy in His very character that prompts this lovely statement. It is not a hard boasting that she belongs to the One who is the loveliest of all. Too often we find this spirit among His followers. They look down their righteous noses at those who have not met Him. They feel superior somehow. Surely it is not God's doing that we should ever feel superior. "Learn of me," said the One who is "as the apple tree among the trees of the wood." And then He went on to remind us that He is "meek and lowly in heart."

No pumped up fervor here. She speaks out of the overflow of her own knowledge of what He's really like. She has seen Him as *He is.* She knows that He is "as the apple tree among the trees of the wood" because she has "sat down under his shadow with great delight." She knows He is the One for whom she has longed because "his fruit was sweet to [her] taste." Can we witness so quietly and tenderly and with such disarming certainty to the delight of belonging to Jesus? Have we stopped long enough to be with Him? To sit down under His shadow? To know that His fruit is sweet to our taste?

O taste and see that the Lord is good . . . Delight thyself . . . in the Lord; and he shall give thee the desires of thine heart.

He brought me to the banqueting house, and his banner over me was love (Song of Solomon 2:4).

HERE is a "green stone" verse too deep with meaning to be touched with words understandable to our minds. Open your *heart* to it.

Perhaps you've forgotten with the passing of the years, what it was like the day the Lord first "brought [you] to the banqueting house." Perhaps you've forgotten that for the first time in your life you were satisfied *after* you had eaten the bread He gave you there. Perhaps you don't remember that your thirst had never really been quenched until you drank the water He handed you. Or you may have forgotten that the *reason* the bread stopped your hunger and the water your thirst was because He had said: "*I* am the bread of life" and "If any man thirst let him come unto *me* and drink." You believed Him that day and you feasted on Jesus and your heart sang because you knew "his banner over you *was* love."

You knew that no matter what He ever asked of you, it would only be because He loved you. Somehow suddenly the blood on "his banner" no longer surprised you. Calvary was very near and very dear to you, personally. Knowing that "his banner over [you] *was love,*" you understood in your heart that He could have done nothing else but die for you! Your heart seemed too small to contain it all. But the big reason for all the glory was that Jesus was there. He is still there. You can know this wonder again. If you've never known it at all, you can know it now. Jesus is here pressing upon our hearts.

. . . **and his banner over [us IS] love.**

Come with me from Lebanon, my spouse, with me from
Lebanon; look from the top of Amana, from the top of
Shenir and Hermon (Song of Solomon 4:8).

IT is well with our souls when we sit down "under his
shadow with great delight." When we finally are willing
to delight ourselves only in God, we find that He does
give us the desires of our hearts.

The true desires of our hearts.

Because when we "delight in Him," when we obey Him,
He works minute by minute, *as* we obey, to change our desires back to what He intended them to be when He created
us in the first place.

Then after He has changed our desires, we find that He
gives us "the desires of our heart." Now and then some of
us have come a way through life which has put us "on the
fringe" of the "multitude." We look about and wonder *how*
He is ever going to give *us* the desires of our hearts! Perhaps He can't for many years, but ultimately He will. Ours
is in one sense, "the better part," because our suffering lasts
longer and we are more helplessly driven to His side. We
know we have to *stay* there too or we are bereft. This is
cause for rejoicing! Anything that drives us to Jesus is cause
for rejoicing. And so, when we do sit at His banqueting table,
we find His fruit sweet, His bread and water eternally satisfying and His banner love. *But,* our Beloved does not leave
us sitting there growing fat and dull. We hear the voice of
our Beloved again, calling us to come on up a little higher.
Stirring us up to leap and skip about the mountain with
Him. We may stumble all the way up Amana, we may weep
all the way up Shenir and Hermon, but He is up there calling and we know we will ultimately *have* to follow.

Come with me from Lebanon my spouse . . . come away.

Come with me from Lebanon, my spouse . . . look . . . from
the lions' dens, from the mountains of the leopards (Song
of Solomon 4:8a-c).

H E does not call us to follow Him always "a little higher"
just for the sake of spiritual exercise.

Spiritual exercise is good, but here in this fragment
of the "green stone" we shared yesterday, we see *why* He
calls us to the mountains with Him. We see *why* it is a
"green stone" verse and cause for rejoicing.

It is actually cause for rejoicing just to be on a mountain
with Jesus. Peter liked it so well he wanted to stay (Matthew 17:4). And Jesus does call us to the top of the mountain
somtimes so that we can see Him in His glory. So we can
be with Him there. He calls us when He knows we need to
go.

"Come with me from Lebanon, my spouse . . . look from the
top of Amana, from the top of Shenir and Hermon, *from the
lions' dens, from the mountains of the leopards.*" Here I believe is the great secret of His call to ever higher ground.
When we follow, we learn to climb, and we also come to
the place of being able to *face* the fact that in this life,
even the lovely mountains not only have rough ways up
their rocky sides, they also are "the mountains of the leopards"!
Leopards are killers. They represent our particular fears
prowling about on our "mountains." Christ calls us to come
with Him right into these "mountains of the leopards" and
let Him prove to us that "perfect love casteth out fear." He
calls us to come *with Him* up into our life-mountains *exactly
as frightening as they are* and following Him, to let the dangers
spring and the temptations roar *in His presence!* He dares
us to stand with Him and "look . . . *from the lions' dens, from*
the mountains of the leopards."

Fear not: for I have redeemed thee. I have called thee
by thy name; thou art mine.

276

Thou hast ravished my heart, my sister, my spouse; thou hast ravished my heart . . . How fair is thy love, my sister, my spouse! how much better is thy love than wine! and the smell of thine ointments than all spices! (Song of Solomon 4:9, 10).

ONLY my *heart* can rejoice at this most precious "green stone"! My voice goes dumb at the thought of it. Could the One who "is altogether lovely" look at *us* and cry: "How fair is *thy* love . . . How much better is *thy* love than wine!" Could this be?

Yes.

There is no indication anywhere that we will *ever* understand love like this toward us, but there is *every* reason why we must *accept* His love. Without it life is tasteless and dry. Without the love of God operative in our lives through Jesus Christ, we are people slowly starving to death!

"He who hath the Son hath life, and he who hath not the Son, hath not life."

Jesus Christ *is* the definition of God's love.

And He loves us even more than our priceless "green stone" verse expresses.

As long as I tried to conceive God as the creator of the vast universe of universes, I could not "accept" Him. As long as I tried to conceive God as the creator of the vast world "not seen" *inside* the atom, I could not "accept" Him. But then He came to me as LOVE, saying "Come with me . . . Come away . . . Come unto me," and I went with Him where He "made his flock to rest at noon," and "I sat down under his shadow with great delight." I knew He loved me and at last I knew it was Christ "whom my soul loveth." He knew His way to my heart, because He created my heart.

My beloved is mine and I am His.

A garden inclosed is my sister, my spouse; a spring
shut up, a fountain sealed (Song of Solomon 4:12).

THIS is a singing "green stone" verse for us, *if* this is
the true situation in our lives with Him.

He rejoices in this verse. Here again is the mystery
of God rejoicing in us.

And yet He tells us "my delights were with the sons of
men." He rejoiced "in the habitable parts of the earth."
The earth, where we live. God rejoices in it because *we* are
here.

And when He can sing "A garden inclosed is my sister . . .
a spring shut up, a fountain sealed," His own dear Heart
moves in love poured down to woo us into loving Him more
and more.

But *are* we "a garden inclosed"?

Are we "a spring shut up"?

Are we "a fountain sealed"?

Are we sealed against all else but our Beloved? The Holy
Spirit desires to "seal" us. We are to "grieve not the Spirit
whereby ye are sealed . . ." God knows those who have been
sealed by His Spirit. Our questions concern our willingness
to keep ourselves from opening our "gardens" to any but the
Lord Jesus Himself! We are to choose and our choice is to
be toward Him and His lovely purpose in our lives. Is He,
Himself first? Can we *honestly* declare:

To me to live is Christ?

By night on my bed I sought him whom my soul loveth:
I sought him, but I found him not. I will rise now, and
go about the city in the streets, and in the broad ways I
will seek him whom my soul loveth: I sought him but I
found him not (Song of Solomon 3:1, 2).

IS there reason for rejoicing in this "green stone" passage?
At first we might see nothing but quiet desperation. Sleepless nights, spent envying those we know who are at
peace with God. Sleepless nights endured, as we toss back
and forth fuming with discontent.

Looking more closely we see even more desperation. This
time it isn't even *quiet* desperation. It has turned *frantic.*
"I will rise now and go about the city in the streets, and in
the broad ways I will seek Him whom my soul loveth."

Seeking and not finding.

Seeming to prove Jesus' words false: "Seek and ye shall
find."

We run around in circles from this conference to that church,
to this counselor, to that book! We seek Him but we seem to
find Him *not.*

How could this possibly be cause for rejoicing?

How is it that we have placed these strange, restless verses
among our "green stones" for praise and victory?

The answer is simple. This picture of desperate searching
is a glorious picture to God. This searcher is searching for
the Beloved Himself. She is on a "hunger-march" around the
city streets and the broad ways looking into *every* face for
the one Face her "soul loveth."

God is every minute yearning to fill us with Himself. But
He waits until we see our utter helplessness. He waits for
the time of our true hungering and thirsting after righteousness. Since He "has been made unto us . . . righteousness,"
He waits until we are hungry *enough* for Him!

O God, thou art my God; early will I seek thee: . . . my
flesh longeth for thee . . . My soul followeth hard after thee.

The watchmen that went about the city found me, they smote me, they wounded me; the keepers of the walls took away my veil from me (Song of Solomon 5:7).

HERE again is a strange "green stone" verse. And yet a close look under the guidance of the Spirit shows us the wonder in it.

Who among us has not been smitten and wounded by "the watchmen" who go about in Christendom "keeping order" with a big stick? Have you never been corrected sharply by some dear brother who feels God has called him to be *your* "watchman" going about *your* city?

I well remember once when I was a very new Christian, and quite sincerely trying to find an answer in a certain difficult situation. I believed God's will was to stop the undertaking we had begun. One such "watchman" brother fixed me with a cold eye and snapped: "Who are *you* to decide what God wants?"

I admit I carried the bruise from the "watchman" brother's "big stick" for a while. I rejoice now, because the "big stick" drove me to Jesus.

A woman's veil in Biblical days signified her innocence. Have you never had "the keepers of the walls" take your "veil" away? I can share from my own bumpy first years in Christian service here too. At the very innocent outset I was unaware to the point of stupidity about Christians *not* loving one another. Few people manage to miss it as I had. I remembered fights in the church as a child, but I hadn't been in a church for eighteen years.

Then some very *definite* minded "keepers of the walls" of the *correct doctrine* "took away my veil [of innocence] from me." I was almost blinded at first. But now I rejoice that it was jerked off so soon. Otherwise I might still be looking at those "keepers of the walls" and missing the face of my Beloved! His warning is such a great kindness:

Look unto ME, and be ye saved . . .

I charge you, O daughters of Jerusalem, if ye find my beloved, that ye tell him, that I am sick of love (Song of Solomon 5:8).

ONCE we have been stripped of our innocence about Christendom (and have seen that men and women whom God has saved through Christ, resemble Him *only* as they surrender themselves to Him), we *are* a little frantic at first.

We are discouraged.

We think, "Oh, if they've known Him all those years and are still so unlike Him, is there *any* hope for me?"

In one sense there is more hope. Not ultimately, but for right now. Because nothing slows us up more quickly than to drag the spiritual heels of dogmatism. And it is usually the "dogmatic" brothers and sisters who disillusion us most. As soon as we begin to decide *we're* right, even about His shed blood, we lose some resemblance to Him! We are to believe in His sacrifice. But *not* in order to be "right." Simply because there is nothing else one can believe, if one has seen into the heart that poured out the blood on the Cross.

Those of us who are still amazed that *anything*, even the blood of God Himself, could cleanse *us*, don't have to argue the atonement. We only have to live *at one* with Him. But at first, when our "veils" are stripped off, we have a tendency to run around crying, "Where is Jesus Christ in all this?"

We run up this street and down that broad way, sobbing, "Where is He? What about all this talk of love? Where is Christ anyway?" Now and then we leave our fellow Christians and go to outsiders for the answer! "I charge you, O daughters of Jerusalem, if ye find my beloved, that ye tell him, that I am sick of love." Cause for rejoicing? Yes. *We have seen our need.* "I am sick of love."

Come unto me . . . God is love.

What is thy beloved more than another beloved, O thou fairest among women? What is thy beloved more than another beloved, that thou dost so charge us? (Song of Solomon 5:9).

WE have been running here and there in search of our Beloved. Now as the woman in the Song of Solomon, we have run up to the first people we see and in our desperation to find Him, we cry, "I charge you, O daughters of Jerusalem, if ye find my beloved, that ye tell him, . . . I am sick of love."

I can well imagine that the "daughters of Jerusalem" in your life or mine, might raise vaguely quizzical eyebrows as they look us over somewhat pityingly. We blurt it out again: "I charge you . . . if ye find my beloved, tell him . . . I am sick of love."

We have *annoyed* them into answering now. They know we're "religious fanatics," but here is a chance to back us up against the wall with a question they're sure we won't be able to answer! After all, we left their world "outside" and turned to Christ. Have we come back? Did we not find what we were looking for? They look us up and down. *They* seem quite controlled. *We* are out of breath and nervous and somehow embarrassed. They give us a minute to grow more ill at ease and then one of them asks: "What is thy beloved more than another beloved?" We don't answer right away and she repeats her question, laughing now: "What is thy beloved more than another beloved, that thou dost so charge us?"

Here is a question everyone outside of Christ has a *right* to ask. If it forces us to find the answer, then this is a "green stone" verse about which to rejoice. What is your answer? *Why* Jesus Christ above any other? Jesus asked it Himself.

The voice of my beloved! . . . Whom say ye that I am?

What is thy beloved more than another beloved, O thou fairest among women? (Song of Solomon 5:9a).

THERE is no other way to the Father except through Jesus Christ, the Son. Christians believe this. Those who are "outside" do not.

But the world asks, sometimes with kindly interest, sometimes sarcastically, sometimes angrily: "What is thy beloved more than another beloved?" Why Jesus Christ *only?* Why not another approach?

What do we answer when this question is asked of us? With all our hearts we long to be *able* to answer. Even though we may have been running frantically around in the spiritual doldrums ourselves, still He *is* our Beloved, and when someone asks this question, we long to answer adequately. What we usually do however is what the woman did in the Song of Solomon. She began rather feverishly and with many adjective-laden sentences to *try* to describe Him: "My beloved is white and ruddy, the chiefest among ten thousand. His head is as the most fine gold, his locks are bushy, and black as a raven. His eyes are as the eyes of doves by the rivers of waters washed with milk, and fitly set. His cheeks are as a bed of spices, as sweet flowers: his lips like lilies dropping sweet smelling myrrh. His hands are as gold rings set with the beryl: his belly is as bright ivory overlaid with sapphires. His legs are as pillars of marble, set upon sockets of fine gold: his countenance is as Lebanon, excellent as the cedars. His mouth is most sweet."

And here, I think we are not wrong to sense that like us, she has run out of words. There were none adequate to begin such an impossible task as describing this Beloved who *is* "more than another beloved." I see her stop, catch her breath, and wait for Him to come to her rescue. He does. He is beside her and speaks for Himself.

I am the beginning and the end. I am he that liveth, and was dead, and . . . am alive for evermore . . .

This is my beloved, and this is my friend, O daughters of Jerusalem (Song of Solomon 5:16b).

WORDS failed her, but He did not. When we are challenged with the question: "What is thy beloved more than another beloved?" we can only rejoice, because we have been driven to find out that He *cannot* be described.

We must let Him say, "Before Abraham was, *I am.*"

But there is something we can do with our *lives.* We can do exactly what the woman in the Song does. After her beautiful, but futile attempt to capture Jesus Christ in words, she stops a moment. I can see her look around quickly and I can hear her sigh with relief when suddenly she sees He is there beside her. I believe this is when she said, "Yea, he is altogether lovely." Then she must have simply pointed toward Him as He stood there as only *He* is, and said with no adjectives flying: "This is my beloved, and this is my friend."

Words failed her. Words fail us. I was led to Christ much as these "daughters of Jerusalem" were led. I was being sarcastic and then someone's *life* pointed toward Christ and said: "This is my beloved, this is my friend." That's why I quite understand the question voiced by the "daughters of Jerusalem." After she had pointed to Him so simply as her beloved and her friend, after her *own* personal quiet and peace returned, after *her* eyes were back on Jesus, the miracle occurred. They asked: "Whither is thy beloved gone, O thou fairest among women? whither is thy beloved turned aside? *that we may seek him with thee.*" *They* couldn't see Him standing there with her. Their eyes were still blinded. *But He was there.* And they saw the peace come back into her eyes. He had done His own drawing. He will do it in your life and mine if we let our lives point directly to His altogether lovely Person.

. . . I, if I be lifted up . . . will draw . . .

284

My beloved is gone down into his garden, to the beds of
spices, to feed in the gardens, and to gather lilies (Song
of Solomon 6:2).

A "green stone" verse whose joy content is only reached
as the victory on the Cross was reached — through
suffering. He calls us "a garden inclosed."
What of the gate to the garden of your life? Is it closed
to everyone but Christ? Or is it sometimes closed even to
Him? Are there times at the end of the long, heavy days
when you feel you have a right to rest in the cool of your
own garden and that even Christ has no right to come there
except to comfort you?

But He comes, sometimes, as we have seen, in the *unlove-
liest* of people. And now and then He also comes at the most
inconvenient times. We are told to "be instant in season
[and] out of season." When it is convenient and when it is
not convenient for us, we are to *keep the gate open* to the
Lord Himself. He Himself has become the door to the abundant life, so that we may "go in and out and find pasture."
Can we do less for Him? Does He have access to your garden at any time *He* needs it? Is He free to come and go as
He likes? Are you and I willing to welcome Jesus when we
are so weary or so ill *He* has to help us stand? And when
He comes into our garden, what does He find? Does He find
fruit sweet to His taste?

Does the gate of your secret garden open easily to His
touch? Do we welcome the hard, bitter tasks because we
see that only in those can we really show our love for Him?
Or is the gate now and then locked when He comes with
one of His needy ones? He *is* our Beloved. He gave Himself
for us once and for all. He will never leave us nor forsake
us. But what does He receive from us? Is He always free
to "feed among the lilies" there in your garden? In mine?

. . . If any man will come after me, let him deny himself,
and take up his cross daily, and follow me.

I am my beloved's, and my beloved is mine: he feedeth among the lilies (Song of Solomon 6:3).

HERE the joy hidden in the heart of suffering is revealed. I like to think that the woman in the Song of Solomon was very quiet and very poised when she answered the "daughters of Jerusalem" who wanted to know where they too could find her beloved who *was* so much "more than another beloved."

I am quite *sure* she was poised and quiet and confident. As all those who have finally seen *His right* to the secret gardens of *their* lives *are* poised and quiet and confident. There is no flurry about the saints deep in God. No skidding tires, no jerking of telephone hooks, no slamming of doors. Eternity has begun for them.

They are as willing to let Him "feed among the lilies" in the disguise of a selfish alcoholic at three A.M. when no-one is watching, as they are willing to mount a high pulpit and tell of His love to thousands. Either way, it's all right, because they have not only found out *why* their "beloved is more than another beloved," they have given Him the key to the big gate at the entrance to their secret gardens. And they have given it to Him to keep. They are not their own. They "have been bought with a price." And they welcome the One who bought them. They are free and peaceful and poised and unhurried *because* they are not their own any longer. There is no rush because at last they belong completely to the Eternal, Himself. He can come and go as He chooses. No wonder at all that the "daughters of Jerusalem" wanted to have what she *at long last realized she had possessed* all along in Him. He drew them to Himself through *her* captured life. She belonged to Him and it made her so lovely, they wanted to belong to Him too.

I am my beloved's and my beloved is mine . . . let my beloved come into his garden and eat his pleasant fruits.

I am come into my garden, my sister, my spouse: I have gathered my myrrh with my spice; I have eaten my honeycomb with my honey; I have drunk my wine with my milk; eat, O friends; drink, yea, drink abundantly, O beloved (Song of Solomon 5:1).

THE Lord has been welcomed in the secret garden of her life here. She can rejoice.

If He has been welcomed in the secret garden of your life, you can also rejoice. The fruits and spices of your garden were made available to Him freely. He gathered His myrrh, and He ate His honey and drank His wine with His milk.

The Lord, in telling you this, is giving you a new manifestation of His love for you. If we could imagine it, He is thanking you!

But immediately, He feels free now to turn to His friends who are in need and invite *them* to come into your garden. Up to now this has been a close, love-filled, satisfying intimacy between your soul and the lover of your soul. What will you do now that your Beloved has thrown open the gate of your garden and invited His other needy ones to do as He has been allowed to do?

He calls them "beloved" too. Is this all right with you? Or do you want to hold Him only to yourself and lock the gate against outsiders who might not understand your *particular form* of worship of your Beloved? This will not please Him. He has bought you with His blood and *He has a right to feed you to anyone whom He knows is hungry!*

. . . Eat, O friends; drink, yea, drink abundantly . . .

OCTOBER 1

Who is this that cometh up from the wilderness. leaning upon her beloved? (Song of Solomon 8:5a).

HERE is hidden cause for rejoicing among those of us who know about the "wilderness." Cause for rejoicing for those of us who have not forgotten the terror of the black "wilderness" night. For those who still shudder wide awake from a dream set to an old rhythm. A rhythm heard only in the "wilderness" night.

Here is a "green stone" verse deep with reason for praise to the One who Himself lived through forty "wilderness" nights blacker with torment of soul and body and mind than any we could ever know.

Reason to rejoice here in the One whose desire to "lead us out" finally formed itself into a Cross, so that we would be given a weapon to "withstand the evil one."

Christ's temptations in the wilderness were *not checked* by God. "Himself He *could* not save." All the demons of Hell were loosed upon Jesus during those forty black nights. But we can rejoice. Somehow because they *were* loosed on Him, we can know in our "wilderness times" that "God . . . *will not suffer* [us] to be tempted above that [we] are able to endure." Temptations were *not* curbed for Jesus, so they could be curbed for us!

Reason in this "green stone" to rejoice in the One who also walked willingly into the "wilderness" of Gethsemane and Calvary so that we *could* be led up from the "wildernesses" of our blackest hours. We can all be driven *to* the wilderness to be tempted, but if we are His, as completely as He is ours, we will be willing to let Him lead us out again.

The wonder is not that He is able to lead *anyone* out of *any* "wilderness." The wonder is that He longs to do it! And for *us*.

> **Who is this that cometh up from the wilderness, leaning upon her beloved?** . . . **Ye have not chosen me, but I have chosen you.**

288

I sleep, but my heart waketh: it is the voice of my beloved
that knocketh, saying, Open to me, my sister, my love . . .
for my head is filled with dew, and my locks with the
drops of the night (Song of Solomon 5:2).

THIS "green stone" verse is unusually precious to me
and without my realizing it, I find we are sharing it
on the anniversary of the day He first took me to Himself.

On October 2, 1949, I heard "the voice of my beloved . . .
saying, Open to me, my sister, my love . . ."

My heart will be singing forever because I was given the
power to open to Him. I have found Him to be "altogether
lovely."

I have found Him every day to be "my beloved and my
friend."

If only we would realize how marvelous it is that God calls
us as He does.

Think of God's own voice, saying, "Open to me, my sister,
my love . . ." God needs to have access to all that is intimate
and dear to us. Surely, He has full right to this access, but
being God, He always knocks first.

"It is the voice of my beloved that knocketh, saying, Open
to me."

God has need of *you*.

God has need of *me*.

Wonder to end wonders, that *He* could need and want us,
and yet, He continues to draw us by explaining that "[His]
head is filled with dew, and [His] locks with the drops
of the night."

Could it be that the Eternal needs shelter in the warmth
of our inner selves? Yes, He does. In the earthly sense,
He "has no place to lay His head" and so He calls to us to
let Him in.

Behold, I stand at the door and knock . . .

OCTOBER 3

I have put off my coat; how shall I put it on? I have
washed my feet; how shall I defile them? (Song of Solomon
5:3).

"IT is the voice of my beloved that knocketh, saying, Open
to me, my sister, my love . . ."

She well recognizes His voice. And yet she answers with
trite alibis: "I have put off my coat; how shall I put it on?
I have washed my feet; how shall I defile them?"

In other words, she has already retired and is not willing
to receive anyone in the Name of her Beloved. Not even the
Beloved Himself!

"I have put off my coat . . ." She's too comfortable to be
disturbed.

". . . how shall I put it on?" Who wants to be disturbed
by getting dressed again?

The Lord is standing at the door knocking, but we know
that someone who is *so difficult* for us, is standing there with
Him and we find all kinds of excuses *not* to answer the door!

Not to be available when He needs us. Not to make that
phone call or write that note of apology. Not to have "them"
to dinner any more because they are not receptive to the
Gospel. Or dull conversationalists. Not to invite the sales-
man in out of the cold rain for a cup of hot coffee and a word
about the Good News. Not to associate with those we feel
are "beneath us."

"I have washed my feet; how shall I defile them?"

How it must grieve the Lord as He stands there knocking,
when those "who have been washed in the blood of the Lamb"
feel that they are "too good" to associate with some of the
unattractive loved ones He brings along. We pull our skirts
aside and fear to get our good clothes soiled by personal contact with those who have fallen into the filth of life. We
prefer to write a check or pray at home where it's clean and
restful. We have washed our feet! How shall we defile them?

Feed my sheep . . . Feed my lambs . . . Feed my sheep.

290

My beloved put in his hand by the hole of the door, and
[I was] moved for him (Song of Solomon 5:4).

SHE was bathed and resting, clean and perfumed in her
bed. Totally taken up with her own comfort and ease,
she made excuses not to open the door to her Beloved
who stood there knocking in the rain, *needing* to come in.

He had need of her, but she was not available. She was
too comfortable and self-righteous. "I have washed my feet;
how shall I defile them?" What He wanted was no doubt
difficult and might cause her great inconvenience. And she
was ready for a night of rest. But, the love of God, being
what it is (even in her selfishness), she was just about to be
taught a lovely eternal lesson by her Beloved. At her most
self-righteous and stubborn moment, His love moved *toward*
her.

"My beloved put in his hand by the hole of the door . . ."
She had been refusing him entrance. But He did something
to get her attention. He "put in his hand by the hole of the
door" and immediately she was moved with love for Him.

Up to that moment she had been conscious only of *herself*.
Of her own comforts and of the luxuries she loved so much.
Her clean linens and her "sweet smelling myrrh." But then
she saw just His *hand* and her heart came alive toward *Him*.

I cannot count the times I have been "too comfortable" to
open the door to Jesus when He has needed me for Himself
or for one of His needy ones. But then, in the midst of my
alibis, now and then He has showed me His hand! There is
only one hand like His. No other has nail-prints in it. When
I see it I have no more alibis. Anyone who has been washed
in His blood, recognizes His hand. And it's all right if we
have just "washed [our] feet." We can "defile them" easily
and joyfully for Jesus! There are marks on His feet too.

[I] Rejoice in the Lord always . . . [and] bear in my
body the marks of the Lord Jesus.

I rose up to open to my beloved; and my hands dropped with myrrh, and my fingers with sweet smelling myrrh, upon the handles of the lock. I opened to my beloved; but my beloved had withdrawn himself, and was gone . . . I sought him, but I could not find him; I called him, but he gave me no answer (Song of Solomon 5:5, 6).

ONCE He put His hand in at the lock of her door, she wanted Him to come in. Her attention was on Him and no longer on herself and the comforts of her life. "I rose up to open to my beloved . . ."

Myrrh and sweet smelling ointments dropped from her fingers unnoticed to the floor as she threw open the door to Him. Just the sight of His hand had caused her to remember that He is "altogether lovely."

But He was gone!

"I opened to my beloved; but my beloved had withdrawn himself, and was gone." Then began another frantic search.

Does this sound familiar to you? Has God called to you at a most inconvenient time and found you *not* "at home" to Him? But has something, perhaps a word of Scripture or a song, a thought of His eyes or His hands, sent you running to the door to let Him in only to find that He "had withdrawn himself, and was gone"?

He had not forsaken her. He does not forsake us. "I will never leave you nor forsake you." But He will withdraw the *sense* of His presence in order to cause us to "search for [Him] with *all* our hearts." Up to the time of *this* new, reckless search, we have wanted Him with *almost* all of our hearts. All except the part reserved for our own comfort and ease. Now, she is beside herself with longing for Him and "charges" anyone she sees to tell Him she is "sick of love." Comforts and intellectual achievement and good deeds and morality are fine but they do not satisfy our hearts. When we see *Him*, we are "sick of love" and that is cause to rejoice! There is healing in His hands and . . .

God is love.

I am my beloved's, and his desire is toward me. Come, my
beloved, let us go forth into the field; let us lodge in
the villages (Song of Solomon 7:10, 11).

AFTER she has searched with all her heart, she has found
Him, little knowing that all along, *He* had prompted
the search.

There would have seemed no reason to give thanks if, when
she finally stopped making excuses, she opened her door to
find Him gone. And yet, there is much about which to rejoice. The lovely lesson has been learned.

They are together again. "I am my beloved's and my beloved is mine." In a deeper way, they are *one*. I can easily
see that perhaps for the first time, His *love* dawned on her!
". . . his desire is toward *me.*" This seems almost too good to
be true. And yet, as someone declared: God's love is too
good *not* to be true.

Up to then she had obeyed Him *most* of the time. But
part of it must have been from fear or duty, because now
there is a new *oneness.* "I am my beloved's and his desire
is toward me." Once resting in this new intimacy, she makes
what now seems a natural suggestion to Him. Instead of making excuses, she wants to go with Him wherever He goes.

"Come, my beloved, let us go forth into the field."

Anything to be with Him every minute *forever.* She longs
for a new and unbroken fellowship. Oneness. Union with
her Beloved.

"Let us lodge in the villages." Live together as one in all
our daily lives. She is ready now, to obey His command. Her
longing to be in *Him* as "one with Him" forever, is a result
of His longing to be with *her,* as one with her forever.

Abide in me, and I in you. . . . Without me, ye can do nothing.

Christ in you, the hope of glory (Colossians 1:27b).

THIS glorious "green stone" verse is, tragically, one of the last to become real to so many of us.

Union of this intimate kind *is* inconceivable to our human minds. But we are given the power to possess it by faith. Christ *does* "dwell in our hearts by faith." Our part is to realize it.

To realize it and make use of it.

We have not been given the chance to make a new start.

We have been given an entirely new life!

And this life is the very life of Christ Himself. When we receive Him as our Saviour, He comes. But there is more to follow.

"My little children, of whom I travail in birth again until Christ be formed in you."

There has to be more, or Paul would not have spoken this way of his beloved Galatian "problem children." Christ comes in when we open the door to Him. We have His own word for that. ". . .if any man will open the door, I will come in . . ." But we need to "decrease that He might increase." Sin is, after all, *resistance* to God. And as we continue to resist, we continue to hinder the creative power of this new and glorious life within us. The Creator God Himself has come to indwell our mortal bodies.

And His highest will is to turn His full creative energy toward *re-creating* us in the very depths of our beings. But He waits for us to stop *resisting*. And somehow the *realization* that He is there in us causes us to want to let Him have His lovely way in all things. Ask the Holy Spirit to make it real to you that He is *in you*.

Nevertheless not I, but Christ liveth in me.

OCTOBER 8

And grieve not the holy spirit of God . . . (Ephesians 4:30).

WHAT does this really mean? Why would an admonition like this be among our "green stone" verses for rejoicing?

Let's look at what "grieving the Holy Spirit" means in a practical, daily way. The Holy Spirit and Jesus Christ and the Father are One. We cannot understand this, but we can accept it. And when we begin to act on our acceptance of it, we begin to *know* it is true.

They are One and cannot contradict one another.

The Holy Spirit would never instruct us to do *anything* that would be unlike Jesus. Jesus and the Father are One. So, grieving the Holy Spirit of God, is grieving God Himself. It is grieving Jesus Christ who saved us. If your heart "is moved" toward your Beloved, Jesus Christ, you do not want willingly to hurt Him. To grieve Him.

Just a few minutes ago as I was writing this page, a call came from someone who asked me for help. Someone for whom I had been praying. But he asked for my help at the exact time I intended to have six or seven full hours free to work on this book! I *tried* to refuse the request. I did a year of rationalizing in thirty seconds. Then I picked up the telephone and said "All right. We'll talk as long as you need to talk."

I wanted to talk to this person. He had simply asked to see me at the "wrong" time. But "the voice of my beloved" called to me in this troubled voice. Christ *in* me let me know that this was from Him and *He* has *captured my heart*. He has been "formed" in me sufficiently so that most of the time I recognize His voice. If He were remote from me, I would not. His presence increases my love for Him. It hurts *me* now, to grieve Him.

Behold, I stand at the door and knock . . . I rose up to open to my beloved . . . his banner over me is love.

295

Many waters cannot quench love, neither can the floods drown it. . . (Song of Solomon 8:7a).

BEFORE the mountains were brought forth, or ever thou hadst formed the earth and the world, even from everlasting to everlasting, thou art God."

Our "green stone" verse above catches flame in the fact that God is from "everlasting to everlasting" and that this God *is love*.

And this God is *in us*.

In us, gently, firmly, relentlessly pressing us to love Him in return. Christ will never stop urging us to respond to His love. He cannot. He *is* love. And He is "from everlasting to everlasting." We only hold back our own enjoyment of the quality of the life He died to give us when we refuse to respond to Him. "Many waters cannot quench [His] love" because He *is* that love and He is *in us*. "Neither can the floods drown it" because He has promised that He will never leave us nor forsake us. "Lo, I am with you alway." Jesus Christ *is* love. He cannot be drowned! He is alive forever now. And as we open ourselves to this *everlasting love* which for all eternity will be calling us closer, we will find response becomes as natural to us as breathing. But the habit must be formed of remembering that *He is in us*. It is His presence that calls us to love. Not the "feeling" that He is near. But the *knowledge* that He is never going away again. We can grieve Him, by refusing to accept each thing that comes as from His lovely hand. The choice is ours. We can *complain* about the hardships which are not of "our making." Or we can *respond* with joy to the One who will use them *for our remaking*.

God is love . . . I and the Father are one . . . I am he that liveth and was dead, and am alive for evermore. . . . Abide in me, and I in you.

For I reckon that the sufferings of this present time are not worthy to be compared with the glory which shall be revealed in us (Romans 8:18).

I make no attempt at scholarly interpretation. I am not a scholar. But I am a witness to the power of this verse to give us victory in the daily "sufferings of this present time."

I am sure that the sufferings of our earthly life *will* fade from our memories when we see Jesus. "That will be glory for me." I have never longed for Heaven, except to see Jesus as He is. In His glory.

But my heart sings and places this verse among our "green stones" for rejoicing because I have found very practically, from my own experience, that it also has to do with "glory which shall be revealed in us" *now*. In this earthly life. Not that we will be glorified. But that we shall *experience* glory because of Christ *in us*. And most particularly have I included this verse among our "green stones" because as each day goes by in the sharing of these verses, I am more and more convinced that God reveals His glory through *suffering*. When my own heart aches it is not quite enough consolation for me to remind myself that nothing is permanent but change, and that one day I'll go to heaven and this struggle on earth will be over. That is true. But more is true which helps me *now*. If Christ is in me now, "glory [is] . . . revealed in us." Glory is not merely a blaze of light. Henry Drummond calls it the "character" of God. Heaven would be dark without Christ. His *character* is the light. And it shines now in me, because *He* is in me. And He is "revealed in me" as I stop resisting the "sufferings of this present time" and see them for what they are: letters of introduction to His glory!

Heirs of God, and joint-heirs with Christ; if so be that we suffer WITH him, that we may also be glorified together.

297

The glory of the Lord shall endure for ever: the Lord shall rejoice in his works (Psalm 104:31).

SO that you will understand completely why this verse has been included among our "green stone" verses to praise God, will you please read all of Psalm 104? Open your heart and your mind *and your emotions* to its glory-filled words as you read and ask the Holy Spirit to open the depths of its message to you. And once you have grasped its lovely truth, you will be grasped *by* it forever. This has been my own experience with this Psalm and I ask this same Holy Spirit now to enable me to make clear to you what He has shown me in it.

If you read Psalm 104 you know it is a Psalm of praise. If you are in fellowship with the Lord Jesus, I know your heart is singing. If you are not close to Him, He is close to you and longs to gain entrance to your heart. He longs to give you a closer look at His *intention toward us* in this magnificent Psalm which rolls from "glory to glory" declaring God's infinite *care* about every living creature! About every part of the earth from the "beams of his chambers in the waters" . . . to "wings of the wind" that blows over the earth which He created and which He loves. On and on rolls the Psalm, singing of God's care manifested in "drink to every beast of the field" and sap for the trees and nests for the birds.

This God cares for every part of His creation. And in the last verse, we see that He cares *so infinitely* for "the man [who] goeth forth unto his work" that He wants the "sinners consumed out of the earth." He wants peace for everyone. *There is only one way to "consume sinners" and that is by consuming the sin from them and only the holy fire of the Spirit of God can do this!* My heart sings and shouts for joy. God *wants* to "consume the sinners" by turning them into saints!

Bless thou the Lord, O my soul.

He brought me up also out of an horrible pit, out of the miry clay, and set my feet upon a rock, and established my goings (Psalm 40:2).

THIS is a true emerald among our "green stone" verses. It is a witness for me. My heart sings that Jesus Christ does not wait for us to crawl out of the pit and walk to Him.

He reaches down *into* the "pit" and puts His strong arms under us and lifts us *out*. With the same arms He "sets our feet upon a rock" and the rock is Himself.

But because our feet have been set upon a rock, we are not made stationary as I used to fear. We are *stabilized* but not *stationary*. He "established my *goings*" the Psalmist sang.

"He established my goings" I also sing. Now, for the first time in my life, I can go. And I am "established [in] my goings." Who can travel far in a "pit"? No-one should attempt to describe that "pit" because actually, although it is "an horrible pit" to us, God blessedly never lets us see *how* horrible it really is! I am sure we would have broken under it before He lifted us out if we could have seen all of it. The literal translation of "an horrible pit" is *an horrible pit of noise*. As I write this page, I am "writing over" a very noisy radiator near my desk. Perhaps there is a "noise" in your life as you read, far more annoying or crushing than my "noisy radiator." Constant noise can be devastating and destructive. I can witness to the destructive "noise" in the "pit" from which Christ lifted me. In fact, so great and so constant was the noise and the confusion down in that "pit" that for a long time after He lifted me out, I missed it! Check yourself if you *have* to have sound around you constantly. A radio or a television or incessant telephone conversations. God has lifted us up out of a "pit of noise." Let us learn to be with Him in the quietness of our spirits.

Be still and know that I am God.

God was in Christ, reconciling the world unto himself, not imputing their trespasses unto them . . . (II Corinthians 5:19).

I F you know Christ, your heart sings with joy at this "green stone" verse. But only His loved ones know His love as it is.

How often we should repeat and repeat that He is *love.*

"God was in Christ" on that Cross, "reconciling the world unto Himself." We've already seen that to be reconciled means to be *harmonized.* To be made to "sing together."

God hung on the Cross so that His whole world could be harmonized with Himself. So that we could all sing together with Christ forever.

Mahalia Jackson sings ". . . and with Jesus, I'm going to sing redemption's story"! How glorious, when Mahalia and Jesus and Paul and you and I and *all* who will hear the song of reconciliation, can dance around the throne and sing together in a heavenly-harmonized eternal life!

"God was in Christ, *reconciling . . . not* imputing their trespasses unto them." God was in Christ, making harmony, *not* pointing a finger! He could not have pointed a finger as He hung there. He had given *both* His hands to be nailed to the Cross.

He did not point a finger to condemn. He opened His arms to save. Not charging us with our sins. But embracing them *for* us.

There is therefore now no condemnation to them which are in Christ Jesus.

**Acquaint now thyself with him, and be at peace . . .
(Job 22:21a).**

A LL we need to do to find peace is to become acquainted
with God.

Knowing Christ brings peace because He is peace.

He left His own peace on earth and then He comes to deliver it *personally* when He comes to live within us at our
new birth. We're not always aware of the peace within us
in Christ, but it's there.

Because He is there.

Unfortunately most of us are not enough aware that *He is*
there. And this is because we have not really become *acquainted* with Him as He is.

This is because we do not really know His ways. We
know that He said "My ways are not your ways," but we
need to know *how* they are not like ours.

We will know His ways when we know His heart. And
we know His heart when we open ourselves to His love.
When we acquaint ourselves with His love in the daily round.

We find that His love is not like ours. Our love *excludes*
those who don't please us. His love *includes* all. "For God
so loved the world."

We find that our love grows strong on *response*. His grows
on *suffering*. The more they mistreated Him on the Cross,
the more love He poured down upon them. He knew they
needed it. Much the way a mother pours out her love upon
an afflicted child.

We find that our love depends upon our *moods*. His love
is "from everlasting to everlasting."

We long for human love to bring us peace. At times it
brings great peace and great joy. But only the love of God
brings peace and joy *in all things and under all circumstances.*

God is love . . . Acquaint thyself with him, and be at peace.

From the first day that thou didst set thine heart to understand, and to chasten thyself before thy God, thy words were heard . . . (Daniel 10:12).

GOD'S great daughter, Mrs. Charles E. Cowman, once said to me: "Genie, all great books are born in the furnace." I do not believe writing "in the furnace" is a guarantee that a book will be great, but I take hope that it means a book may be *useful*. And I take that hope from the flames which have leaped almost joyfully about me as I have written much of this book!

The flames leaped with joy because they knew what they were doing *for* me. But I confess, I fought them and tried to escape for the first few days. And then I had to put this verse among our "green stones" for rejoicing, because although the flames have not all gone out around me, I see what they are doing.

And in the seeing, I have been willing, on one particular point, to "set [my] heart to understand" for the first time. This conflict of mine, like yours, I had "surrendered" and "surrendered" and "surrendered." Back it kept coming to haunt me. At last, God seemed to say ". . . set thine heart to understand what I am trying to do in you and for you. Be willing *not* to feel a victim of this thing. Open your heart to *understand* what I have to say *in it*, even though the words may sound strange to you at first."

I set my heart to understand, and to my amazement, I began to get God's point. At first, I didn't want to get it, because it meant I had to let go of one of my most beloved symptoms! But God is faithful. And once I opened my heart to understand *without resisting* Him, I saw that it was good "to chasten [myself] before . . . God." In other words, to be willing to be changed even at the place where I least wanted to be.

From the first day thou didst set thine heart to understand, and to chasten thyself before thy God, THY WORDS WERE HEARD.

The Lord thy God in the midst of thee is mighty; he will save, he will rejoice over thee with joy; he will rest in his love, he will joy over thee with singing (Zephaniah 3:17).

THIS verse tumbled of its own nature into our collection of singing "green stones." Read it again. There it is, in God's written down Word, and yet it is almost too glorious to believe!

Those of us who have begun to open ourselves to see what God is about *in us,* know that "The Lord thy God in the midst of thee is mighty . . ." We who have reached for Him in time of trouble or temptation or trial have found Him always to be "in the midst." Right there to help and to save and to protect.

But to think of God *rejoicing* over us!

This is almost impossible to believe.

We bring "great joy" to the heart of God when we *let* Him save us. He doesn't require payment for dying for us. He just rejoices that we take the gift of His life. "He will rejoice over thee with great joy, He will joy over thee with singing," if you *let* Him bring you out of your "wilderness time" *victoriously.* Perhaps *you* won't be singing immediately. Healing often takes time. But "The Lord thy God in the midst of thee" will rejoice. If you don't feel a song at once, go on in faith because of what you know His heart is *really like.* Let God do the singing. He can see the whole picture. Once we let Him lift us out of rebellion, we may still feel bruised and songless, but that's all right. God knows what He has done for us. "He will rejoice over thee with joy." He knows what His heart is like toward you, "He will rest in *his* love." Even when we don't feel *we* are resting in *His* love, He will rest in it for *us!*

I know the thoughts that I think toward you, saith the Lord . . . He will joy over thee with singing.

OCTOBER 17

At that time Jesus answered and said, I thank thee, O Father, Lord of heaven and earth, because thou hast hid these things from the wise and prudent, and hast revealed them unto babes. Even so, Father: for so it seemed good in thy sight (Matthew 11:25, 26).

FOR this *I* rejoice and hasten to place these words of the Lord Jesus among our "green stone" verses. Those of us who are completely untrained theologically *feel* the impact of joy in these words and cannot help giving thanks.

Just a few years ago I didn't know in which Testament Matthew could be found. But, "Father . . . so it seemed good in thy sight" to reveal Your truth even to me, and I thank You.

This does not mean those who are "the wise and prudent" can't know it. It is the childlike *heart* God seeks. He is definitely in favor of trained minds. By giving me eternal life, he has taught me to think more clearly than I learned to do in almost seven years of university life. And I enjoy using my mind as never before. This is no discrimination against education on God's part as some who are uneducated would like to think. God does *not* love the "down and outer" one bit more than He loves the "up and outer." "While we were [all] sinners, Christ died for us." We must never forget that the ground is level at the foot of His Cross.

The mind is not directly involved at all in this point Jesus is making. Except that He saw, as anyone sees, how much more difficult it is for a trained mind to *receive* "revealed truth." My friend who led me to Christ suggested wisely just minutes before my conversion, that I "stack my intellectual blocks in the corner and try *Him*." I did, and of course, when Christ came, truth came too. "I am the . . . truth . . ." Academic degrees or lack of them are beside the point. Is your *heart* an expectant, receptive, trusting *child's* heart?

Verily I say unto you, Whosoever shall not receive the kingdom of God as a little child shall in no wise enter in.

304

All things are delivered unto me of my Father: and no man
knoweth the Son, but the Father; neither knoweth any man
the Father, save the Son, and he to whomsoever the Son will
reveal him. Come unto me, all ye that labour and are heavy
laden, and I will give you rest (Matthew 11:27, 28).

THESE magnificent words of Jesus are usually not quoted
together. But there is cause for great rejoicing here
if we realize that they are *not* separated by the Holy
Spirit as He directed Matthew to set them down. We separate "Come unto me, all ye that labour" and group it with
the closing verses of Matthew 11 to make up the great-hearted
invitation of Jesus to all suffering mankind. To all weary
mankind. To all burdened mankind. This is one of my
favorite passages as I'm sure it is one of yours.

But there is new cause for rejoicing when we look at the
verse preceding "Come unto me."

In it Jesus declares His divinity and emphasizes His right to
speak *for* the Father in revealing His intentions toward us. He
is the only One who *can* reveal the Father to *anyone*. ". . .
neither knoweth any man the Father, save the Son, and *he to
whomsoever the Son will reveal Him*." In other words, I can see
that this means Jesus will reveal the Father to whomever
He pleases. If the Son does not choose to reveal the Father
to you, you cannot know the Father. Dare we be this literal?
Yes. We must be. "No man cometh unto the Father *but by
me*." Either Jesus is right or He is *not* who He claims to be!
But, here is the reason for singing: In His own words Jesus
includes *me* in the very next line. He includes *you* in the
very next line. "Come unto me, *all* ye that labour and are
heavy laden, and I will give you rest." Oh, that glorious "all"!
God's arms are open even to us. And we have Jesus' own
word for it.

Behold, I stand at the door, and knock; if ANY MAN hear
my voice, and open the door, I will come in to him . . .
even so, Father; for so it seemed good in thy sight.

305

And when they had sung an hymn, they went out into the mount of Olives (Mark 14:26).

IF you read on in the Gospel of Mark, you find that Jesus immediately begins to tell them that the Shepherd will be smitten and the sheep will be scattered in just a few hours.

Jesus knew, of course, what Peter would do in those hours ahead. He tried to tell Peter, but I'm sure Peter kept on arguing his devotion. Like us, Peter only stopped protesting his "spirituality" in words, when Jesus looked at him after the *third* blasphemous denial. Peter stopped vowing his love then. He was weeping too hard for words. We make large claims of loyalty to Christ until the temptation to disobey and deny Him sweeps over us as it swept over Peter that night. But Jesus *knew all along what Peter would do*. And this is the main reason this verse is among our "green stones."

"And when they had sung an hymn, they went out . . ." I'm sure Jesus led the hymn. And He did it knowing not only that He was about to die, but that Peter would do what he did. He still goes right on with us too, as He went right on with Peter. Knowing what vile thing we may do tomorrow or ten years from now. This melts me. When we displease earthly loved ones, they often grow angry with us. Not the Lord Jesus. His is a *different kind* of love. He woos all the more strongly, until we come back. Only Jesus can "sing a hymn" *knowing* what is up ahead by way of disobedient, broken hearts. And He can do it because He knows His own intention to *restore*. He knows about *us*, and He knows about *Himself*.

While we were yet sinners, Christ died for us.

> At that time Jesus went on the sabbath day through the corn; and his disciples were an hungred, and began to pluck the ears of corn, and to eat . . . For the Son of man is Lord even of the sabbath day (Matthew 12:1, 8).

MY heart can only sing as I picture Jesus standing there beside that cornfield with His disciples munching a handful of corn and the haughty Pharisees confronting Him with their "sin" of breaking the Sabbath!

My heart sings every time I think of the authority of God in the voice of Jesus throwing those poor old legalistic "religiosos" into more fits of frantic garment-rending. My heart sings because what He was saying to them, did not only cut them down to size, it gave them a way to be lifted up too.

He stood there, with the power of the simplicity of His singular place as the Son of God *and* of Man and showed His love for *us*: "For the Son of man is Lord even of the Sabbath day." If we are His, nothing possesses us. *We possess all things.* Even the sabbath. "And he said unto them, The sabbath was made for man, and not man for the sabbath" (Mark 2:27).

This shows me His love for me.

This shows me His love for you.

This shows me that He did come to show us a "better way." Jesus came being more fully "God's explanation" of *all things*. And He came particularly to show us God's great Creator *regard* for His creations. The dignity of man will save no-one. But anyone can be saved if he opens himself to seeing to what extent God regards this human dignity He, Himself placed in us. Any man can be saved if He looks at Jesus and believes what God is saying *in Him*. And seeing God's regard for us *above* religious practices and holy days, we begin to see His Heart. And seeing His heart, we begin to long to be close to that heart. We come *first* with God. Calvary proves this, and a longer, more honest look at Calvary causes us to stop resisting and let Him come first with us.

Looking unto Jesus, the author and finisher of our faith.

As soon as they were come to land, they saw a fire of coals there, and fish laid thereon, and bread. Jesus saith unto them, Bring of the fish which ye have now caught . . . Come and dine . . . (John 21:9, 10, 12a).

THE bewildered disciples, unable to cope with the glorious fact of His resurrection, yet knowing He had risen, decided to "go fishing." They caught nothing all night. But when morning came, "Jesus stood on the shore, but the disciples knew not that it was Jesus."

But it was. And the first question He called out to them from the shore, had nothing whatever to do with what they believed about His resurrection. He showed His deep concern for their *physical* well being! "Children, have ye any meat?"

Not only did He tell them where to cast their nets in order to find fish, He had brought bread and fish with Him and began to build a fire on the shore in order to cook for them. My joy overflows as one after another of the bright facets of this "green stone" verse come to life. God Himself, their Master, their Redeemer, who had just died for them had risen from the grave and had breakfast waiting! But more than that, He showed His great caring for their human dignity once more. He showed He cares that we *do* succeed in our efforts. He called out to them, "Bring of the fish which ye have now caught." He wanted them to feel *needed*. "Bring of the fish which ye have now caught . . . [and] Come and dine." One more cause for rejoicing packs this "green stone" passage and that is the fact that Jesus not only brought bread and fish, built a fire, told them how to succeed, let them feel needed, *He served their breakfast to them!* He was the glorified, resurrected Christ, but His heart remained the same. It is the same today.

Take eat; this is my body. Drink ye ALL of it, . . . this is my blood . . . the good shepherd giveth his life for the sheep.

For what if some did not believe? shall their unbelief make the faith of God without effect? (Romans 3:3).

I did not believe in Christ until I was thirty-three years old. For this reason, I place this verse written by one who also "did not believe" for most of his adult life, in the collection of "green stones" for rejoicing.

"For what if some did not believe? Shall their unbelief make the faith of God without effect?" The more accurate translation of the word "faith" here is "faithfulness." Those of us who "did not believe" know that our unbelief did not affect God's faithfulness in any way. And we rejoice that it did not.

No one denies that the lack of belief among the peoples of the earth breeds more unbelief. Over and over we hear: "But so few people believe that Christ died for our sins."

That's right. Pathetically few believe it. But according to the Word of God that doesn't make one bit of difference. "Shall their unbelief make the faithfulness of God of none effect?"

I remember well one sharp, isolated moment when I argued: "But I don't *believe* that." My friend looked at me and smiled and said: "I know you don't. But that doesn't mean it isn't true."

It was true. Whether or not I believed it.

Now that I do believe, I know. And have "entered in." And rest.

So we see that they could not enter in because of unbelief.

Believe on the Lord Jesus Christ and thou shalt be saved.

And at midnight Paul and Silas prayed, and sang praises unto God; and the prisoners heard them (Acts 16:25).

I have put this verse among our "green stones" because I am so thankful that there is a dependable law in operation here. If you and I rejoice in the midst of suffering, *someone will hear.*

Other "prisoners" will hear.

Perhaps other "prisoners" of the same suffering as ours. Perhaps not. But others *will hear.*

This does not mean we are to sing songs and pray in loud voices to show off our faith in God. This does not mean we need to make a sound with our voice at all. But we have been born into a human *family.* God created a family, all interdependent upon one another and therefore all touching one another. There is no true isolationism because God said "It is not good that . . . man should be alone." Man is not alone.

No-one can live without in some way being "heard" by others.

My *attitude of heart* in the midst of trouble and hardship sings or complains far more loudly than my voice could sing or complain. And someone will always hear. Someone will be affected by the attitude of your heart and mine *today.* There *is* a law in operation here: ". . . at midnight Paul and Silas prayed, and sang praises unto God; and the prisoners *heard* them."

You and I will be "heard" too.

Let this mind be in you, which was also in Christ Jesus . . . who . . . humbled himself and became obedient unto death, even the death of the cross.

And suddenly there was a great earthquake, so that the
foundations of the prison were shaken: and immediately all
the doors were opened, and every one's bands were loosed
. . . But Paul cried with a loud voice, saying, Do thyself
no harm: for we are all here (Acts 16:26, 28).

THIS time God did not open the prison doors only in
order to let His beloved disciples escape. He opened
them primarily so that the Philippian jailer and his family
could be set free from their sin.

The "other prisoners heard" Paul and Silas singing but the
jailer had evidently heard too. And if he didn't quite understand how it was that prisoners could sing and praise God at
midnight, he found out when Paul and Silas put their "praise
and singing" into action.

"Suddenly there was a great earthquake . . . and everyone's
bands were loosed. And the keeper of the prison, . . . seeing
the prison doors open, he drew out his sword, and would
have killed himself, supposing that the prisoners had fled."
But Paul stopped him by shouting "We're all here." So impressed was the jailer with this unusual behavior, that he
knelt before Paul and Silas and cried "What must I do to
be saved?"

Sometimes God permits "a great earthquake" which opens
our prison doors, so that we can take the easy way out. We
decide at this point. Remaining in prison can sometimes lead
to a greater fulfilling of God's purpose than for us to go free.
If Paul and Silas had escaped, the Lord would have loved
them just as much, but they would not have shown us nor
the jailer how much they loved Christ. After Paul and Silas
led the jailer and his family to Christ, they even went back
to prison. Paul could do this. Jesus Christ was his reason
for living. And he knew Christ means every word He speaks.
If it seems you are not to leave your "prison," even though
the doors are open, the word of the Lord Jesus is for you too.

My grace is sufficient for thee . . .

311

. . . and the foundations of the prison were shaken: and immediately all the doors were opened, and every one's bands were loosed (Acts 16:26).

ONE more look at a small, but very bright facet of this same "green stone," because it is eternal cause for rejoicing. This fragment above describes the opening of actual prison doors and the breaking of the chains that bound Paul and Silas.

I am sure both of them would have liked to have walked out of that prison, free men.

But they could not.

They could not become free men by walking through a door, because they were already *free!*

If you are behind the bars and locked doors of some new pressure upon your life, nothing basically will be changed, if that pressure suddenly is released. If you are chained with the iron of a deep loss or a new grief, nothing eternal will be changed if your chains fall off, because you, if you are Christ's, are already *free.*

Perhaps your heart is too torn to grasp this today. That's all right. Just go on. It is still true. Perhaps you are too new a Christian to understand. That's all right too. Jesus knows that. Just go on. It is still true. And one day you will know it. But until you do, it is still true. Jesus has done for you what He did for Lazarus at the grave. He has "loosed you and let you go." In or out of trouble, you are free.

If the Son therefore shall make you free, ye shall be free indeed.

And there sat in a window a certain young man named
Eutychus, being fallen into a deep sleep: and as Paul was
long preaching, he sunk down with sleep, and fell down from
the third loft, and was taken up dead. And Paul went down,
and fell on him, and embracing him said, Trouble not yourselves; for his life is in him (Acts 20:9, 10).

ALL real humor comes from God. I am convinced that
God is overpoweringly in favor of laughter. Only those
who have experienced the holy hilarity of the saints of
God as against the hysterical hilarity of the world, know the
tremendous difference between the laughter of heaven and the
laughter of earth. In this "green stone" is heavenly humor.

Paul preached so long, a sleepy fellow named Eutychus
"drifted *off*" and then down from a third floor window!

As people do, they gathered around the prostrate body of
the boy and "he was taken up dead." They didn't just think
he was dead. He was. The accident stopped Paul's disserta-
tion, but it gave him one more chance to prove that we *can*
give thanks *for all things*. To prove that the Lord to whom
he was a bond-slave, *was* at that moment a redeemer, "Paul
went down, and fell on him, and embracing him said, Trouble
not yourselves; for his life is in him."

What might have happened had Paul been *insulted* at the
boy's falling asleep in the middle of his lengthy sermon?
God would still have had the power to bring the boy to life,
but could that power have gotten through Paul if he had
been suddenly filled up with wounded pride? Paul might
have gone through the same procedure with the boy, but
nothing might have happened further. A tragedy would have
been left a tragedy. And there would have been no rejoicing and no holy laughter in heaven or on earth. As it was,
Paul was even able to finish his sermon! "Paul talked a long
while, even till break of day."

And they brought the young man alive, and were not a
little comforted.

And now, brethren, I commend you to God, and to the
word of his grace, which is able to build you up, and to
give you an inheritance among all them which are sanctified
(Acts 20:32).

WHEN a minister uses this verse as a benediction
after I have spoken in a church, I am always glad.
Not once have I ever been too tired for my heart to
speed up a little with sheer joy that it is true.

God *is* able to build us up.

If He weren't, where would we be?

Daily torn *down*, even as we would be trying to build ourselves up!

As long as we are "working *on* ourselves" for any reason,
we are, in a sense, tearing down. We are to work *with* God.
To co-operate with Him in our "building up" process. We
are to let Him plainly show His own life in us through our
actions. But we are not to waste our precious energies on
the futile performance of trying to *improve ourselves* spiritually. We are merely to expose ourselves to Him.

God is able to build us up.

We do not have to labor for our inheritance among the
saints. We are *given* that too. We respond to the gift with
obedience. By doing God's will we say "thank you" for this
amazing "gift," but it *is* a gift. And only when we realize
this, do we begin to fall into the dynamic rhythm of the
"hid" ones. He is our life. We receive it breath by breath
from Him. And respond breath by breath in obedience to
the Giver. This is the rhythm of those who walk the earth
to the music of heaven. Receive from Christ and give back
to Christ. Receive from Christ and give back to Christ. This
is the grace-filled rhythm of the true walk.

Come unto me . . . O God, thou art my God . . . Come
unto me . . . O God, thou art my God.

314

And thine ears shall hear a word behind thee, saying,
This is the way, walk ye in it, when ye turn to the right
hand, and when ye turn to the left (Isaiah 30:21).

EVEN when the pressure on my heart is a dark one, this
verse reminds me that joy is not necessarily for laughter.
Especially when the dark shafts strike one upon one
and merge to surround me with confusion, I am reminded
of the joy in this "green stone" verse. This kind of joy can
live in the dark.

There is joy in this verse because God is in it.

In it to tell us whether we are to turn to the right or to the
left. God Himself, not only being lovingly detailed in His
directions to us, but proving His love as He does so.

Somehow to me, if God had only said ". . . thine ears shall
hear a word behind thee, saying, This is the way, walk ye
in it," it would have been cause for cringing and fear of never
being able to do it.

But God said, I'll tell you exactly "when ye turn to the
right hand, and when ye turn to the left."

If you are in confused darkness now, *wait*. God has promised to give detailed instructions. He is not "the author of
confusion." Be still and wait, God will show you clearly and
simply, *if* you are willing to follow His instructions. He knows
whether or not you and I are willing. He knows what it is
that He will tell us to do. So, if He knows us to be *unwilling*
in some perplexing matter, what would be the point in giving directions until He has brought us by a means of His
own, to the point of willingness? He will never add to your
confusion. He will be quite simple about it. No need to
agitate. We can rest.

For God hath not given us the spirit of fear; but of
power, and of love, and of a sound mind.

Looking unto Jesus, the author and finisher of our faith (Hebrews 12:2a).

THIS emerald clear fragment of "green stone" sets me praising more each time I think on it. And I find myself thinking on it more and more, as the days turn into other days, filled sometimes with new confusion and new heartaches and new conflicts.

I find this "green stone" truth coming, seemingly of its own accord, when the old confusions return.

Coming to clarify *me.*

God doesn't always clarify things *for* us at once. Sometimes we need the felt-darkness around us in order to be freshly reminded that He is in that too.

He does not always clarify things *for* us.

But He will always clarify *us,* if we turn to Him. And there is no other way to turn to God except by "Looking unto Jesus."

Everything is here in the few words of this "green stone" verse. The way to salvation is here but also the way to victorious living is here. All in this one small fragment: "Looking unto Jesus, the *author and finisher* of our faith."

He began it, why do we refuse to let Him finish it?

An author *begins* a thing. He *began* new life by placing a seed of His life in yours.

We stop there and struggle through the years. And wring our hands and our hearts in needless anxiety for growth and peace, when all the time God has reminded us that *He* is the "finisher." He began it, let Him finish it!

> Being confident of this very thing, that he which hath begun a good work in you will perform it until the day of Jesus Christ.

I have just told you this before it takes place so that, when it does happen, you may have faith. I shall not talk over many things with you any more; for the world's ruler comes. He has no claim on Me; but I act as I do in order that the world may learn that I love the Father and act in full agreement with His orders . . . (John 14:29-31, Berkeley).

EVERY facet of this "green stone" is heavy with reason for rejoicing. Too often overlooked, perhaps is Jesus' *intimate approach* to us. "I shall not talk over many things with you any more . . ." How wonderful that He *does* "talk things over" with us.

But look more deeply into this "green stone" and see still more glory. Glory for God *even* in the coming of the "world's ruler"!

The enemy is about to bring Jesus down in what he hopes is defeat. But, on His way to the Cross, where the "world's ruler" will perform, Jesus makes a statement that lifts our hearts under any circumstances, *if* we want them lifted. On the way to Calvary, Jesus declares with that singular authority that "he has no claim on me." If the "prince of this world" has no claim on Jesus, then he has no claim on us either! He can attract our attention, but if we are Christ's, no-one but Christ has a *claim* on us. We are given power over any trick of the enemy. We can leave the power unused, or we can choose to use it. But it is there. He has no possible way of defeating us unless we help him.

But perhaps most joy-filled to me is Jesus' *reason* for going to the Cross. He makes it clear that the "prince of this world" has no claim on Him whatever. But that He is going through with it to *prove* the Father's intention toward *us*. "I act as I do in order that the world may learn that I love the Father *and* [that I] act in *full agreement with His orders*." God's love toward us is so great that He orders it proven by the death of His own beloved Son!

For God so loved the world, that He gave His only begotten Son, that whosoever believeth in him should not perish, but have everlasting life.

317

Now thanks be unto God, which always causeth us to triumph in Christ, and maketh manifest the savour of his knowledge by us in every place (II Corinthians 2:14).

THIS light from the last "green stone" verse falls upon each of the others causing us to look in new wonder at the One who Himself *is* that light.

"Now thanks be unto God, which *always* causeth us to triumph in Christ . . ."

Not "thanks be unto God," for victory in every area of my life *except one.* But because God *always* causeth us to triumph in Christ. If, as you read these words, you are in a time of dark defeat, this verse is still true and it is still true for *you.* There are no half-way measures with God. We can triumph *in all things* in Christ, if we want to.

If we want to and *when* we want to.

During the times of honest confusion when we don't seem to know how to lay hold of this triumph in Christ, the very desire of our heart to know it, will open the door to the triumph. If it is your heart's true desire to overcome the defeat at any cost, "he will give thee the desires of thine heart."

Always.

Under any circumstance and in the face of any temptation. And He will make manifest the "savour" of our new found intimacy with Him "in every place." Each time we allow God to cause us to triumph in Christ, we know Him better.

And it is God's pleasure to make it plain to all with whom we come in contact, that He is causing us to live abundantly through Christ. We don't need to broadcast our victories. God will not only give them to us *always* in Christ, He will let it be known in His way. A much higher way than ours.

Thanks be to God, who invariably leads us on triumphantly in Christ and who evidences through us in every place the fragrance that results from knowing Him (II Corinthians. 2:14, Berkeley).

MANY—COLORED STONES

During the last two months of this year, no ONE KIND *of stone will be shared, as in the other months. I have found that some of the "pleasant stone" verses in the Bible do not seem to fall into singular, separated meanings, but rather, are so many-sided in their truths that I have placed them in the collection called "many-colored stones."*

We may find verses which are like a certain kind of true quartz. And others like chalcedony, are merely quartz-like, waxy of surface and easily missed, if we are not aware they are there.

Again, there will be verses which attract our attention suddenly as ordinary chalcedony when its name changes to carnelian, and its color to orange red because it happens to be streaked with iron. Some of these verses appear "attractive" to us, until we discover the "iron" in them and almost wish we had passed them by! Quartz can be chalcedony, carnelian, sard, jasper, bloodstone, onyx, or agate. All beautiful, all differing in marked ways. And all, in their original form of quartz, useful in BUILDING *as well as in* ADORNING.

We will find "opal" verses among our "many-colored stones" too. Lovely stones of the same chemical composition as quartz, yet so different that they are distinct in themselves. Opals may APPEAR *perfectly hard, solid and dry, but they* ALWAYS *contain some water. Enough to vary their appearance and color to an amazing degree. So it is with our "many-colored" verses, all containing the water of life to those of us who seek it.*

Endless varieties of many-colored crystals God has put in the earth; endless shapes, endless formations, endless colors. Endless meanings in the endless varieties of "pleasant stone verses" God has put into His Word. And for us, endless joy and eternal life, IF *we are open to them. For the remaining two months of this year and forever, share my "pleasant many-colored stones."*

But now, O Lord, thou art our father; we are the clay, and thou our potter; and we all are the work of thy hand (Isaiah 64:8).

HERE is a "many-colored stone" which we can only see in part now, because "we see through a glass darkly." "But now, O Lord, thou art our father . . ." Isaiah *foresaw* Christ more clearly than most of us *see* Him now that He has come. But the prophet did not, I believe, refer to the place we have as sons and daughters *now*, by faith in Christ. This would not have surprised old Isaiah, I'm sure. Anyone to whom God revealed His future actions as clearly as He revealed them to Isaiah (Isaiah 53) would not have been at all surprised to learn that God had this *intimate* Father-son *relationship* in His lovely plan for us through Christ.

And yet, Isaiah *is* declaring our *general child-position* because God, the Father, created us. I have heard that Christians have bitter arguments over this point. How this must hurt the Father's heart! Because whether or not Isaiah meant a Father and creation relationship, or a Father and son relationship, the Father's *heart* remains the same.

I am no authority on these points of theology. But I do know that "we are all the work of [His] hand" and that even though we are now *in Christ*, we are *still* much in need of being worked over by His creative and re-creative touch.

Our closeness to God through faith in Jesus Christ should only cause us to long to be *more like* the Creator-God's original desire for us. He did create us. He is still longing to bring us to perfection. Hand Him your heart. The pressure of His dear fingers on the hard places may bring pain at first. But if we are not willing to bear this pain at the touch of His *hand*, we are *wasting* the Calvary-pain in His *heart* for us.

It is the Lord; let him do what seemeth him good.

I am sought of them that asked not for me; I am found of them that sought me not: I said, Behold me, behold me, unto a nation that was not called by my name. I have spread out my hands all the day unto a rebellious people, which walketh in a way that was not good, after their own thoughts (Isaiah 65:1, 2).

WHAT can it mean that the God who loved us even to the Cross, should have to stand before us and cry "Behold me, behold me"? How can we reconcile this with our own heart's cry to God to "hear my voice: let thine ears be attentive to the voice of my supplications . . . O Lord, O Lord"?

At least I believe if we were to let the Holy Spirit show us the side of God's heart which cries to us, "Behold me, behold me," we would not *have* to cry for God's attention. On the Cross, God proved that we already *have* His attention. Christ has come. We no longer have to plead for God's mercy. He has given it forever in Jesus' life poured out. It is so clear in Christ that we never need to beg from God. *God has already given.*

And my shame is great when I realize that so often, this same God still stands before me saying: "I have spread out my hands all the day . . . I have spread out my hands all the day . . . Behold me . . . behold me."

My shame grows greater when at last I behold Him and see again what I seem to forget so quickly, that in those hands spread out "all the day" are still the nail-prints from the Great Giving on Calvary. Did I really *forget?* Did you really *forget?* Spread out your own hands right now in your imagination toward someone you love. Try to conceive no response at all. See that person pass you by once and twice and then "all the day . . . in a way that was not good, after their own thoughts . . . *rebellious.*" Then hear God's words . . .

I have spread out my hands all the day unto a rebellious people . . . the good shepherd giveth his life for the sheep . . . yea, for the rebellious also.

321

NOVEMBER 3

Ye are my witnesses, saith the Lord, and my servant whom
I have chosen; that ye may know and believe me, and understand that I am he; before me there was no God formed,
neither shall there be after me (Isaiah 43:10).

THERE is depth under depth in this "many-colored stone."
Too many depths for us to see now.

But we *are* His witnesses, and if we are to be convincing
witnesses, we must know something of the *fact* of the unseeable
depths of God.

What does it mean to you that Jesus declared Himself to be
"the beginning and the end"?

Alpha and Omega.

Our earth and time bound minds cannot comprehend that
there has never been a beginning that *was not God Himself!*
God did not come from *anywhere.* He seems to care very much
that we know this. It must have a great bearing on our concept of Him, because over and over we are reminded that there
was no other God before Him.

". . . understand that I am he; before me there was no God
formed."

He wants us to know also that He is the end.

". . . before me there was no God formed, neither shall there
be after me."

He *is* the first and the last.

All of creation is God's idea. If we know God, we know all
there is to know now. We will not necessarily have well-worded
answers to all questions. But if we know God, we are willing
to let the questions wait. After all, He will not only be there
at the end. He *is* the end. Add this to the knowledge of His
love we have gained together in this sharing, and rest.

I am the first, and I am the last; and beside me
there is no God . . . God is love.

822

I have declared, and have saved, and I have shewed, when
there was no strange god among you: therefore ye are my
witnesses, saith the Lord, that I am God (Isaiah 43:12).

GOD is reminding us again that we are His witnesses. And
it seems enough to witness to the fact that *He is God.*

Being God, He says of Himself, "I have declared, and
have saved, and I have showed . . ."

He has done this because He is God.

And because *only* He is God.

No-one else can *declare* and know that the declaration is absolute and final. Because no-one else is God.

No-one else can *save,* because no-one else is a Saviour.

No-one else can *show,* because no-one else knows the beginning and the end and all that lies between.

This is all in the "many-colored" verse at the top of this page, but there is one streak of strong color not to be missed, if we are to be sure in our *own* hearts of God's identity. He has *declared,* He has *saved,* and He has *shown.* He will continue to declare and to save and to show. *But,* even though He and He alone can do these things for us, He *cannot* do them except "when there [is] no strange god among [us]."

We don't build idols of gold and stone to worship as did the ancients, but we *do* build idols. Strange gods among us to cloud our vision of God as He really is in Jesus Christ. Subtle "strange gods" which seem to be a part of Him. Points of doctrine, denomination, service, even witnessing can become "strange gods" if we are witnessing for witnessing's sake. We are to witness, not *for* the sake of our "witness" but for the sake of Jesus Christ.

I am the Lord thy God . . . Thou shalt have no other gods
before me . . . they shall go in confusion together that are
makers of idols.

I form the light, and create darkness: I make peace, and create evil. I the Lord do all these things (Isaiah 45:7).

THE formation of some natural stones is so strange as to cause confusion even to the expert when he tries to identify them.

This must be true of this "many-colored" verse.

Being no expert, I dreaded the verse for a long time. In one sense part of it frightened me. I know God is light. I know He said "let there be light" *and* darkness. Day and night are not sources of confusion. There must be night before there is day. Night does not *produce* day, but it *defines* it. Night is merely the *consequence* of our part of the earth *leaving* the light.

No cause for confusion either when God says "I make peace." We who belong to Jesus Christ, know that He is our peace.

But my heart tightened at the next statement of God. ". . . and [I] create *evil.*" Did God *create* the very thing that caused Him to send His Son to earth to die? Did God create a monster which got so out of His control that He had to take a step as drastic as Calvary to defeat His own fiendish creation? *No.*

God created all things *for His own Son* (Colossians 1:16). He created joy and comfort and love. All good. All desirable. *But* because they are so good and so desirable, their *absence* creates sorrow and misery and hate! The absence of joy means sorrow. The absence of comfort means misery. The absence of love means hate. No, God did not *willfully* create evil, except as He created its opposite, *good.* He did not *create* evil, but He has taken *full responsibility for it* when He took sin into His own heart on the Cross. He is —

The God of all comfort . . . Comfort ye, my people.

Bel boweth down, Nebo stoopeth, their idols were upon the
beasts, and upon the cattle: your carriages were heavy laden;
they are a burden to the weary beast. They stoop, they
bow down together; they could not deliver the burden, but
themselves are gone into captivity (Isaiah 46:1, 2).

CAN we look into the rather unusual depths of this "many-
colored stone" and find some of the reason why our
Christian service eventually takes us "into captivity"?
Here is a vivid picture of utter exhaustion and weariness.
Physical exhaustion comes to everyone now and then. But
for this day's sharing, consider the exhaustion of spirit, mind
and soul in some who serve so sincerely. I can witness to
periods of such exhaustion in my own life. And *from* them
and *through* this verse, I have found the reason and the way
out for most service-fatigue. Remember, we are not speaking of physical tiredness now. And the soul and spirit weariness of which I write is not limited only to those who work
in what we call "full-time Christian service." We are called
to serve Him whatever our profession, and the same weariness comes over those who work at a secular profession all
day and serve actively in their churches at night.

The Holy Spirit has shown me in these verses, that my
"idols" are too heavy! Even the "beasts of burden" which
I use to carry on my work (the mind God gave me, the talents,
etc.), are unable to deliver as they should because of the
burden of "idols" I have forced them to bear. Such "idols"
can be anything from ego to self-effort, to pride in my work,
to misdirected zeal. Zeal to accomplish what *I* want to be
able to tell about instead of zeal simply to obey the Lord
when there is *nothing* to tell. I have found that sometimes
He asks me to do *nothing* but belong to Him. If I am not
willing to do this, demanding no results, I am overburdening
both the carriages and the cattle. My "idols" are too heavy.

Come unto me, all ye that labour and are heavy laden, and
I will give you rest. I have made, and I will bear; even I
will carry, and will deliver you.

Therefore hear now this, thou that art given to pleasures, that dwellest carelessly, that sayest in thine heart, I am, and none else beside me (Isaiah 47:8).

THIS "many-colored stone" has a sharp edge that pierces my own heart.

I lived that way.

Given to pleasures, dwelling carelessly and saying in effect in my heart *and* aloud, if I could get anyone to listen "*I am,* and [there is] none else beside me."

I not only said this in my heart and aloud, I *lived* it.

And every day since the moment I first looked at Christ hanging on the Cross for me and *believed,* I have had to guard against the return of such an attitude!

Could we as Christians who have been washed in the blood of God Himself, poured out for our sake, really defy God as this verse claims? Could Christians be "given to pleasures" above the One who gave Himself for us? Could Christians dwell carelessly, caring only for themselves and their families? Could we as Christians who know in our hearts that it is only by the grace and mercy of God that we are not lost, *defy* the God who saved us? Could we who have been cleansed and given eternal life by the heart of God broken on the Cross shake our fists at the sky and declare "I am, and none else beside"?

That list of questions needs no answering. We *know* the answers. And God knows them also. The *antithesis* of this attitude *is* the attitude of the Cross.

Father, forgive them; for they know not what they do.

NOVEMBER 8

I shall not sit as a widow, neither shall I know the loss of children; But these two things shall come to thee in a moment in one day, the loss of children, and widowhood. . . . thou hast said in thine heart, I am, and none else beside me (Isaiah 47:8c, 9a, 10c).

LOOKING at this "many-colored stone" I see also the faces of Christian women here and there, who have come to me almost annoyed after I have spoken on the attitude of our hearts toward tragedy and suffering. They say, "Time enough to worry about the death of my husband later. I can't face it now!"

I had not recommended "worry" at all. I had recommended a *prepared heart*. And a prepared heart is a heart which has opened itself to the attitude of the heart that opened itself to our sin on Calvary. These women are standing behind their phony barricades saying, "This won't happen to me. Maybe to my neighbor, but not to me."

"*I* shall not sit as a widow, neither shall *I* know the loss of children."

Refusing to face reality. How can they *embrace* tragedy in the name of Jesus if they have refused even to face its possibility? "But these two things shall come to thee in a moment, in one day, the loss of children and widowhood," warns God. God will not send them as a punishment for our self-centeredness. He warns that they come to anyone and everyone and only those who have stopped *resisting* the attitude of Christ survive victoriously. Those who stiffen their necks and say, "I'm *safe* in the circle of my family and friends, and I'll stay here" *will stay* there growing old and bitter and hard when tragedy breaks that circle. Check yourself. Are you smug in your precious "safe" circle? Do you ever invite some "undesirable" person to dinner with your family? If not, God wants to help you.

A new heart also will I give you . . . and I will take away the stony heart out of your flesh, and I will give you an heart of flesh.

327

Unto Adam also and to his wife did the Lord God make coats of skins, and clothed them (Genesis 3:21).

GOD warned Adam and Eve. God warns us. But as with the couple in the garden, we "take over" and ignore God's warning. He attempts to convince us in every way possible that He has formed things a *certain way.* If we obey, we live in peace. If we disobey and ignore His warnings, we reap the consequences.

By nature, after the original self-assertion in the garden, we have *no power* to obey God. But not only has God provided this power in Christ, He began to show us His heart in the altogether gracious way in which He cared for Adam and Eve right there in their first shame!

God's heart did not *become* like Jesus' heart on the Cross during the hours Jesus hung there. *God's heart has always been that way.* And here is tender proof of it.

Just minutes after He saw their disobedience, and heard their feeble explanations, He *began to minister to them.* He merely acted like Himself in the garden when, after clearly setting forth the inevitable *consequences* which would follow their sin, He began to serve them. God will always make the consequences of our sin plain to us. This is part of His nature too. Not the vindictive part as we so wrongly think. Rather a lovely proof of His fairness. He was not a vengeful God. He was a loving Father. He was like Jesus. He made coats for them to hide their shame. Caring as He still does, for human dignity and suffering. He acted like Jesus. They were One then, as they are now.

> . . . Then I was by him, as one brought up with him . . .
> I and the Father are One.

> ... I am the Lord thy God, that divided the sea ... And
> I have put my words in thy mouth, and I have covered thee
> in the shadow of mine hand ... (Isaiah 51:15a, 16a).

HERE is a treasure for you among our "many-colored stones" if you are tongue-tied when you get up to speak in public. It is one I can promise will work if we are willing to give God His way in the *timing* of it.

We must also be *willing* to prove Him.

We must be willing to get to our feet and begin.

I had been a Christian about six months when I was given my first job before a microphone. Up to then I worked on the director's side of the control room window. But here I was with an open microphone before me and a wooden tongue which would do nothing but chip off splinters when I tried to use it!

Day after day I listened to myself on tape and wanted to die. I felt my listeners must be longing for my extinction even more than I longed for it. And after a few painful weeks, I came to realize radio *couldn't* be too difficult for Jesus Christ, even with *me* at the microphone! After all, if He "divided the sea," can't He put words in our mouths? Didn't He create our mouths in the first place?

Following the radio ordeal, I then had to begin *facing* crowds of various sizes. This was my very first attempt at public speaking and I was thirty-four years old. He kept His promise here too. *He covered* my embarrassment and my self-consciousness *as* I let Him. As I became more certain that He would cover *me* in the shadow of His hand, I became more and more willing to put myself *in* His hands at those difficult times. He will speak through you, according to *His* need of you. He makes absolutely no exceptions when He promises a thing.

> The Lord God will help me; therefore I shall not be confounded ... I know that I shall not be ashamed.

Therefore hear now this, thou afflicted, and drunken, but not with wine; Thus saith thy Lord the Lord, and thy God that pleadeth the cause of his people, Behold, I have taken out of thine hand the cup of trembling . . . (Isaiah 51:21, 22a).

HAVE you ever been "afflicted" with fear? Have you ever been "drunken" with anxiety?

Before getting up to speak, has your chair seemed to be fastened to a section of the floor which is set to revolve at an increasing speed in an ever widening circle? Are you "drunken" with fear for *any* reason at all?

Are you trembling with nervousness right now because a certain letter has not come? Or because you just don't know what you are going to say when the phone rings and the time arrives when you just have to say something?

Are you literally sick ("afflicted") with anxiety over some loved one?

God spoke of the Israelites through Isaiah in this "pleasant stone" verse, but He is also speaking of us through him. And since He loves you and since fear and anxiety can damage not only your peace of mind, but your health as well, God wants you to listen.

If you feel "drunk" with fear and worry and anxiety and nervousness, God has something to say to you, and He is asking for your attention in a very personal way: "Thus saith *thy* Lord the Lord, and *thy* God that pleadeth the cause of his people . . ."

> Behold, I have taken out of thine hand the cup of trembling . . . Fear not, for I am with thee.

And when the ark of the covenant of the Lord came into
the camp, all Israel shouted with a great shout, so that
the earth rang again . . . And the Philistines fought, and
Israel was smitten, and they fled every man into his tent
(I Samuel 4:5, 10a).

HERE is a "many-colored" passage which seems contradictory at first glance.

We will, of course, not attempt to step into the scholar's domain and fit it into context in the historical progress of Israel toward God. But there seems to me to be a definite word for us in it. One which we might very easily miss.

"When the ark of the covenant of the Lord came into the camp, all Israel shouted with a great shout . . . [but] the Philistines fought, and Israel was *smitten,* and they fled."

Have you been in a predicament from which you cried out with a "great shout" to heaven for help, and even after your "great shout" and declaration of faith, the enemy still ran you down? Did you still yield to that temptation? Did you still fail?

Did it seem as though God didn't hear you at all?

Do you think it seemed that way to the Israelites too, as "they fled every man into his own tent"? But what did the account say they did? They shouted with a "great shout . . . when the *ark*" came in! We do not condemn them. Christ had not come. The veil over the holy of holies had not yet been torn from the top to the bottom.

But I could not help making application to myself as I read of their apparent lack of response. Had they perhaps been shouting at the *ark* and not at God? Do we sometimes almost superstitiously cry to *heaven* instead of to God Himself?

Let Israel hope in the LORD: for with the LORD there is
mercy, and with HIM is plenteous redemption. Come unto
ME. If any man thirst, let him come unto ME and drink.

Seek ye the Lord while he may be found, call ye upon him while he is near; let the wicked forsake his way, and the unrighteous man his thoughts: and let him return unto the Lord, and he will have mercy upon him: and to our God, for he will abundantly pardon (Isaiah 55:6, 7).

PERHAPS you need to "return unto the Lord."
If you do, you can. Anyone can "return" who wants to return. Jesus said He would be with us always. God has assured us that He will never leave us nor forsake us.

"He may be found" *right now*.

He is there. Seeking you. Urging you to seek Him. Urging you to *forsake* this thing that is keeping you and your Lord from the fellowship He longs to have with you.

This thing that keeps you from the fellowship you long to have with God is the thing *you are to forsake*. Forsaking your sin is part of "returning."

"Him that cometh to me, I will in no wise cast out."

There is no question here, as I see it, of God's refusing to be found. He is simply aware that if we refuse to forsake our sin and continue to nurture it, we reach the place of near-blindness again. Seek Him while *you can* still find Him.

You are to forsake your sinful ways and your unrighteous thoughts.

I am to forsake my sinful ways and my unrighteous thoughts.

When we do this and "return unto the Lord" then we will find that He will have mercy and will *abundantly* pardon.

He tells us in the next verse that His thoughts are higher than our thoughts. Why are we so stubborn about forsaking our unrighteous thoughts? Why do we seem to doubt that God's thoughts for us *will be* more satisfying, more fulfilling than our own?

Let him return unto the Lord . . . and . . . he shall go out with joy, and be led forth with peace: the mountains and the hills shall break forth before you into singing, and all the trees of the field shall clap their hands.

332

But I trusted in thee, O Lord: I said, Thou art my God. My times are in thy hand (Psalm 31:14, 15a).

HAVE you ever considered that patience is a consistent display of love?

And that impatience is a display of unlove?

Do you agree that impatience is lack of love? A lack of love toward others or excess of love toward ourselves. Either way, it comes out in impatience. In tapping fingers. In heavy sighs. In cross words. In pacing the floor. In clock-watching. In inattention to other people's conversation. In more concern for ourselves than for anyone else at one time in particular. *Coldness begins when impatience becomes an attitude of life.*

The "many-colored stone" above has a streak of crimson through it, if we look closely.

"But I trusted in thee, O Lord; I said, Thou art my God." If we have received Jesus Christ as our own personal Saviour, we have received the right to call God, "*My* God."

If I have the right to call the Christ of the Cross, *mine,* do I also have the right to pace the floor if I'm kept waiting? To dart quick *apparently* casual looks at the door in full view of a lingering guest because my own blood pressure is mounting? If my times are really in His hand, wouldn't it be more Christ-like for me to be perfectly honest and excuse myself, thereby showing only the necessity to be excused in order to get on with the next thing, instead of impatience?

If I really trust in the One who took time to hang on a Cross in order to give me eternal life, am I blind to the blood-red thread of color in this odd little "pleasant stone" verse? The next time I feel my own nerves tense with impatience, I will remember that the pain I *feel* and the pain I *inflict* are in His heart too. The heart that loved me enough to break for me on a Cross.

In all our afflictions, he is afflicted.

Thou shalt hide them in the secret of thy presence from the pride of man: thou shalt keep them secretly in a pavilion from the strife of tongues (Psalm 31:20).

MANY, many colors thread this "pleasant stone" verse. Two attract me in particular.

One, a lovely promise that we will be hidden "in the secret of [His] presence from the pride of man." I see the "color" of joy just from realizing that there *is* "the secret of [His] presence"!

". . . your life is *hid* with Christ, in God."

He has promised never to leave us, and so since He is always with us, we always have a hiding place. Dear and simple and familiar to those of us who have tried this hiding place and found it always there. Especially when we have run to it "from the pride of man."

We can be insulted *in public* when we know about the "secret of his presence."

How it glorifies Him when we remember that we don't need to strike back. We can simply "hide in his presence."

In the "open secret" of His presence.

And so much a redeemer under all circumstances is Jesus Christ, that He even redeems criticism, *if we* remember the hiding place.

". . . thou shalt keep them secretly in a pavilion from the strife of tongues."

We may be the recipients of many lashes from many tongues. Nothing unusual about that.

But it *can* be glorious! I can permit the indwelling Christ to make me so creative that the very tirades against me will be gathered up with joy and used to get *for me* my heart's deepest desire — to be closer and still closer to Christ Himself.

. . . Be of good courage, and he shall strengthen thine heart . . . Be of good cheer, I have overcome the world.

Blessed is he whose transgression is forgiven, whose sin is covered. Blessed is the man unto whom the Lord imputeth not iniquity, and in whose spirit there is no guile (Psalm 32:1, 2).

NO other religion offers forgiveness. Only those who have experienced the forgiveness of Christ, know the freedom forgiveness brings.

Only those of us who are forgiven by the One who will never point a finger at us and remind us of what He has done, know the *rest* of being free. God never points a finger at us for any reason. "Blessed is the man unto whom the Lord imputeth not inquity." Blessed is the man who knows Christ did not come to condemn, but to save.

God could not condemn because of what His heart is like. But He also is far too wise to point a finger at *us* for *any* reason. He knows that's what most of us want, *to be noticed!* We want to be pointed *out*, therefore many of us are willing to be pointed *at*, if only someone is directing attention toward us. It is a pathetic and humanly disgusting spectacle to see an adult (in years) sit and squirm through an entire evening clinging to and building up a problem in order to get attention. But think of the patience God has had to have with us. Think of the patience He must still show us. And be thankful that He shows it so wisely. If He kept pointing at our sin, He would keep *our* attention on it. And He knows that whatever attracts our attention, also attracts us. So, God in His lovely wisdom, points to *Himself*.

When He has our attention, He also has us. And one good way for us to know how much of us He really possesses, is to see how much guile we still possess. If we are still full of tricks and devious conversation, there is need for cleansing. Need for much cleansing. The simplicity of no guile captures us when we are completely captured by Christ.

Blessed is the man . . . in whose spirit there is no guile.
Learn of me, for I am meek and lowly in heart.

> But if we walk in the light, as he is in the light, we have fellowship one with another, and the blood of Jesus Christ his Son cleanseth us from all sin (I John 1:7).

GOD never points a finger at us, that is true. He has put our sins behind Him forever. ". . . as far as the east is from the west."

He has forgotten them.

He *knows* about the blood of Jesus Christ. It is His own blood. We hold *theories* about it, but God *knows* about it. Therefore, He knows that it cleanses and keeps us cleansed.

There is no question about God's acting in accord with His own knowledge. We can rest here. He will never act in discord with it.

He knows about the cleansing power of the blood of Christ. So, of course, He *forgets* what has been utterly cleansed away. If you send a suit to the cleaners and they remove the ugly spot which caused you so much concern just the day before, you're not likely to continue to worry about that spot the next time you wear it. The cleaners got it out!

It's gone.

Why waste time remembering how terrible it looked?

We are the ones who hang on to our worry patterns. God is *not* neurotic. He lets it go and goes on with us *keeping* us clean, as we keep ourselves "in the light as He is in the light."

We need to stay in the light because spots and stains don't show up in the dark. "The blood of Jesus Christ his Son *cleanseth* us from all sin" *as* we see our stained up lives and take them to Him for cleansing. That is our part. He keeps us and He *keeps cleansing* us. If He is first, the stains do not appear. If He is pushed into second place, back they come. But, God is all light, and "in him is no darkness at all." The stains show up at once and they can be cleansed away at once.

> . . . the blood of Jesus Christ his Son, cleanseth us from all sin.

NOVEMBER 18

He shall not be afraid of evil tidings: his heart is fixed, trusting in the Lord. His heart is established, he shall not be afraid . . . (Psalm 112:7, 8a).

HERE is a "many-colored pleasant stone" which often causes distress rather than rest.

First of all, most of us don't even want to be reminded that evil tidings might come. And here God is saying that we will not be afraid of them.

It so happens that over the years of my life, my family and I have exchanged long distance phone calls and telegrams with rather too much abandon. For that reason, telegrams and calls at odd hours have never frightened me. But I well understand the fear that tightens your heart, if they frighten you. The fact that the phone rang often long distance for me did not mean that I was *not* afraid of bad news. The call itself did not frighten me, but I always made a quick appraisal of the tone of my mother's voice during the first few seconds of the call, just to be sure everything was all right.

What does God really mean here?

He doesn't say I won't *dread* to hear "evil tidings." He doesn't say you won't *dislike* hearing bad news. He simply says we don't need to *fear* it. And He *is* quite simple about it, for which I am thankful. God says we don't need to fear bad news, because of the fact that we are *fixed on Him*. Not because of the fact that we are "fixed." Not because of the fact of Himself. But because we are *fixed on Him*. Nothing that can happen to you and nothing that can happen to me can in any way, change Jesus Christ. This is our *rest*. This is our *poise*.

His heart is established, he shall not be afraid. . . .
Fear not, it is I.

337

Then Paul and Barnabas waxed bold, and said, It was necessary that the word of God should first have been spoken to you: but seeing ye put it from you, and judge yourselves unworthy of everlasting life, lo, we turn to the Gentiles (Acts 13:46).

HERE is an interesting "many-colored stone" which looked so much like its historical surroundings in the book of Acts, that I passed it by as having practically nothing to do with me.

And then I caught a new flash of color on it near the end of the verse: ". . . but seeing ye put it from you, and *judge yourselves unworthy of everlasting life . . .*"

In one sense there is humor here.

Most persons who reject Christ, do it in an arrogant manner. For some reason they manage to feel superior about the whole thing. It is "child's stuff" or "old woman's stuff" or fantastic or not logical. It has no "verifiable data." No scientific proof, etc., etc. Whatever the reason given for rejecting Him, it is usually for some felt sense of personal esteem. So it was with the Jews in Paul's day. They were "sons of Abraham." They knew God's plan and it had nothing whatever to do with this crucified carpenter Paul talked about! But here God's Word strikes to the heart of such rejection, in a surprising way. God says they judge themselves *unworthy* of everlasting life. Actually they *prove* themselves unworthy. Unworthy because *unable* to receive a gift. There is always a moment of humility involved when something is truly received. We may "take" a gift, or "grab" it, but if we *receive* it, there is always that moment when we really mean that we "just don't know what to say."

. . . before honor is humility.

And when Peter was come to himself, he said, Now I know
of a surety, that the Lord hath sent his angel, and hath
delivered me out of the hand of Herod, and from all the
expectation of the people of the Jews. And when he had
considered the thing, he came to the house of Mary the
mother of John, whose surname was Mark; where many were
gathered together praying (Acts 12:11, 12).

PETER had just been delivered from prison by an angel
of the Lord. Delivered completely and lovingly. The
angel even took time to remind Peter to put on his coat
and shoes. ". . . bind on thy sandals . . . cast thy garment
about thee." Our God delivers completely and cares for *all*
the details important to our well-being *as He does it.*

Peter is out of prison, standing in the street, a free man.
The angel has gone and it is just dawning on Peter what has
happened. *He has been delivered.* "Now I know of a surety,
that the Lord hath . . . delivered me."

Here is the word to *us.* We need to "come to" and realize
and declare, *first to ourselves,* what God has done. If He has
just given you eternal life, express it to *yourself.* If He has
just delivered you from a sinful habit, remind yourself what
He has done.

Then, "consider" it. Meditate upon it. Let it become a
part of you. The sin was a part of you. Now, let the joy-
filled fact of the deliverance become a part of you too. Begin to get accustomed to it. Dwell on it. Rejoice in it. "And
when he had considered the thing, he came to the house . . .
where many were gathered together praying." Here is the
next personal word to us. Once we let deliverance become
a reality to *us,* no-one has to tell us to go where other Christians meet together. It takes varying lengths of time for the
realization of deliverance to "soak in" on us, and human beings must not push. But once it is real, we do as Peter did.
We simply go where people pray.

For where two or three are gathered together in
my name, there am I in the midst of them.

... the people ... having stoned Paul, dragged him out of the city, supposing he had been dead. Howbeit, as the disciples stood round about him, he rose up, and came into the city: and the next day he departed with Barnabas to Derbe (Acts 14:19b, 20).

THERE is a shaft of deep, encouraging "color" in this "pleasant stone" which is often missed in our amazement at Paul's being able to get up and go back "into the city" after he had been stoned and left for dead.

His enemies stoned him to unconsciousness, dragged his body from the city and left him lying there, "supposing he had been dead."

The next day, Paul was able to "depart with Barnabas to Derbe" to continue spreading the Good News about Jesus.

But here is the lovely stripe of "color" in this "pleasant stone" which has meant much to me: ". . . *as the disciples stood round about him*, he rose up . . ."

Jesus had promised that where two or three of His disciples were gathered together in His Name, He Himself would be right there in the midst. The Lord proved that with Paul that day outside the city limits of Lystra. When the disciples gathered around Paul, unusual power was released! And Paul was *enabled* to rise up.

I have experienced the dynamic of this truth of the "gathered disciples" in the writing of this book. Some of the Lord's dear ones in many parts of the world are gathered "round about" me in prayer as I work. Because of this and because of this *only*, have I been adequate to the task. We only need to be adequate. Paul must have been bruised and broken and stiff. But he was able to get up and go back to the city. And he was able to leave for the next task the next day. He was adequate. His need had been met by the "gathered disciples" agreeing as they "stood round about him."

Again I say unto you, That if two of you shall agree on earth as touching any thing that they shall ask, it shall be done for them of my Father which is in heaven.

340

One woman, named Lydia, a purple-seller from the city of Thyatira, a worshiper of God, listened, and the Lord opened Her heart to pay attention to Paul's messages. So, when she and her family had been baptized, she begged us, "If you consider me faithful to the Lord, come to my home and stay with us." And she just made us come (Acts 16:14, 15, Berkeley).

LYDIA was the first convert in Europe. And those who are converted today are still reacting much as Lydia did. Lydia already worshiped God. The new life comes *only* when we begin to see that love, as it is made plain in Christ, is *not* "what can God do for *us?*" but, "what can I do for *God?*" It is in His life poured out on the Cross that we see the transforming love that *cannot* stop giving. The love that lifts and does not expect to be thanked. The love that gives *more* when it is receiving *nothing*. The love of God.

Many believe in God as a "higher power." But only as we are "converted" to Him in *Christ*, can *this* love be "shed abroad in our hearts." We don't even suspect that there is love like this until our hearts are opened, as was Lydia's, to "pay attention" to the heart of the Cross. This changes us. This turns us from laggers to lifters. All new Christians are not immediately lifters. All do not begin at once as Lydia, to give. Some of us will go to any lengths to *remain* "problems" in order to *retain* the attention of those who care!

This is not a pretty thing to admit. But it is well to admit it. And to be aware that in most cases, when someone "just can't get the victory" it may be because that person still does not want to lose the limelight. Lifters often work in the background. The attention is never on the counselor. Always on the one in "need" of counseling. How shameful to force others to keep on feeding *us*, when Jesus commands:

Feed my sheep . . . Feed my lambs . . . Follow me.

341

And she just made us come (Acts 16:15c, Berkeley).

H ERE is a tiny, but potent streak of color in this "pleasant stone" fragment which I cannot resist sharing with you. The King James version reads: "And she constrained us."

Now most people know how to give gifts and kindnesses. I know from experience that this is true, because for all the years of my Christian life, God's people have showered me with kindness, and almost all of it "had no strings attached" whatever. But being *showered* with kindness is one thing and being *stormed* with "kindness" is another!

Perhaps Lydia, as we said of her yesterday, *did* become a "lifter" at once. But God's humor comes through His saints in the Bible now and then, and it could be that Luke smiled and clapped a hand to his head when he wrote: ". . . she just *made* us come."

Now and then someone invites us to dinner with such urgency that we somehow feel guilty if we refuse.

It is a joy to meet God's relaxed saints who can receive your refusal of their kindness as graciously as they offer it to you in the first place. For the sake of those who led Lydia to a knowledge of Jesus Christ as her own personal Saviour, I sincerely hope she was one of those who "joined the team" immediately.

I quite agree "It *is* more blessed to give than to receive." But it might be well now and then if those of us who *insist* upon "being more blessed" would take the *lesser* blessing. Especially if we are determined to "give" our newest culinary creation or an evening of *our* favorite home movies to someone who is tired and would rather be alone and not eat at all!

Blessed are the merciful; for they shall obtain mercy.

And some believed the things which were spoken, and some believed not (Acts 28:24).

WE can use this little "pleasant stone" to remind us that human nature is human nature.

Things happen to us and then things don't happen.

We succeed and then we fail.

Some believe and others do not believe.

But God goes on about His amazing purpose and we are simply to go on about our little part in fulfilling this purpose.

We are to keep our egos out of the picture and just go on "about [our] Father's business." It isn't ours. It's His. We are to go on about His business, relying utterly on the fact that Jesus Christ began our faith and that He will finish it. That God sent us and He will see us through anything that hinders our going.

If He doesn't get us *through* it, He will somehow lead us *around* it and we will be able to go on doing all that we need to do. And all we need to do is to belong to Him and leave the results *and* the consequences entirely in His hands.

The sooner we realize we are not able to handle even the results (when some *do* believe), the sooner we see that of course, we can do nothing about the *consequences* (when some do *not* believe). Running ourselves down is not humility, it is self-attention. If some do not believe, God will not stop pursuing them and it is all right (and sometimes for us, better!) if He reaches them at last through someone else. We very much need to accept life as it is and just go on following Christ. The Bible is always perfectly blunt about stating facts as they are.

Some believed the things which were spoken, and some believed not.

For they that are after the flesh do mind the things of the flesh; but they that are after the Spirit the things of the Spirit (Romans 8:5).

H ERE, out of the great eighth chapter of Romans, is a single "pleasant stone" whose subtle "colors" we often miss, because we are reaching for the larger truth in the chapter itself.

We have already seen that what gets our attention will ultimately get us.

This, of course, is exactly what this verse declares: "For they that are after the flesh do mind the things of the flesh; but they that are after the Spirit the things of the Spirit."

There is great value in group therapy. Power is released in the coming together of the members of any group. Not supernatural power necessarily, certainly not the power of the Holy Spirit, unless it is a Christian group. But power *is* released and it can be dangerous power as well as creative power. For example, when a group of people assemble around their old sin, even if it is to keep them from partaking of it, the sin or the weakness still has their attention! So often this is true even of Christian groups made up of people of various professions. I learned just last night of one sincere young woman whose card was "torn up" by the secretary of a "professional women's" group because it was learned that she worked in a factory. And this was a Christian group and my friend is also a Christian. We dare not gather exclusively around anything but the Cross of Christ!

They that are after the flesh, do mind the things of the flesh . . .

344

NOVEMBER 26

> But God, who is rich in mercy, for his great love where-
> with he loved us, Even when we were dead in sins, hath
> quickened us together with Christ (by grace ye are saved;)
> and hath raised us up together, and made us sit together
> in heavenly places in Christ Jesus (Ephesians 2:4-6).

STRIKINGLY vivid at the close of this *"many*-colored pleasant stone" is one line, and one spot of strong "color" in that line, which I overlooked for a long time.

". . . and made us sit together in heavenly places in Christ Jesus."

Of course, I knew this verse and the glorious truth in it. Of course, I believed even though I did not understand, that God had raised me up so that I could be seated "in heavenly places in Christ Jesus." I knew this. I believed it, but except for personal consolation and comfort, it had no real bearing on my *daily* life.

Then I caught the glint of light in this "color spot" among the other high "colors" in the same "pleasant stone." At last I saw the dreadful futility of trying to live up to *human heritage* as a slap in the face of God! It isn't royalty and the names on the pages of the Social Register who alone "try to live up to their high standing." Look around you in your own church or community. Look in your own family. People are exhausting themselves trying to "live up to" ancestry or means or acquired position in human life.

Beacon Hill in Boston is the *most* charming place in America as far as I'm concerned. And it retains its charms as long as one retains one's sense of humor about the exhausting *effort* still straining up and down its quaint winding streets, proving itself to be a stout, hardy "proper Bostonian" *effort* in all kinds of weather. Old line Bostonians are not alone in this futility of living up to a heritage. But how "alone" are the few Christians among us who "live up to" our heavenly position!

> Blessed be the God and Father of our Lord Jesus Christ,
> who hath blessed us with all spiritual blessings in heavenly
> places in Christ.

Then said Jesus unto them, When ye have lifted up the
Son of man, then shall ye know that I am he, and that I
do nothing of myself; but as my Father hath taught me,
I speak these things (John 8:28).

ONE subtle "color" here has brought me to a *new* place
of obedience.

The more obvious "colors" tell us that Jesus and the
Father are One. That "God was in Christ" on the Cross that
bright-dark day.

With sure, clear strokes, the Holy Spirit has drawn fine,
highlights of eternal truths back and forth through the many
colors of this "pleasant stone." But there is one shade of truth
among them which, only within the past few weeks, as I
have written, has caused me to dread *disobedience* in a way
I have never dreaded it before.

Too often, we make exceptions, when "just a little disobedience" seems justified. Or perhaps under the high pressures
of a great temptation, we say "*this* time I'm sure God will
understand."

Yes, He will.

That's the crux of the matter. He understood sin so well,
He died because of it. Here is the fragment of this "pleasant
stone" verse which broke my heart in a new place: "When
ye have *lifted up* the Son of man, then shall ye know . . ."

When we hurt Him (lift Him up) *we know*. We hide our
faces at the thought that we might have been among those
who stood watching Him on the actual Cross. And yet, because He *is* the Lamb of God, "slain *before* the foundation
of the world," we *do* still lift Him up on a cross every time
we disobey Him! Alibis and rationalization do not keep us
from "knowing." Disobedience hurts no-one as much as it
hurts the Lord Jesus.

Against thee, thee only, have I sinned, and done this
evil in thy sight . . .

So that ye were ensamples to all that believe in Macedonia and Achaia. For from you sounded out the word of the Lord not only in Macedonia and Achaia, but also in every place your faith to God-ward is spread abroad; so that we need not to speak anything. For ye are our glory and joy (I Thessalonians 1:7, 8; 2:20).

WHAT a really gay "color" the Holy Spirit has worked into this "pleasant stone."

It is one of my favorite "colors" because I know the feeling of light-hearted thanksgiving to God because some of you who are reading this page today have proven "your faith to God-ward" so that I "need not to speak any thing."

There is no joy to compare with the joy of seeing the great contagion of Christianity at work, shining out from the victorious lives of *new Christians* who, even when they stumble, always stumble God-ward!

I stumble too. But when I fall into the "paralysis of too much self-analysis," the Lord causes me to think of one and then another whom I have watched Him take unto Himself forever. I remember *you*, if you are one of these, and "ye are examples to all that believe," including me.

This is a bright, clear-colored "pleasant stone."

A gift, directly from the hand of God.

For ye are our glory and joy.

> . . . we beseech you, brethren, that ye increase more and more; and that ye study to be quiet, and to do your own business, and to work with your hands, as we commanded you (I Thessalonians 4:10b, 11).

IN this "pleasant stone" is a subtle streak of "color" which is easily missed, unless we look closely.

It is very easy to see ". . . we beseech you, brethren, that ye *increase* more and more." Everyone loves "increase." The human thing is to think in terms of "numbers." God is interested in numbers too. He proved it on the Cross, where He died for *everyone.*

Not just several thousand, but "everyone that thirsteth."

But here, in the verse, is a secret to the *true* increase. The "increase" God gives. The "increase" that lasts. Here, in this "pleasant stone" is the method God recommends: ". . . that ye study to be quiet, and to do your own business, and to work with your hands."

Nothing exciting or glamorous or pretentious about this at all. How many of us think we have to make a big noise and fly many banners and blow many trumpets and include many "special numbers" and a three-color mailing piece with photographs before we can "increase" as God commands us to do!

This is fine in its place. *If* God guides that way. But even in the midst of the "promotion," we desperately need *quiet.* God knows most of us have to "*study* to be quiet," and so it is not at all surprising that He included that in the same verse with His instruction to "increase." Well to remember also that we are "to do [our] own business." I know of three men whose wives and children suffer because *they* insist upon "serving God" instead of *obeying* God's admonition to "do your own business, and to work with your hands."

> That ye may walk honestly toward them that are without, and that ye may have lack of nothing.

**That ye may walk honestly toward them that are without
. . . (I Thessalonians 4:12a).**

HERE is a "pleasant stone" fragment which many do not
think so pleasant.

"That ye may walk *honestly* toward them that are
without" *Christ.*

No better place to apply this than the "time when all [go]
to be taxed." Our income tax reports seem somehow to be so
private and so personal and so utterly "no one's business but
our own," that we are tempted to exclude the Lord too!

It is a tragedy, but it is also a truth, that *some* Christians
do exclude Him here. And yet, honesty is not only the "best
policy," it is the *only* one which does not cloud our fellowship
with God.

One man who is a successful tax consultant and not a
Christian, only smiled at me when I told him I had become
a Christian. He had three Christian clients. At least only
three made a point of giving him tracts and witnessing to
their own "salvation." He smiled at *me*, unimpressed, because for years he had been helping to juggle the accounts
of *two* of his three "saved" clients.

When we juggle our tax report, or "shade the truth" in
order to clear ourselves with someone socially, we are only
telling "those without" that He is *not* quite sufficient. He
can't quite take care of His own. We need to check ourselves.
At "the time when all go to be taxed" or at the time of
hating to be *misunderstood* so much that we lie to avoid it!

**He is able to succour them that are tempted . . .
he is able to keep you from falling.**

Our Lord Jesus Christ, Who died for us, that, whether we wake or sleep, we should live together with him (I Thessalonians 5:9b, 10).

LET this bright "pleasant stone" take you by the heart with its full and lovely meaning.

It can change your entire heart-life toward Christ and toward all humanity. Love like this makes tender. Love like this reshapes into its own image.

This is the love of God as it is explained to us in ". . . our Lord Jesus Christ, who died for us [so] that whether we wake or sleep, we should live together with him."

So that we *could* live together with Him. Dr. Verkuyl in the Berkeley version translates the "should" which so often misleads us as "might." ". . . that we might live together with Him."

The word "should" has come to be coated all over with the dust of *duty*. We sigh and say "Oh, I *should* call her today." But it is something we evidently dread. Or at least something which we are not anticipating with joy. But here in this deeply poignant verse we are reminded that Jesus did what He did on the Cross of agony and shame and blood so that *we* might (be enabled to) live *together* with Him. Can you conceive wanting so much to be *with* your enemies that you would suffer the death of the Cross for the privilege of being with them? No. We can't conceive this. But that is why we cannot counterfeit the love of God. It must be *shed abroad* in our hearts by the Holy Spirit. There is no other way. He will begin melting your heart so that He *can* come in bringing this kind of love to *you*, if you open to the Heart that prompted this verse right now. If you open yourself to the One who prayed, just a few hours before they killed Him, that He could be with you forever.

> **Father, I will that they also, whom thou hast given me, be with me where I am.**

DECEMBER 2

Rejoice evermore. Pray without ceasing (I Thessalonians 5:16,17).

HERE are two bright little "pleasant stones" which seem to many to have sharp corners. Actually, they do have sharp corners, but for a reason. For purposes of cutting away the confusion which surrounds them.

They are not orders, so much as *results*.

Results of a life indwelt by the One who lived His earthly life rejoicing in the midst of trouble and holding His heart ever toward His Father, in an open, childlike attitude of prayer.

Nothing which happened to Him really upset Jesus. He lived in an attitude of praise and prayer. But, the glorious thing about this to me, is that it only made Him *normal*. He was sane and balanced and did not call attention to Himself as a fanatic. He was *not* a fanatic. The Christians you know who make themselves conspicuous by cluttering their conversation with religious clichés and pious-sounding references to themselves and *their* Lord, are not *easy* people to be with. *Their* Lord always seems to be giving *them* special instructions to do more amazing things than you could dream up in your wildest moments of dreaming, but *they* do *not* show forth Christ as He is! They are eccentric. He has been pushed to the margin of their lives and their own idealized image of themselves reigns squarely in the center, repelling rather than drawing. I personally feel ill at ease with the type of Christian who narrows her eyelids and speaks in syrupy tones about the "messages that came to her from God this morning." God does speak to us. But it never leads to anything queer. It is always attractive and balanced. *Rejoicing* is being ready to accept *anything* that comes in His Name and Nature. He *is* perfect balance. *Unceasing prayer* is an ever open heart toward God. Every "voice" we hear does not come from God.

Prove all things; hold fast that which is good.

351

DECEMBER 3

I will not leave you comfortless: I will come to you
... At that day ye shall know that I am in my Father,
and ye in me, and I in you (John 14:18, 20).

WHEN Jesus Christ says a thing, it is true.
He said that if we open to Him, He will come in
(Revelation 3:20). In the "pleasant stone" verse
above He declared His willingness to come and live His life
in us just *before* He was killed.

And then He declared the same wonder-filled intention
again *after* He had ascended to sit at the right hand of the
Father among the glories He had known before He visited
our little planet to show us His heart. In John's glorious Revelation He showed Himself to His beloved disciple in such
brilliance and light that John fell on his face as though dead!
But even back in this eternal glory, Christ's *heart* had not
changed.

He is reminding us through John that He is *still* the same
Lord. Still humbly standing at the door of the human heart,
knocking, and promising to come in if we will only open to
Him.

He does come in when we open to Him.

And when He does, He acts like *Himself*. His influence on
our lives, as He lives day by day *in* our mortal bodies, causes
us to resemble Him more each day, if we have given Him
freedom to live His life as He would live it. As we obey His
promptings, as we allow Him to "be Himself" in us, He
proves again and again that He is not only more than
adequate to every circumstance, but that He is wise and
balanced and *never* eccentric and strange.

All the words of my mouth are in righteousness;
there is nothing froward or perverse in them.

352

The fruit of the Spirit is . . . longsuffering, gentleness
. . . temperance . . . (Galatians 5:22, 23a).

WHEN Christ comes to indwell us, these facets of this "pleasant stone" verse gradually begin to show up in our lives. Bearing "fruit" does not always mean winning people to Christ. Winning people to Christ is a natural *result* of bearing the fruit of the Spirit in our daily lives.

I watched authentic Christian behavior one rainy morning when my good friend, Lois Warrens, who was driving me home from a speaking engagement the night before, didn't have *time* to remember to "act Christian." Everything happened too fast for that. With just enough time to reach my house before Lois opened her Christian bookstore that day, we stopped at a traffic light, seconds before an old jalopy banged into the back of her new yellow car with such force that the entire side where I sat, had to be replaced.

Lois looked back at the smashed front of the offending jalopy, grinned and said, "Well, by the way he looks, guess I'd better get out and see what happened to us." The driver of the other car had been admiring his new infant son, and it had come as a complete surprise to both him and his young wife, that we had been up ahead waiting some fifteen seconds for a red light to turn green. Lois operated her bookstore alone in those days and there was no-one to open it. But not once during the almost four hours in which we waited at the police-station for a particular "type" of officer who was in some mysterious way specially equipped to write up our accident, did I see one wrinkle of annoyance or rebellion in my friend Lois Warrens. This was *not* natural for Lois, but it *was* for the One who had come to live *His* life in hers. *Patience* and *self-control* are both fruits of the Spirit. They are "natural" only to God.

. . . As the branch cannot bear fruit of itself, except it abide in the vine; no more can ye, except ye abide in me.

> Then certain philosophers of the Epicureans, and of the Stoics, encountered him. And some said, What will this babbler say? other some, He seemeth to be a setter forth of strange gods: because he preached unto them Jesus, and the resurrection (Acts 17:18).

THE Epicureans, who had abandoned the search for truth through the process of reason, had begun to live solely for the experience of *pleasure*.

The Stoics, whose entire philosophy centered in complete self-sufficiency, lived by the stern rule of *self-repression*.

How mad these two schools of thinkers must have thought Paul!

Their two philosophies divided the entire period of thought at that period, although they obviously held an intellectual respect for each other. But even though the Greeks were always open to new thought or the possibility of a lengthy discussion, they certainly quite understandably thought Paul a "babbler."

After all, he preached "Christ and him crucified." He "preached unto them Jesus, and the resurrection."

It sounded so simple, they thought him foolish. From the intellectual viewpoint, I quite understand their verdict. The ancient Greeks, like myself, up to the time of my conversion to Christ, and like every other modern-day "greek" who demands to grasp the Gospel *intellectually,* is insulted at the simplicity of "believing" that Jesus was God showing us His heart!

It is more than foolish for those of us who have *received* the truth, to condemn those who still demand to *understand* it. They are still in spiritual darkness and we only increase that darkness by not *understanding* them. God's Word attempts to make this very clear to us:

> For the preaching of the cross is to them that perish foolishness; but unto us which are saved it is the power of God . . . we preach Christ crucified . . . unto the Greeks foolishness.

December 6

These that have turned the world upside down are come
hither also . . . these . . . do contrary to the decrees . . .
saying that there is another king, one Jesus (Acts 17:6b, 7).

JESUS Christ *was* king in the lives of those early disciples
and for that reason their ordinary daily lives literally de-
fined holy boldness.

They *did* turn the "world upside down."

Anyone who truly follows Christ lives in a world viewed
from the *other* end of the glass. From the viewpoint of God
Himself. Jesus Christ walked into human history and literally turned the world's philosophy upside down!

To the Epicureans who lived for the experience of pleasure,
He cried ". . . except a corn of wheat fall into the ground
and *die*, it abideth alone." They were *grabbing* life according to their own pleasurable desires. He stood before them
and told them to lose their lives for His sake! He turned
their "world upside down."

To the Stoics who stood with their chins out saying, "We
can take anything, therefore we will find truth by self-suppression and discipline," He said *He* had come to give a more *abundant life*. "By me if any man enter in, he shall be saved, and
shall go in and out and find pasture." He turned their "bloody
but unbowed" world of human endurance and self-suppression
upside down and poured His own blood over it that *they*
might *live!* Abundantly.

The Israelites had *cursed* their enemies. Jesus turned their
world upside down too by telling them to "*bless* them that
persecute you."

Everything about Him turns everything about us "upside
down" and it makes us dizzy until we realize that *His* way
is the way we were intended to live "in the beginning" when
God created! Only sin is "upside down" from God's point of
view.

Lord, I believe . . . Lord, I believe.

355

> Then Peter said, Silver and gold have I none; but such as I have give I thee: In the name of Jesus Christ of Nazareth rise up and walk. And he took him by the right hand, and lifted him up: and immediately his feet and ankle bones received strength. And he leaping up stood, and walked, and entered with them into the temple, walking, and leaping, and praising God (Acts 3:6-8).

THIS "many-colored pleasant stone" passage is a crystal-clear, step-by-step procedure for becoming whole again. It may be followed by anyone who has been touched by the power of Jesus Christ. A power which can heal a spirit or a body. A power which can heal a mind or emotions.

It is the same power which brought the dead body of Jesus of Nazareth up out of the tomb that first Easter morning.

It is the same power that "saves" a man and keeps him day by day. And if any man is disposed to take all Jesus Christ has for him in the way of emotional healing, he will unconsciously follow much the same procedure this beggar followed. Peter "took him by the right hand, and lifted him up: and immediately his feet and ankle bones received strength." *But,* the man *could* have sunk back down again, just as soon as Peter dropped his hand! Many do. Instead, "leaping up [he] stood, and walked, and entered with them into the temple, walking, and leaping, and praising God." This man *wanted* to be healed. He *wanted* to "join the human race" again! He was tired to the very *death* of his ego, of being "a certain man lame from his mother's womb [who] was carried, whom they daily laid at the gate of the temple." He wanted to be rid of his "beloved symptom" and so he stood up and began to *walk* and to leap, and doing this, he "entered *with them* into the temple." He was willing just to be another member of the human race again, doing what everyone else did and requiring no more special attention.

I am crucified with Christ, nevertheless I live.

And all the people saw him walking and praising God (Acts 3:9).

THIS facet of this "many-colored pleasant stone" from yesterday, must be examined alone.

It is more than a witness to a physical healing. It concerns the healing of any condition. This man's healing was complete and the reason was that he was willing *not* to be a "special case" any longer. He jumped up and began doing what the others were doing. He dared to believe that something had happened. There must have been a long moment of seemingly nothing. But then "his feet and ankle bones received strength."

Jesus told Paul that *His* strength was made perfect in weakness. Paul didn't wait to *feel* the strength. He acted on what he *knew* was there because Christ was there. How many of us who have known this Christ through year upon year, still wait for a *feeling!*

If we do, then no-one ever sees us "walking and praising God." The only way to find out if God has done something for us is to begin walking. And a courteous warning is shaded into this "many-colored" fragment at the top of this page, when the Holy Spirit reminds us, through this exciting story, that the people see us, no matter what we're doing. "And all the people saw him walking and praising God." When "the people" see *our walk*, do they see us "praising God" in it?

Go ye into all the world ... ye are witnesses of these things.

Ye are a chosen generation, a royal priesthood, an holy nation, a peculiar people: that ye should show forth the praises of him who hath called you out of darkness into his marvelous light (I Peter 2:9).

NO matter who you are, if your faith is in Jesus Christ, this brilliant "many-colored pleasant stone" is *yours*.

It is mine too, for the very same, simple reason that it is yours. *We* who belong to Christ, are a "chosen generation, a royal priesthood, an holy nation, a peculiar people."

Peculiar among our fellow human beings whose lives have not yet been invaded by the life of God in Christ.

Webster's definition of the word "peculiar" is this: *Belonging to an individual; privately owned; not common.*

We are not to be peculiar in the sense that we call attention to *ourselves*. We are peculiar in that we belong to Jesus Christ and *no longer* to ourselves. *Anyone* still outside of Christ belongs to himself. A man can retain self-ownership and follow any other religion. But we are to be "privately owned," if we are Christians. The *private possessions* of no-one in heaven or on earth, but Jesus Christ. He shares us lovingly. But we are not to *divide* ourselves. We are to be *His*. The common thing is to own oneself. We are to be "not common" in this sense at all. We have been "bought with a price."

And we are to be a "chosen generation, a royal priesthood, an holy nation, a peculiar people" (privately owned by Christ) so that we *can* "show forth the praises of him who hath called [us] out of darkness into his marvelous light."

I am come a light into the world, that whosoever believeth on me should not abide in darkness . . . for he that walketh in darkness knoweth not whither he goeth.

Jesus cried and said, He that believeth on me, believeth
not on me, but on him that sent me, And he that seeth
me seeth him that sent me (John 12:44, 45).

JESUS *cried* and said . . ."

He seems always so eager that we get hold of the truth
that He has *not* come to show Himself, but "him that
sent me." There must have been a particular urgency in His
voice as He spoke the words that make up our "many-colored
pleasant stone" verse at the top of this page. Christ shows
a passion to be understood by those He understands so well.

A passion to be understood and received as He *is*, not as
some would have Him be. Jesus *is* God. Come straight from
the Father with, *nothing between them but love.* The bonds
of love that make them One. Jesus was so intent upon having
us know that He did *not* belong to Himself, that He "cried,
and said, He that believeth on me, believeth not on me, but
on him that sent me."

Later in a dark, shadowy Garden alone, Jesus cried again,
"O Father . . . not as I will, but as thou wilt."

Not *once* did the Lord Jesus act independently of the
Father. "I and the Father are one." When we act independ-
ently of Christ, we simply show that we are *not* one with
Him, as He prayed we would be.

As thou hast sent me into the world, even so have I
sent them into the world . . . that they may be one in us
. . . I in them, and thou in me.

. . . Behold how he loved (John 11:36).

THE "pleasant stones" we will share in these days leading up to Christmas, are "opal-like stones" to me. Common opal is uniform in color, but certain deposits within
it flash and gleam with every color of the spectrum. Yet,
these are not true colors. They are reflections of *light* caused
by tiny cracks or fissures in the opal and they act like numberless little prisms separating the white of pure light into
its various colors.

All colors are contained in white light and since Jesus, whose
birthday we remember at this time of year *is* "the light of
the world," it seems right that our verses and fragments of
verses related to His first visit to earth, should be in our
"many-colored" collection of opal-like stones *reflecting* pure
light.

Look at the lovely fragment at the top of this page. "Behold how he loved." This was spoken by the Jews who had
come to mourn the death of Jesus' dear friend, Lazarus.
They said it as Jesus stood before Lazarus' grave and wept.
Making Himself one with *their* weeping. Making Himself
one with *our* weeping.

"Behold how he loved."

That is the motive that moved God's heart *toward* the
manger at Bethlehem on His way to the Cross.

For God so loved the world . . .

He took not on him the nature of angels; but he took on him the seed of Abraham . . . In all things it behoved him to be made like unto his brethren, that he might be a merciful and faithful high priest in things pertaining to God, to make reconciliation for the sins of the people (Hebrews 2:16, 17).

JESUS did not come to earth to save angels. "Christ Jesus came into the world to save sinners." And only *people* are sinners. All people. "There is none righteous, no not one."

And if you think that is an unpleasant thought to be suggesting at the Christmas season, perhaps we had better go into the glory side of it.

The glory side is simply this: *until* we realize in a *personal way* that we have sinned, that God visited this earth to save *us* individually, we will miss all there is in store for His own. You are not His personally until you give yourself to Him personally. He won't grab you.

I was not His, until in repentance I gave myself to Him.

But seeing our need for a Saviour, we can rejoice that "he took *not* on him the nature of angels." We can rejoice that God became *perfectly human* in Jesus of Nazareth. We can rejoice because this has directly to do with us. Being God, He saw that "in all things" He had to become *like us*. Even though God created us and knows us, still His heart prompted Him to come down here and find out just what it *feels* like to be one of us. To become "personal" with us. He retained His divinity, but He did become *perfectly human*.

. . . That he might be a merciful and faithful high priest in things pertaining to God, to make reconciliation for the sins of the people.

A N "opal" passage whose markings reflect color after color to those who will see.

Perhaps you are thinking this a strange verse about which to think at Christmas time. I find it deep with Christmas meaning. After all, did not Jesus stoop to being born in a stable so that no-one could ever believe Himself "not good enough" to be a Christian? Didn't Jesus "take on" the infirmity of the "bad background," the "lowly beginnings," so that anyone from anywhere can know that He *feels* their infirmities?

We have already looked at the wonder in the fact that the Word of God tells us the Lord Jesus was "in all points tempted like as we are, yet without sin." How it reassures me to realize He too was tempted *as I am!* And here in this "many-colored" stone at the top of this page, is reassurance of a still deeper kind.

God came to earth in the lowliest surroundings as the most helpless being, a newborn infant. He knows how it *feels* to be a baby. He knows how it *feels* to be a ten-year-old child. He knows how it *feels* to be a teen-ager. He knows how it *feels* to be an adult who is disappointed and hurt and alone.

His heart was broken again and again before it broke in the Great Agony of the Garden and the Cross. Jesus knows how it *feels* to be brokenhearted and grieved. Open yourself to know in a deeper way that the One who came that first Christmas was . . .

. . . touched with the FEELING of our infirmities . . .

> . . . I have loved thee with an everlasting love . . .
> (Jeremiah 31:3b).

THROUGHOUT the Old Testament we read of God's attempts to show His people about His love.

Over and over He said to them "Yea, I have loved thee with an everlasting love: therefore with lovingkindness have I drawn thee."

Over and over again we saw them turn away to worship idols.

And still God watched over them and waited until He knew it was the "fullness of time."

In the fullness of time, God visited the earth *as* one of His people. God became a human being. A life of a quality and kind never before seen in man, came to be among men in the Person of Jesus of Nazareth. And this Coming showed God's love in a way it had never been shown before.

Jesus did not come proclaiming God's love.

He came *defining* it.

He came *as* love.

He came demonstrating the things Isaiah wrote of the One who "was wounded for our transgressions . . . bruised for our iniquities." He did not do what He did to prove Isaiah right. Isaiah had simply *been* right in what He saw of God's heart. The little Baby in the manger at Bethlehem *was* this One who "poured out his soul unto death . . . who bare the sin of many, and made intercession for the transgressors." All in the spirit of love. Because He is love.

> I was not rebellious, neither turned away back. I gave my back to the smiters, and my cheeks to them that plucked off the hair: I hid not my face from shame and spitting . . . I have loved thee with an everlasting love . . .

DECEMBER 15

Herein is love, not that we loved God, but that he loved us, and sent his Son to be the propitiation for our sins (I John 4:10).

FOR years and years I sang the beloved Christmas carol, "Hark the Herald Angels Sing" and sang right past the line "God and sinners reconciled" as though it had nothing more to do with me than the line about Yankee Doodle sticking a feather in his hat!

Herein was love. But I didn't know it.

There in that manger lay love. But I didn't know it.

The point is not whether or not we love God. The point is that God loved us so much that He came Himself to *become* sin for us. "For God so loved the world that he . . . sent his Son to be the propitiation for our sins."

Christmas carols still mean little more than peaceful feelings and a vague, general form of goodwill to most people in this same world which God loved enough to die for. To many they are colorful, sacred folk songs sung in celebration of an ancient legend about a baby and its mother and some wise men who saw a star and brought gifts in pretty oriental brass urns and caskets lined with silk.

But therein that night lay love.

There in that manger in the Person of the Christ child. The baby "Christ Jesus came into the world to save sinners." But I sang "God and sinners reconciled" and didn't know what I was singing! I might have shuddered and thought you unpleasant if you had reminded me that those same little baby hands were nailed to a Cross for *me* thirty-three years later. There in the manger lay love. But this Christmas, remember also that there on the Cross *hung* love.

. . . Christ Jesus came into the world to save sinners . . .

364

Who did no sin, neither was guile found in his mouth:
Who, when he was reviled, reviled not again; when he suffered, he threatened not; . . . Who his own self bare our sins
in his own body on the tree . . . (I Peter 2:22-24a).

WHO his own self bare our sins in his own body on
the tree." This is not symbolism. Christ *did become
sin*. From the moment in the Garden of Gethsemane,
when He let His own will break into the will of the Father,
Jesus *felt* the dark down-pull of sin. He carried that load
of darkness and desperation in His own body to the Cross.
It was still *in His body* as He hung there on that ugly tree
bearing our sin and asking forgiveness *for* us!

Think of the heavy, depressing down-pull in your own
heart when you are experiencing sin in your life. When you
are filled with bitterness and defying God with it. Nothing goes
right. There is never enough fresh air. You want to throw
things and hurt people and all the time you are experiencing
the nerve-cracking weight of the down-pull of sin in your
heart.

Jesus felt this for the whole world from that moment of
surrender to the Father's will in the Garden. He "gave [His]
back to the smiters and [His] cheeks to them that plucked
off the hair" and not once did He hide His "face from shame
and spitting," but He still carried that dreadful *weight*. Jesus was sinless. And yet He became sin for *all* of us.

When we think of the crush of the sin in our own hearts
in our times of disobedience, we don't dare to try to think
what the weight must have been in His heart. And yet,
"when he was reviled, [He] reviled not again." This is the
Spirit Jesus showed as He hung on that other tree, bearing
our sin in His heart. What spirit do *we* show as we hang orna-
ments on our family Christmas tree, if someone happens to
"get on our nerves"?

Christ . . . suffered for us, leaving us an
example, that [we] should follow his steps.

Who, when he was reviled, reviled not again; when he suffered, he threatened not; but committed himself to him that judgeth righteously (I Peter 2:23).

MANY of the tiny crevices of an opal hold varying amounts of moisture which causes the brilliance of the "fire" in the stone.

Living water is contained in all of God's Word. We see it clearly, adding to the "fire" in the opal-like fragment at the top of this page. When we begin to be held by the dynamic of Christian behavior, we see the "fire" and take it to our hearts for further cleansing.

Christmas preparation at your house or the mad, scramble of Christmas shopping at the store where you work, or shop, will give you excellent opportunities to take the "fire" of this little fragment into your own heart. To find out how much you resemble the One who indwells your body during your time of stress and strain.

When you are reviled, do you revile again?

When you are caused to suffer, from tired, aching feet, or a tired, aching heart, what do you do? Do you threaten?

When someone pushes you on the subway or the train or the bus or crowds you to the curb in your car, after a long, hectic day, do you push back? Does something in you stamp down on the foot that stamped down on yours getting off that packed elevator? Do you revile? Do you threaten? Or have you learned the lovely secret of the Son, "who committed himself to *him* [to the Father] that judgeth righteously"? Only He knows about the person who stepped on you. Only He knows about *you*. Commit yourself to Him "that judgeth righteously."

He careth for you.

The angel said unto him, Fear not, Zacharias: for thy prayer is heard: and thy wife Elisabeth shall bear thee a son, and thou shalt call his name John . . . And Zacharias said unto the angel, Whereby shall I know this? For I am an old man, and my wife well stricken in years. And the angel answering said . . . behold, thou shalt be dumb, and not able to speak, until the day that these things shall be performed . . . (Luke 1:13, 18-20).

WHEN old Zacharias doubted that God would send a child to him and his wife in their old age, he lost his power of speech. I don't believe God sent this as a punishment. I believe it is simply a *consequence* of Zacharias' *real doubt.*

Surely, it must have seemed fantastic to the old fellow having the angel Gabriel appear as he did, with such news. And his question: "Whereby shall I know this?" was a perfectly normal question for an ordinary human being.

But the angel's answer was a perfectly normal answer for an angel too. He simply said, "I am Gabriel, that stand in the presence of God; and am sent to speak unto thee, and to show thee these glad tidings." Gabriel stood in the presence of God. That was enough. The message was straight and clear and to him, quite believable. God had said it. Gabriel knew God personally. But Zacharias, living in that still half-dark hour just before Jesus came, wondered and doubted. Zacharias was a priest. Talking was a big part of his work. It was hampered, almost stopped in fact, because of his doubt.

Has your work never been hampered because of doubt?

Has mine never been hampered by doubt?

Zacharias doubted and it stilled his tongue, it greatly inhibited his performance of his duties, but God's purpose rolled right along anyway. The child, John, was born right on schedule.

The glory of the Lord shall be revealed, and all flesh shall see it together: for the mouth of the Lord hath spoken it.

And the angel said unto her, Fear not, Mary: for thou hast found favour with God. And behold, thou shalt conceive in thy womb, and bring forth a son, and shalt call his name JESUS. He shall be great, and shall be called the Son of the Highest . . . and of his kingdom there shall be no end. Then said Mary unto the angel, How shall this be, seeing I know not a man? (Luke 1:30, 31, 32a, 33b, 34).

WHEN the angel Gabriel came to Mary with the "glad tidings" that *she* would bear a son, Mary had a question too.

"How shall this be, seeing I know not a man?"

But Mary did not lose her voice. Nothing uncomfortable happened to her at all. What is the difference between their two questionings? Old Zacharias' question, as I see it, held genuine doubt: "Whereby shall I *know* this?" In other words, "how can I be sure God *can* do such a thing under such naturally impossible circumstances?"

Mary's question had a different inner-ring to it: "How shall this be, seeing I know not a man?" She did *not* question whether or not it *would* or *could* be done. She simply asked *how?* Zacharias wanted to know how he could be *sure*. Mary just asked *how* it would be done. There is no doubt in her inquiry at all.

This great, childlike simplicity "found favor with God." In order to verify his news to doubting Zacharias, Gabriel said: "I am Gabriel, that stand in the presence of God." He had to present his credentials to Zacharias. To Mary, Gabriel could simply say: ". . . thou art highly favoured. The Lord is with *thee*."

Are we like Zacharias or Mary? Both were faithful servants of God. But one was struck dumb and confused by his own doubt. By his own refusal to be simple with God. But Mary didn't have to remember to be simple and clear and uncomplicated. She was. That is why she found favor with God.

. . . blessed art thou among women.

... and the virgin's name was Mary (Luke 1:27b).

HERE in this "opalescent pleasant stone" fragment is more loveliness than words should disturb.

It is a singular verse. Choice. Chosen of God.

Setting apart one, simple, devoted woman to the Lord Himself *first*. Mary was lovely in her purity of life and her devotion to Jehovah. No one could think that God had made a hasty choice. He must have looked long and carefully at the women of the earth before He selected one through whom He *could* send His only begotten Son, Jesus. She couldn't be a proud lady, however beautiful and gifted. His Son was coming to earth to save *all* the people who would come unto Him by faith. Mary had to be just one of the people down here, but one who "found favour with God" because of her life and because of His own secret requirements known only to Himself.

How it must grieve God's heart that so much bitterness and accusation swirl around our concept of this woman whose "name was Mary." To me it is inconceivable that she was *not* a virgin. She had to be. As someone has said, Jesus could not have been born in the same manner in which you and I were born. He was *God*.

But Mary was no goddess. She was a simple, lovely, obedient young woman and God chose her to be the quite *human* mother of Jesus. She had *not* known a man when Jesus was born. But she went right on to be a good wife to Joseph and a good mother to Jesus and her other children *after* God's will had been fulfilled in her life. But Jesus *was* born of a virgin. How else could it be expressed?

For with God nothing shall be impossible.

And the angel answered and said unto her, The Holy Ghost shall come upon thee, and the power of the Highest shall overshadow thee: therefore also that holy thing which shall be born of thee shall be called the Son of God . . . And Mary said, Behold the handmaid of the Lord; be it unto me according to thy word (Luke 1:35, 38).

HERE is another "opal-like" verse, shot through with "fire." Let it hold your attention. There is so much here for *us* today.

Mary was a virgin when the angel told her these amazing things. She had lived a clean, moral, lovely life. A life deep in the things of God. And yet, here was the angel Gabriel telling her quite bluntly that "thou shalt conceive in thy womb and bring forth a son . . ."

Mary knew God was in this. She lived so close to Him that she recognized His voice. But what courage and what devotion she must have had not to complain or at least try to reason with God. Mary knew God was *in* the heavenly visit, but what about her husband-to-be? What about Joseph? What about her family and her friends? Mary would be a social outcast! Her child would have no legal father.

But what did she do? Did she run to Joseph and ask his advice? No. Did she run to her mother or to her friends? No. She loved God so much she was *willing to be misunderstood,* if He asked it of her. She would obey and trust Him with the consequences.

The coming of the Holy Ghost upon us, follows normally as a beautiful result of obedience like this. We will be overshadowed by Him when we *want* to be. When we are, at last, willing to stop defending ourselves. When we are at last willing to obey *before* we have all the answers from God. When you and I are simple enough to obey, *regardless of the consequences,* "the power of the Highest shall overshadow" us.

. . . be it unto me according to thy word.

And it came to pass, that on the eighth day they came to circumcise the child; and they called him Zacharias, after the name of his father . . . And he [Zacharias] asked for a writing table, and wrote, saying, His name is John. And they marvelled all. And his mouth was opened immediately, and his tongue loosed, and he spake, and praised God (Luke 1:59, 63, 64).

GOD'S purpose moved on and the child was born to Elisabeth and Zacharias, but when they were about to name the baby after his father, old Zacharias had his chance. And he took it. Elisabeth said his name was to be John. But women never had the last word legally in those days. And when they gave Zacharias a writing table, he obeyed God. He wrote "His name is John."

This must have cost the old couple something. After all, they were not likely to have another child and they must have longed to call this one Zacharias after his father. But both obeyed God's instructions. The miracle of the child's birth had convinced them.

I do not think Zacharias obeyed that day at the writing table *so that* his power of speech would be returned to him. I believe he obeyed because he had become *obedient* and because he had stopped doubting God.

When peace lays hold of us, we are "loosed." Set free.

God takes care of all the big and little signs that point us along our way. Our part is to obey first, as Mary did. Being perfectly willing to be misunderstood and gossiped about, she obeyed God. And He gave her a lovely sign that He had everything under control for her. When she went to visit her cousin, Elisabeth, instead of reprimand or scorn as she might have received from an older woman, she looked at Mary and said, "Blessed art thou among women, and blessed is the fruit of thy womb." Mary obeyed and Elisabeth understood.

Zacharias obeyed and his tongue was freed. We *can* leave all the consequences and results to God. Joyfully.

My times are in thy hand.

For in him dwelleth all the fulness of the Godhead bodily (Colossians 2:9).

IN the Child which Mary conceived by the Holy Ghost, was "all the fulness of the Godhead bodily"!

In the helpless Baby lying in the straw of a Bethlehem stable was "all the fulness of the Godhead *bodily.*" How can we take this in? We can't explain it. Most of the world still does not believe it. And yet it is true.

This "pleasant stone" verse is true as God is true.

We either believe it or we disbelieve it. We accept it as coming from the mind of God and let it be unto us according to His word, as Mary did, or we reject it. Mary showed the greatest wisdom when she did not try to *understand* God's message to her. "The fear of God is the beginning of wisdom." Mary simply obeyed.

That "all the fulness of the Godhead" could be *in* that Baby is utterly inconceivable to us. But it is still true. And when we are wise enough *not* to try to understand, we find out that it is true. As long as the fight is on against accepting anything we cannot explain, we will remain in darkness. Recently I have watched an old friend, one of the most brilliant and gifted men I have ever known, come to the end of himself and turn, as a child turns, to follow Christ. If any human mind could understand, his could. But his personal life crumbled and he reached the glorious place of desperate need! There was no other turn left to make. He had no choice but to turn to Christ. His insights and understanding now that he has *received* Christ by faith, are breathtaking. He still doesn't understand, but he *knows*. He has taken this life-giving fact as his own. He *belongs* to the One in whom dwells "all the fulness of the Godhead bodily." The Son of God has been born *in him*. There is no other way to grasp the miracle in the manger except to let it happen to you.

. . . Ye are complete in him . . .

And the angel said unto them, Fear not: for, behold, I bring you good tidings of great joy, which shall be to all people. For unto you is born this day in the city of David a Saviour, which is Christ the Lord (Luke 2:10, 11).

TONIGHT is a "Silent Night" for those of us who remember the birthday of Jesus. There is a depth about this night (even to those who do not know Him personally), which causes one distinct note of response never struck again all year long.

Only on this "silent night."

In the "many-colored stone" passage at the top of this page we see why this is true. "And the angel said unto them, Fear not: for behold, I bring you good tidings of great joy, which shall be *to all people.*"

The warm hearts and the one distinct note of response never heard again all year long, are simply the inevitable *results* of God's all-embracing intention toward "all people." "For as in Adam all die, even so in Christ shall all be made alive." God's intention is *all.* He would not turn *any* away. "Him that cometh to me I will in *no wise* cast out."

Good tidings of great joy which shall be to all people.

The great heart of God beat there in that makeshift cradle that night, the first night of Jesus' life on earth. God's intention toward *all people* came into the world the first "silent night" and began to move *toward* us with a love that will never, *never* turn back.

Unto us a child is born, "a Saviour, which is Christ, the Lord." He came *unto us.* He was given *unto us.* In the birth in the little Bethlehem stable that first "silent night" God began a new movement *toward us.* A new attempt to show us His heart. To give *unto us* His own Son. Those of us who have received Him know *this* night about the heavenly song in *that* night.

Glory to God in the highest, and on earth peace, good will TOWARD MEN.

And behold, there was a man in Jerusalem, whose name was Simeon . . . and it was revealed unto him by the Holy Ghost, that he should not see death, before he had seen the Lord's Christ . . . when the parents brought in the child Jesus, . . . then took he him up in his arms, and blessed God, and said, Lord, now lettest thou thy servant depart in peace, according to thy word. For mine eyes have seen thy salvation (Luke 2:25-30).

WE are sharing this "pleasant stone" on this holy day, because in it is the very heart of the Gospel.

Old Simeon was "just and devout, waiting for the consolation of Israel: and the Holy Ghost was upon him." God had told His faithful old servant that He would let him live on earth to *see* "the Lord's Christ." There was no way at all Simeon might have thought to look for this Messiah in a little baby brought to the temple to be presented to the Lord by humble parents. But Simeon "came by the Spirit to the temple" that day. God directed him. And the minute the old man took the Baby Jesus in his arms, he *knew.*

"Then took he him up in his arms, and blessed God, and said . . . mine eyes have seen *thy salvation.*"

The glorious simplicity of the Gospel broke on Simeon "by the Spirit" that day. He saw what so few of us see, that salvation is not a *process*, it is a Person!

". . . mine eyes have seen thy salvation."

God instructed Mary and Joseph to call His name Jesus, because He was to "save His people from their sins." Simeon saw the Lord's *salvation* when God allowed him to see "the Lord's Christ."

For unto you is born this day in the city of David a Saviour, which is Christ the Lord . . . for it pleased the Father that in him should all fulness dwell.

And they came with haste, and found Mary, and Joseph, and the babe lying in a manger. And when they had seen it, they made known abroad the saying which was told them concerning this child (Luke 2:16, 17).

THERE is no reason at all why Christians should be "let down" on the day after Christmas.

If we are, it is because we have allowed the holy day to become merely a holiday. We have centered our attention around gifts and family and decor. It is no wonder we are "let down."

Toys are usually broken by the day after Christmas.

Gifts are on their way to be exchanged.

The tree is dropping its needles and the lights are burned out except in a few spots and somehow no-one cares any more.

Women sit in beauty shops and vow they'll "never do it again." Not one more year will they wait "till the last minute" to do all that shopping.

Men and women everywhere (even Christians) sigh and say they're glad it's all over for another year.

But it isn't over. "Unto you is born . . . a Saviour."

It's just beginning!

And it will go on forever. The "Saviour which is Christ the Lord" has given you eternal life. *With Him.* Christmas is forever and ever because He Himself *is* the end.

Glory to God in the highest . . . Glory to God in the highest.

Then cometh the end, when he shall have delivered up the kingdom to God, even the Father ... (I Corinthians 15:24a).

I do not pretend to know very much of what this "pleasant stone" fragment means.

It is "opal-like" in that it is filled with the water of the Spirit, as an opal is filled with water drops. Its meaning has to be flashed to us by the Spirit within it. Human understanding must fall "at his feet as dead" at any attempt to grasp its deepest meaning.

"Then cometh the end, when he shall have delivered up the kingdom to God, even the Father."

"Then cometh the end . . ."

What this means, I don't need to know, because Jesus has said He is the end. "I am alpha and omega." That is enough for me. If *He* is the end, it is all right. If *He* is the end, it will be lovely and right and perfect.

"Then cometh the end, when he shall have delivered up the kingdom to God, even the Father."

That will be lovely and right and perfect too, because Jesus also said "I and the Father are one."

Perhaps then we will see Father and Son in even more union than we now see them.

However it is, it will be the very best.

We shall see him as he is.

. . . He must reign, till he hath put all enemies under
his feet (I Corinthians 15:25).

HERE is another "opal-like" stone which shoots "fire"
from its depths. What does it have to do with us today?
Where do *we* come into it?

Is it so remote and so infinite in content that we cannot
possibly know? Perhaps. Oh, I'm sure there are many who
sincerely believe that they know. And there may be some
who do know.

I am sharing it with you, however, because it has come to
mean much to me in a personal way. It has, more than once,
turned my eyes from the world to God, and made me willing
to go on when all about me as far as I could see, was nothing but confusion.

"He must reign, *till* he hath put all enemies under his feet."

No-one has any idea how long this will take. No-one needs
to know. *He* knows. And now that we have shared almost
an entire year of looking at "pleasant stone" verses which
have given us deeper insight into what *His heart* is like,
don't you think we can trust *Him* to know about all these
"enemies"? Aren't you convinced that *our* enemies are *His
enemies* too? Don't you see that He *means us well?* That
when *His* enemies are conquered, *ours* will be too? We can
rest. Today and when "cometh the end."

For he must reign, till he hath put all enemies under his
feet . . . I am the beginning and the end.

The last enemy that shall be destroyed is death
(I Corinthians 15:26).

THIS is a darkly shaded "pleasant stone." One resembling a shadowy "fire opal" to me.

One I cannot fully look into.

One I would not fully want to look into. But one which I cherish among my "pleasant stones" and will cherish until I have experienced it myself.

In one sense death has already been destroyed. Surely its sting is gone for those who know in their hearts that Jesus Christ *is* "the resurrection and the life."

Some disagree, but I believe quite simply that I will not even lose consciousness when I die. The essential "me" will go on at once, uninhibited by my body, and my mind, into the presence of the One who has given me eternal life.

This is part of my joy in Christ. I believe it for myself and I am prepared to lose my loved ones, sustained by the same certainty that they too, will step at once into His presence. I am not arguing with you if you don't believe this. But the Lord Himself reassures me that "whosoever liveth and believeth in me shall never die." I believe that. And yet, *whatever He does will be right.* If I have a *wrong* conception of eternal life, then I have an *inferior* conception. He will handle it all *perfectly.* And one day dying will be all over. More than the sting of death will be gone. Death itself will be destroyed.

I am he that liveth, and was dead, and . . . am alive
for evermore . . . We shall be like him.

Verily, verily, I say unto you, If a man keep my saying,
he shall never see death (John 8:51).

JESUS shared and understood our horror of death. We cannot repeat too often, that although He was God visiting
this earth, He also became *perfectly human*.

This "many-colored stone" strikes my heart because it shows
me in its bright depths that He longs to make peace for
everyone. Even His enemies. He loved His enemies, even as
they persecuted Him. We think often that He loved even
those who nailed Him to a cross, but here we see that He also
loved the Pharisees who plagued Him all during His earthly
ministry. He spoke to His *enemies* too in the verse at the top
of this page.

He knew that in the very next breath they would call Him
a devil (John 8:52), but in spite of that He offered them
eternal life! A way *not to die*.

"If a man keep my saying, he shall never see death."

Jesus, the Son of God, stood declaring the way to eternal
life to those who hated Him. He offered it to them, knowing, as He did, that they would murder Him in just a few
months. That very day, in fact, He knew they would take
up "stones to cast at him." But still He stood there telling
them a way not to die. The year is ending. Our earthly life
is ending. But we need not *die*.

The Saviour has come, bringing eternal life, "to as many
as received him."

... I am the way, the truth, and the life: no man cometh
unto the Father, but by me ... Come unto me, all ye
that labour and are heavy laden ... If a man keep my
saying, he shall never see death.

For here have we no continuing city, but we seek one to come (Hebrews 13:14).

OUR earthly life is ending with the passing of every day and every year.

Another year is ending now.

Perhaps it has been a good year, as we think of "good years." It may have been a "bad year." Whatever it has been, in it, God has given us the opportunity to learn many lessons.

Some we have learned. Some we have refused to learn.

No doubt, right now, as this year is actually in motion toward its ending, we are more aware than usual that "here have we no continuing city."

Christians are not at home here.

Christians are at home with God.

"Here have we no continuing city," but that does not mean we are not *going to the Father.* This earthly life is a school. We are learning to speak the language of heaven. We are in the process of being re-made in His image, so that we will feel "at home" when we step out of the fussiness and confusion of earth into the glory and clarity of heaven. If we have not been good students during the year just ending, we *can* be in the one just beginning. With Him, life is to be one constant new beginning. Nothing changes Jesus Christ. If we have been unteachable in the year now ending, we will find Him just as willing to repeat the lessons in the year about to begin. He is just the same today as He was yesterday and He will be just the same tomorrow. We have no "continuing city" here on this earth, but because He is the beginning and because He is the end, by His Grace, we can always go on.

. . . Continue ye in my love . . . Continue ye in my love.

Thanks to
Lillian Mangles and Lucy Kormos
for keeping in check
the mechanics of the manuscript.
And to
Easter Straker and Ellen Riley
for keeping the author in check.

SCRIPTURE INDEX

SCRIPTURE INDEX

Scripture Index

Printed in the United States
73006LV00003B/101